Ginkgo Village

TRAUMA AND TRANSFORMATION IN RURAL CHINA

Ginkgo Village

TRAUMA AND TRANSFORMATION IN RURAL CHINA

Tamara Jacka

Australian
National
University

ANU PRESS

For my mother

Australian National University

ANU PRESS

Published by ANU Press
The Australian National University
Canberra ACT 2600, Australia
Email: anupress@anu.edu.au

Available to download for free at press.anu.edu.au

ISBN (print): 9781760466411
ISBN (online): 9781760466428

WorldCat (print): 1428686499
WorldCat (online): 1428762338

DOI: 10.22459/GV.2024

Cover design and layout by ANU Press

This book is published under the aegis of the China in the World editorial board of ANU Press.

WARNING: Readers are advised that Chapters 1-5 of this publication describe traumatic experiences including violence and killing, starvation, the death of children and suicide.

Contents

List of illustrations

Maps

Table

Plates

Language and naming conventions

Language

As I discuss in Chapter 1, Ginkgo Villagers speak a subdialect of Jiang-Huai Mandarin. However, my research assistants and I communicated with them primarily in standard Mandarin. Chinese words in this book are in standard Mandarin, Romanised according to the Pinyin system. The glossary at the end of the book provides the Chinese characters and English translations.

Naming conventions

Several places are mentioned in this book. I have fictionalised the location and other details of Ginkgo Village, Red River Township (under whose jurisdiction Ginkgo Village sits), all the hamlets within Ginkgo Village and nearby villages. The names of these places are pseudonyms, used to protect the identity of Ginkgo Villagers. All other places and placenames, including Xin County—the county in which Red River Township and Ginkgo Village are located—are real.

Li Wei (my research assistant) and all the villagers mentioned in the book are fictionalised characters and their names are pseudonyms. Other people and names are real.

I have named a few village adults with a title followed by a surname, but most are given a full name, written according to the Chinese convention, with the family name appearing before the first name. Children are given a first name only.

Acknowledgements

I am an Australian anthropologist and this is a book of tales based on my ethnographic and life-history research in Ginkgo Village, a rural community in central-eastern China. In what proved to be the last research project I undertook before retiring, two assistants and I visited this village five times between 2015 and 2018. As part of the same project, my assistants also went to Ginkgo Village without me on four occasions, in 2014, 2017 and 2019 (for details, please see the Appendix).

Living in Ginkgo Village was an enormously rewarding experience. Getting a feel for village life, interacting with locals daily and hearing their often heart-wrenching life stories didn't just strengthen my knowledge of rural Chinese society and history. It also transformed my outlook and sense of self and deepened my understanding of what it means to be human. And it sharpened my appreciation of how enriching and challenging efforts to build empathetic understanding across cultures can be.

Sadly, the current political climate in China and tensions between the Chinese and Australian governments make it unsafe to reveal the identities of the numerous Chinese friends who helped me conduct my research. In the following expressions of gratitude, as in the rest of the book, 'Ginkgo Village' is a pseudonym, as are the names of villagers and my research assistants. Other Chinese citizens to whom I'm indebted must also remain anonymous.

Above all, my heartfelt thanks go to the people of Ginkgo Village for accepting me and my assistants into their lives. I could not have completed the research underpinning this book without the willingness of so many villagers to spend so much time with us and respond to so many questions about their lives.

I am particularly indebted to our host in the village, Yang Yurong. Thank you, Yurong, for having us in your beautiful home, for cooking such tasty meals for us, for including us in your family's activities, for introducing us to your relatives and friends and for teaching us so much about village life. Thank you, too, to Yurong's parents, mother-in-law and two sons for tolerating our intrusions into their lives. And thank you to her husband, Wu Jianfu, for devoting so much time to us while he was home on leave. Thank you, too, to Yurong and Jianfu for staying in touch on WeChat and continuing to answer our questions years after our last visit to the village.

I am also deeply grateful to the Chinese university colleagues who hosted my research and organised each trip to Ginkgo Village, and to the local officials who gave permission for me to visit. Special thanks go to the Ginkgo Village leaders for enabling me and my research assistants to move about the village unhindered and unsupervised, and for talking with us so fully and frankly about local circumstances.

I owe a huge debt of thanks to my Chinese student–research assistants, not only for accompanying me to Ginkgo Village but also for undertaking fieldwork trips on my behalf in 2017 and 2019, when I couldn't go myself. In this book, I have merged these two fine researchers into one character, named 'Li Wei'. Thank you, Li Wei, for joining me in conversations with villagers, for helping me to understand older villagers' dialect, for sharing your copious daily fieldnotes, for your research in local county archives and the interviews and survey that you conducted on my behalf and for our numerous discussions about what we encountered in our fieldwork. Thank you also for your assistance before and after each fieldwork trip in preparing interview questions, checking my interpretation of data and conducting further documentary research. I'm particularly grateful to my primary research assistant for ferreting out historical county gazetteers and other difficult-to-access materials and for checking drafts of my writing. Her advice and corrections saved me from many mistakes and infelicities. Of course, I take full responsibility for any remaining flaws.

While Li Wei and I were in Ginkgo Village, two other Chinese students and two colleagues paid visits. I thank them for sharing their understandings of various aspects of village life. Thanks also to my primary research assistant and two other Chinese assistants for collating and analysing survey data and transcribing handwritten archival materials, and to Anna Buckley and my primary research assistant for help translating passages from local county gazetteers and genealogies.

Thank you to the Human Research Ethics Committee of The Australian National University for giving ethics approval for my research in Ginkgo Village.

I completed most of the writing for this book between 2019 and 2022 while at home in Canberra, Australia, on colonised land belonging to the Ngunnawal and Ngambri peoples. I am deeply grateful to Ngunnawal and Ngambri elders, past and present, for their ongoing custodianship of this land, over which sovereignty has never been ceded.

Many thanks to my colleagues in the Department of Political and Social Change at The Australian National University for enabling me to work part-time in 2019, take early retirement in 2020 and shift to emeritus status thereafter. This gave me the time and flexibility to experiment with a new form of writing.

Even so, I couldn't have undertaken this book without the inspiration and support of a great many people. I'm indebted, first and foremost, to Biff Ward for encouraging my early attempts at creative writing and to Jan Cornall for her Draft Busters online workshops. Twice-weekly online sessions with Jan, Biff and other Draft Busters were my lifeline. They gave me invaluable insights into the craft of writing, constructive feedback on oral excerpts of my drafts and a fantastically supportive community of fellow writers.

Thanks to Li Wei for some of the photographs and to Karina Pelling at CartoGIS Services at The Australian National University for the maps.

Huge thanks to Helen Williams, Maxine McArthur and Jan Borrie for editing and to the following people for invaluable feedback on drafts of the manuscript: Jan Cornall, Kerry Dwyer, Helen Williams, Andra Putnis, Suzannah Salojarvi, Li Wei, Tan Yu (a pseudonym), Wu Ling (a pseudonym), Sally Sargeson, Eleanor Jacka, Marcus Jacka, Misha Petkovic and Vidya. Thanks to my two anonymous reviewers for their constructive suggestions for revision. I'm also grateful to Kirin Narayan, Nick Cheesman, Robert Cribb, Jacob Eyferth, Andrew Kipnis, Yan Yunxiang, Jeffrey Wasserstrom, Arthur Kleinman, Jan Cornall and Jennifer Moore for reading recommendations and advice on various aspects of the manuscript and its publication.

Many thanks, also, to the China in the World editorial board of ANU Press for accepting my manuscript, and to the production team at ANU Press for their patience and care in preparing the manuscript for publication.

Finally, I'd like to thank my family and close friends for nurturing and sustaining me over the many years it has taken to produce this book. In particular, I dedicate the book to my mother, Eleanor Jacka. Thank you, Mum, for your generous response to my writing and for your continuing love and support. I don't have the words to express how much I love and admire you and how grateful I am for our relationship.

Introduction

Li Wei and I are chatting with grizzled old Widower Yang. He's a distant relative of Yang Yurong, the woman with whom we live each time we visit Ginkgo Village. The three of us sit on wooden stools outside Widower Yang's small general store on the main road, slouching together in the warm afternoon light. Li Wei and I, either side of Widower Yang, haven't bothered with our notebooks. They remain in our daypacks on the ground. Widower Yang is weaving a wicker basket. His twig-like fingers deftly bend each strip. The village government office compound across the road stands empty, the gate chained and padlocked. All is quiet.

Widower Yang is talking about trees. 'Once,' he murmurs, 'there were tall forests all around here.'

We peer up at the dark mountains looming in the distance.

Li Wei tilts her head in puzzlement. I frown.

'There are still trees everywhere,' I say. 'Were there more before?'

Widower Yang nods. 'The big ones have all gone. See those ginkgos?' He waves at two bright trees opposite. 'They're only young. Planted in the 1990s.'

'When I was a child, we lived up the hill.' He gestures with a thumb behind us. 'There weren't so many houses then, and a lot more trees. There was a ginkgo tree this wide.' He holds his hands up, a metre apart. His eyes briefly sparkle.

'It's gone now.' He squints at the half-made basket in his lap. 'All the trees were cut down in 1958 for the steel-smelting furnaces. One furnace stood over there.' He points his chin at the village government buildings. 'They threw all our iron in the fire—woks, knives, everything. And they chopped the trees for fuel. Some were hundreds of years old.'

The three of us slump on our stools. All week, Li Wei and I have been learning about the horrors of the Great Leap Forward (1958–61). But even knowing about the failed attempt to smelt steel, we hadn't thought to ask how they fuelled the furnaces. All those beautiful trees!

Li Wei is staring at the road. Suddenly, she cries out: 'Laoshi, look!'

I lift my head, just as a posse wearing sleek helmets, gaudy lycra suits and riding thin-framed bicycles streaks past. My mind flips from the Great Leap Forward to racing cyclists. This road wasn't even sealed until 2010. That's only five years ago. I blink and glance at Widower Yang. He, too, looks dumbstruck.

'City folk,' he grunts.

Li Wei and I peer after the bikes.

'Where do you think they're going?' I ask.

Widower Yang shrugs and resumes his weaving.

***

This is a book about trauma and transformation in the lives of Chinese villagers in the twentieth and early twenty-first centuries. Ginkgo Village is a scattering of hamlets under the jurisdiction of Xin County, Xinyang Prefecture, in central-eastern China's Henan Province. It lies in the south-eastern corner of Henan, in a mountainous border region known as Eyuwan.[1]

Through the twentieth and early twenty-first centuries, this region experienced extreme human violence[2] and radical political, economic and social change. In the early 1930s, the Eyuwan Soviet, centred on Xin County, was a key revolutionary base for the Chinese Communist Party (CCP). Its people were slaughtered. At the end of the 1950s, Xinyang led the Great Leap Forward and was devastated by the Great Famine. During the following three decades, Ginkgo Villagers and others in Xin County remained desperately poor. But that changed in the 1990s, when they became early enthusiasts of rural labour outmigration, travelling in huge numbers both within China and overseas.

---

1   The name Eyuwan is shorthand for Hubei–Henan–Anhui. Hubei's provincial capital, Wuhan, is 170 kilometres to the south of Xin County's seat of government, Xin County City. Anhui's capital, Hefei, is 301 kilometres to the east. Zhengzhou, the capital of Henan, is 440 kilometres to the north.
2   In fact, Eyuwan has a centuries-long history of extreme human violence. See William T. Rowe, *Crimson Rain: Seven Centuries of Violence in a Chinese County* (Stanford, CA: Stanford University Press, 2007), doi.org/10.1515/9781503626195.

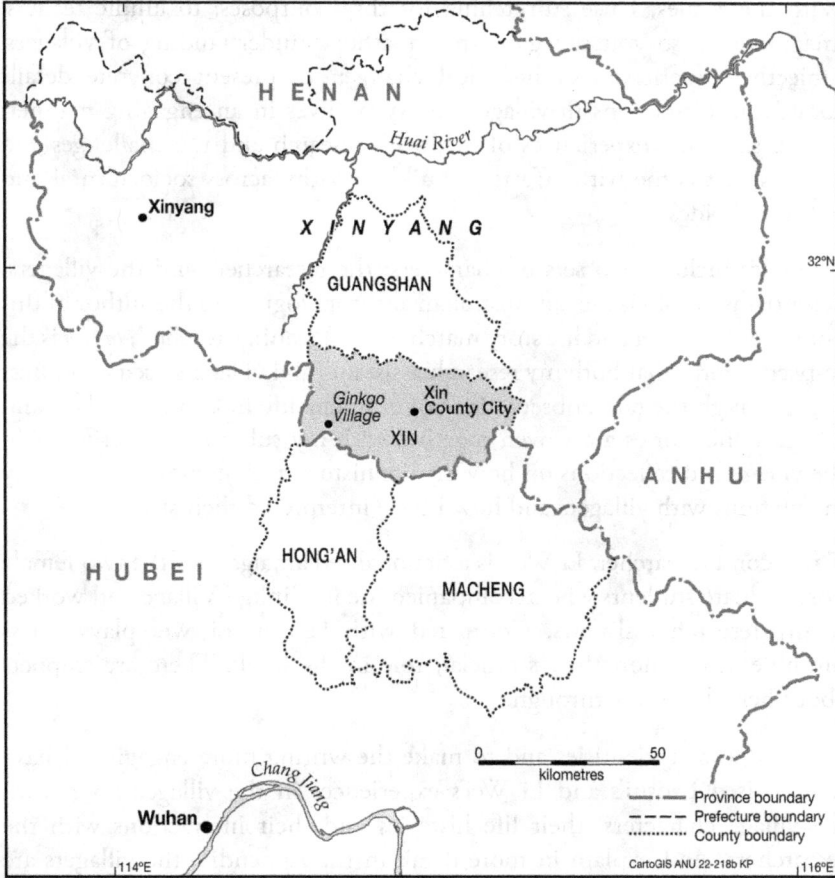

Map 1 Location of Xin County and Ginkgo Village
Source: CartoGIS ANU.

This book draws on ethnographic and life-history research that research assistants and I conducted in Ginkgo Village. But it is not a conventional ethnography or historical text. Rather, it's a melding of ethnographic storytelling, social history and personal reflection. The first chapter provides some information about Ginkgo Village and Xin County and outlines the region's recent history. The remaining chapters—the heart of the book—are a collection of eight interlinked tales offering intimate insights into Ginkgo Villagers' lives and life histories.

With these tales, I use storytelling for three purposes: to kindle readers' imaginations, so you can gain an empathetic understanding of villagers' subjective experiences of historical change;[3] to present concrete details about transformations in villagers' everyday lives in an engaging manner; and to share my experiences of fieldwork research and the challenges and rewards that come with efforts to build empathy across sociocultural and political divides.

The tales include two sets of characters: the researchers and the villagers. Essentially, Laoshi is me, an Australian anthropologist and the author of this book; her character and life story match mine. Meaning 'teacher', *laoshi* is the respectful term that both my research assistants and villagers used to address me. Through the tales, observations of everyday life in Ginkgo Village and villagers' life stories are woven together with my subjective experiences in the village and reflections on how my life history and memories shaped my interactions with villagers and how I have interpreted their stories.

The second researcher, Li Wei, is a fictionalised amalgam of the two female postgraduate students who accompanied me in Ginkgo Village and worked as my research assistants. Compared with Laoshi, Li Wei plays a less prominent, but nonetheless crucial, role in the book. There are snippets about her all the way through.

Both to protect identities and to make the writing more engaging, I have fictionalised Laoshi's and Li Wei's experiences in the village, along with the village characters, their life histories and their interactions with the researchers. As I explain in more detail in the Appendix, the villagers are fictional composite characters, but their personalities, circumstances and life histories are drawn from fieldwork findings and are true to life. The drama of their stories is not exaggerated; it's typical of the place and times.[4]

Each tale includes one or two fictionalised villager protagonists and revolves around these characters' life histories, as well as their lives in the present and their interactions with the researchers. Most are arranged chronologically according to the age of the villager protagonist and are best read in sequence,

---

3   I use the term 'subjective experience' to refer to perceptions, interpretations and emotional responses to events or circumstances.

4   For other examples and discussion of ethnographies variously positioned on a spectrum from nonfiction through to fiction, see Kirin Narayan, *Alive in the Writing: Crafting Ethnography in the Company of Chekhov* (Chicago: University of Chicago Press, 2012), doi.org/10.7208/chicago/9780226567921.001.0001.

as each one builds on those that precede it. Each tale is focused on a different set of topics of importance in daily village life. The main topic or topics are reflected in the tales' titles.

∗∗∗

Two themes are threaded through this book. The first relates to trauma and transformation.

As a collective, Chinese villagers living today have survived multiple episodes of extreme violence, dislocation and deprivation, including the Civil War (1927–49), the Great Leap Forward (1958–61), the Cultural Revolution (1966–76) and the forceful imposition of the One-Child Policy for birth planning (1980s – 2010s). My own and others' historical and anthropological research suggests that these episodes have been extremely traumatic for the rural Chinese population. By this I mean both that they were experienced as catastrophic ruptures in the lives of individuals and communities and that they inflicted serious widespread and long-term damage on surviving villagers' psyches and the social fabric of their communities.[5]

On top of this, through the twentieth century, Chinese villagers' everyday worlds were wrenched and buffeted by major state-led changes in the organisation and governance of their livelihoods and social relations, attacks

---

5   In this paragraph, I draw on conceptualisations of individual and collective trauma developed by the sociologist Kai Erikson in *A New Species of Trouble: The Human Experience of Modern Disasters* (New York: W.W. Norton & Co., 1994), 227–33. Aside from the research on which this book is based, several historical and anthropological studies lend weight to my assessment of the Chinese Civil War, the Great Leap Forward, the Cultural Revolution and the One-Child Policy as engendering extreme trauma among rural citizens. See, for example, Gail Hershatter, *The Gender of Memory: Rural Women and China's Collective Past* (Berkeley, CA: University of California Press, 2011), doi.org/10.1525/california/9780520267701.001.0001; Yang Jisheng, *Tombstone: The Great Chinese Famine, 1958–1962* (New York: Farrar, Straus & Giroux, 2008); and Steven Mosher, *Broken Earth: The Rural Chinese* (New York: Free Press, 1983). This book focuses on trauma across the lifespan of Chinese villagers who themselves experienced catastrophic violence, dislocation and deprivation. Only Chapter 3 includes discussion of historical or cross-generational trauma—that is, indirect trauma experienced by one generation as a result of trauma suffered by previous generations. See William E. Hartmann and Joseph P. Gone, 'American Indian Historical Trauma: Community Perspectives from Two Great Plains Medicine Men', *American Journal of Community Psychology* 54, nos 3–4 (2014): 274–88, doi.org/10.1007/s10464-014-9671-1. In Chapter 3, the villager protagonist Gao Xiuhua experienced historical trauma in the sense that her traumatic childhood was significantly shaped by her mother's earlier traumatic experiences during the Civil War years. There are few studies of historical trauma in rural China. See, however, Ralph A. Thaxton, Jr, *Force and Contention in Contemporary China: Memory and Resistance in the Long Shadow of the Catastrophic Past* (New York: Cambridge University Press, 2016), doi.org/10.1017/CBO9781316338094. Thaxton examines the ways in which collective memories of the traumas of the Mao years, especially the Great Leap Forward, shaped villager resistance to later official behaviour and policies, including the One-Child Policy.

on core cultural values and practices, and repeated shifts in state-promoted notions of morality and justice. In the last two decades of the twentieth century and the first two decades of the twenty-first, their lives have also been shaped by unprecedentedly fast economic growth and marketisation, technological change, increases in mobility, industrialisation, urbanisation and globalisation. All in all, it's fair to say, Chinese villagers living through the twentieth and early twenty-first centuries have experienced among the most rapid and radical social ruptures and about-turns the world has ever seen.

At the same time, macrolevel forces for change have always been mediated in rural China, as elsewhere, by local environments, subcultures and social relations, and the agency of local communities, families and individuals. As a result, stubborn continuities, adaptations and adjustments, resistance to change, renewals, novel combinations of old and new ways and the accretion of small, often unforeseen and unnoticed shifts have been as much a part of Chinese villagers' lives in the twentieth and early twenty-first centuries as have rupture and radical change.

This has led to a historical pattern more aptly described as transformation than either revolution (the CCP's preferred term for the history of the 1940s to 1970s) or reform (the CCP's preferred term for what happened after the 1970s). I understand 'transformation' to be an open-ended process of change involving both continuity and discontinuity over time. When something—an entity, practice or relationship—undergoes transformation, some of its elements change or disappear, but others are carried forward.[6]

Through this book, I depict both trauma and transformation in Ginkgo Villagers' lives. I write about how the traumas of the Civil War years, the Great Leap Forward and the Cultural Revolution continue to haunt older villagers. And I write about how younger villagers have been traumatised by the imposition of birth planning policies. At the same time, I write about transformations in villagers' day-to-day material lives and practices and in their relationships with their environment and other beings, both human and non-human. I also share my understanding of how villagers' subjectivities—their feelings, opinions, values, expectations and desires— have transformed over the course of their lives. And I reflect on how villagers'

---

6   Andrew B. Kipnis, *From Village to City: Social Transformation in a Chinese County Seat* (Oakland, CA: University of California Press, 2016), doi.org/10.1525/california/9780520289703.001.0001; Andrew B. Kipnis, *The Funeral of Mr Wang: Life, Death, and Ghosts in Urbanizing China* (Oakland, CA: University of California Press, 2021), 24, doi.org/10.1515/9780520381995.

experiences and memories might have transformed their subjectivities and relationships in the present. For instance, how did their experiences and memories of trauma, hardship and suffering shape how they talked about their lives and life histories with Li Wei and me?[7]

The second of the book's themes relates to empathy, interpretation and knowledge-building. One of my aims in weaving together ethnographic storytelling, social history and personal reflection is to challenge conventional notions of what constitutes 'knowledge' and of how best to build and communicate it. In particular, the centrality of tales in the book is underpinned by my conviction that empathy is a vital form of knowledge, built more effectively through storytelling than through factual analysis or argument. I'll say more about empathy as knowledge shortly.

Beyond this, each tale explores questions about knowledge-building: What is knowledge and how do we build it? Where are the boundaries between what we can know and what we can't? And what's the role of subjective experience and interpretation in knowledge-building?

I don't believe it's possible for people to acquire or construct objective knowledge that is separate from ourselves. Rather, knowledge is always filtered through our interpretations, which are contingent on several factors.[8]

Some of these relate to in-the-moment emotions and bodily sensations. In each of the book's tales, as in the vignette above, I depict moments of heightened emotion or bodily sensation felt or witnessed by Laoshi and Li Wei. In the fieldwork that my assistants and I conducted, moments such as these critically shaped our experiences in the village, our relationships with villagers and how we interpreted them. In the book, I have highlighted the effects they had on how Laoshi built knowledge.

Longer-term aspects of our identities, subjectivities and experiences are even more important. A whole host of things comes into play. Throughout the tales, I invite readers to consider how Li Wei's and Laoshi's family histories, life experiences and memories shaped our experiences in the village, our interactions with villagers and how we interpreted those experiences and

---

7   For more on this question, see Hershatter, *The Gender of Memory*.

8   The following discussion builds on scholarship that takes an 'interpretativist' approach to epistemology and calls for 'reflexivity'. See Dvora Yanow and Peregrine Schwartz-Shea (eds), *Interpretation and Method: Empirical Research Methods and the Interpretive Turn*, 2nd edn (New York: Routledge, 2015), doi.org/ 10.4324/9781315703275.

interactions. I also make reference to the impact on our interactions with villagers of language, cultural differences and clashes and convergences in values, expectations, desires and preferences.

Social positioning is another factor shaping interpretation and knowledge-building. In Ginkgo Village, the differences and similarities in social positioning between Li Wei, Laoshi and different villagers were shaped by our respective ages, gender, place of origin, level of education, material wealth, sociopolitical status (for example, professor, student, village leader, farmer) and family status (for example, patriarch, mother, daughter-in-law). References to the impact of Li Wei's, Laoshi's and individual villagers' social positioning are scattered through the tales.

Let's now return to my understanding of empathy as a vital form of knowledge. Scholars have more commonly defined it in terms of emotions or experience: as a type of emotional 'resonance' or 'fellow feeling', like sympathy,[9] as 'emotion sharing' or 'co-experience'[10] or as a 'first person-like, experiential understanding of another person's perspective'.[11] In my view, these definitions neglect the role of cognition and learning. I suggest it's more useful to equate empathy with empathetic understanding and see both as a form of knowledge that is learnt and constructed through cognitive, imaginative and emotional processes.[12]

I define empathy as a first-person–like, visceral, emotional and cognitive understanding of others' subjective experiences, underpinned by respect and care for their wellbeing.[13] Through my research and with this book, I strive

---

9   Unni Wikan, *Beyond the Words: Resonance* (Chicago: University of Chicago Press, 2012), doi.org/10.7208/chicago/9780226924489.001.0001; Neil Roughley and Thomas Schramme, 'Empathy, Sympathy, Concern and Moral Agency', in *Forms of Fellow Feeling: Empathy, Sympathy, Concern and Moral Agency*, ed. Neil Roughley and Thomas Schramme (Cambridge, UK: Cambridge University Press, 2018), 3–56, doi.org/10.1017/9781316271698.001.
10   Fritz Breithaupt, *The Dark Sides of Empathy* (Ithaca, NY: Cornell University Press, 2019), doi.org/10.7591/9781501735608.
11   Douglas W. Hollan and C. Jason Throop, 'The Anthropology of Empathy: Introduction', in *The Anthropology of Empathy: Experiencing the Lives of Others in Pacific Societies*, ed. Douglas W. Hollan and C. Jason Throop (New York: Berghahn Books, 2011), 2–5, doi.org/10.1515/9780857451033-002.
12   Ibid.
13   I include respect and care for the wellbeing of others in this definition because, unlike many, I don't assume that these virtues always accompany empathy more broadly defined. Occasionally, emotion-sharing is associated with sadism (Breithaupt, *The Dark Sides of Empathy*, 1–11). This is *not* the sort of 'empathy' for which my assistants and I strove in Ginkgo Village and *not* what I hope to enable in others with this book.

for and aim to build empathy because I see it as vital for countering those who fuel injustice and conflict by constructing 'the other' as 'the enemy' or as lesser than 'us'.

But achieving empathy is a demanding process. It involves learning to imagine what it's like to live as another, while simultaneously learning and appreciating what separates us. Our subjective experiences and an understanding of shared humanity[14] provide a starting point from which to interpret other people's behaviour and, from there, to build an empathetic understanding of their subjective experiences. But this is only a starting point. To understand whether someone's laughter is a sign of amusement, nervousness or something else, for example, we need to learn how each person's subjective experiences and the ways they express them are shaped by their bodies and histories and by the cultures, languages and power relations in which they are enmeshed.[15]

Beyond this, we need to guard against two unhelpful and potentially harmful alternatives to empathy: projection of our own subjective experiences and appropriation of others'.[16] No matter how similar, no two people share the same perceptions, interpretations or emotional responses to events or circumstances.

Striving for empathy takes effort, attentiveness, imagination and a desire to learn. It takes hard work.[17] By writing about myself as a protagonist (Laoshi) in this book's tales and by giving warts-and-all illustrations of my research in Ginkgo Village, I demonstrate both possibilities and challenges in the building of intercultural empathy. I show the flaws in my research practices and the limits of my ability to empathise, as well as the insights I gained. As you will see, I didn't achieve perfect empathy. But empathy is like any other form of knowledge: it's never perfect. It's always partial, provisional and improvable.

14　Non-humans, especially trees, play an important role in this book. But the question of the extent to which humans can and should build empathetic understanding with other beings is beyond the book's scope.

15　This sentence reworks Clifford Geertz's discussion of the interpretation of cultures, in which he gives the example of two boys rapidly contracting their right eyelids: are they twitching, winking or neither? Clifford Geertz, *The Interpretation of Cultures: Selected Essays by Clifford Geertz* (New York: Basic Books, 1973), 6–7. My example of laughter is explored further in Chapter 6.

16　Hollan and Throop, 'The Anthropology of Empathy'; Leslie Jamison, 'The Empathy Exams', in *The Empathy Exams: Essays*, by Leslie Jamison (London: Granta Books, 2014).

17　Jamison, 'The Empathy Exams', 5.

As well as the two main themes—trauma and transformation; and empathy, interpretation and knowledge-building—there are many sub-themes winding through this book. Inequality and injustice, patriarchal family relations, notions of modernity, the impact of labour outmigration and the ongoing centrality in village life of kinship ties, political connections, rituals and gift-giving are examples.

You'll no doubt find others, for meaning and knowledge in stories are constructed by the reader as well as the writer. Stories are journeys through our imagination. They're like a journey through life, full of discovery and transformation. Or they're the stops along the way. This Introduction is a map and Chapter 1 is a travellers' guide. The tales are our destinations: new places, new people. New mountains, rivers and trees. New insights into others and ourselves.

1

Ginkgo Village, Xin County

Place, population and governance

Ginkgo Village's hamlets sit tucked among the foothills of Eyuwan's Dabie Mountains. For many centuries, these mountains have suffered human incursions. At their heart, though, they remain wild and thickly forested, home to wolves, civets, wild pigs and golden eagles. Thousands of plant species grow here: Huangshan pines and China firs, oriental oaks and camphor laurels, several kinds of bamboo and a plethora of edible and medicinal wild plants.

Even ginkgo trees can be found deep in these mountains. Originating in China two million years ago, ginkgos can be found planted next to Buddhist temples, around villages, in gardens and on city streets across the world. But the Dabie Mountain range is one of very few places where they still grow in the wild.[1]

Other species grow in the foothills and around each hamlet. As Widower Yang explained in the Introduction, most trees around Ginkgo Village were cut down at the end of the 1950s. Later, though, villagers planted more. Other trees seeded themselves. Today, in the hills and valleys around each hamlet and along the main road you can see poplars, Chinese toon trees, Chinese scholar trees, willows, chestnuts, China firs and pines, as well as ginkgos. Each time Li Wei and I visited the village, we were struck by its natural beauty.

---

1   Xin County Gazetteer Compilation Committee, 新县志1986–2005 [*Xin County Gazetteer 1986–2005*] (Zhengzhou, China: Zhongzhou Guji Chubanshe, 2012), 69–82.

Xin County, in which Ginkgo Village is located, is a relatively new administrative entity. In 1933, the Nationalist Party created it by carving chunks off three adjacent counties and merging them. The biggest chunk once belonged to Guangshan County, Henan Province; the other two chunks belonged to Macheng and Hong'an counties in Hubei Province.

The village lies in the southernmost part of what was once Guangshan. It's roughly 10 kilometres from the market township of Red River and 30 kilometres south-west of the county seat of government, Xin County City. Guangshan, Hong'an and Macheng are close—the first to the north and the last two to the south.

A web of family ties stretches across this region. Once every few years, Ginkgo men attend large kin gatherings in Guangshan, Macheng and Hong'an. They meet up in a fancy hotel with others who share the same surname, have a large meal, drink far too much liquor and swap cigarettes and business cards. This is the origin of many a business partnership.

Other ties are more surprising. Take the trade in live baby fish. For centuries, live fry have been carried through the mountain passes from Macheng to Xin County to stock local ponds. Even today, the hamlet ponds in Ginkgo Village are stocked with fish born in Macheng.

Plate 1.1 Hamlet with pond
Photo: Tamara Jacka, 2017.

Today, Red River is one of 15 rural townships in Xin County, with a registered population of roughly 25,000 people. Ginkgo Village is one of 14 'administrative villages' (*xingzheng cun*) in Red River. It's made up of 18 hamlets. Officially, the hamlets are referred to as 'small groups' (*xiaozu*), but locals don't call them that. They mostly use language that reflects a common hamlet location next to a stream or river and call them 'small riverbends' (*xiao wan*). Most of the hamlets' given names also reflect the natural world.

The village is typical of Xin County, which locals describe as 'seven-tenths mountains, one of water, one of farmland and one of roads and houses'.[2] In total, the village spans an area of 9,980 mu (665 hectares).[3] Of this, 6,265 mu (417 hectares)—more than 60 per cent—is hilly forest land. This includes 140 mu (9.3 hectares) planted with cash crops of tea, chestnuts and China fir trees. One-tenth of village land—998 mu (66.5 hectares)—is farmland, of which 74 per cent is irrigated 'wet land' (*shuitiandi*) or paddy fields, suitable for planting rice. On average, village households have just 0.4 mu (267 square metres) per person of wet land. They have another 0.1 mu (67 square metres) per person of 'dry land' (*gandi*) on which they plant mainly canola, peanuts, cotton and vegetables. The rest of the village's area is taken up by Red River and its numerous tributary streams, and by houses and other buildings, roads, bridges, irrigation channels and ponds. Each hamlet has a pond.

Altogether, 1,750 people (431 households) are registered in Ginkgo Village. Almost all are of Han ethnicity; only eight women are non-Han.[4] Like most in China, the village is dominated by a patrilineal, patrilocal kinship system. This means that when women marry, they leave their natal family in the hamlet in which they grew up and go to live in the hamlet to which their husband and his family belong.[5] Village men are descended from male ancestors who have lived in the Eyuwan region for 20 or more generations.

---

2   Ibid., 2.
3   Mu is a Chinese unit of measurement, with 1 mu roughly equivalent to 667 square metres or 0.07 hectare. Unless indicated otherwise, the Ginkgo Village statistics in this book are based on 2015 data provided by village leaders. I have slightly modified the size of the village and scaled other figures to match, so that all ratios, fractions and proportions are correct. This means, for example, that the figure for total village landholding is fictional, but the amounts of different types of land per person are real. References for data above the village level are provided. None of these data have been altered.
4   The Han is the largest of modern China's 56 ethnic groups. They make up more than 90 per cent of the nation's total population.
5   Men who marry into their wife's hamlet are commonly stigmatised. In 2015, there were only two such men: one 60-year-old and one in his early forties. Both came from other villages in Xin County.

Most belong to five lineages, the largest of which bear the surnames Wang and Yang. People surnamed Wang make up one-quarter of the village population and those surnamed Yang make up another 20 per cent.

In 2015, most wives in Ginkgo Village came from another village in Red River Township (60 per cent) or another hamlet within the village (20 per cent). Only 10 per cent had married in from elsewhere in Xin County and 10 per cent came from outside Xin County. Of the last, half, including the eight non-Han women and 10 Han, had married into the village from outside the province.

Climate, culture and ancestral origins

In terms of climate, culture and physical location, Xin County belongs to an intermediary zone between the north and south of eastern China, called the Jiang-Huai region. 'Jiang', meaning river, refers to the Yangtze River, which lies to the south. 'Huai' refers to the Huai River, which flows just north of Xinyang City.

The Jiang-Huai region has somewhat milder winters and higher rainfall than the north, but summers are not as hot and wet as in regions south of the Yangtze. Less wheat is grown here than further north. As in regions to the south, rice is the main crop. Unlike in southern China, though, the weather doesn't allow for two crops of rice to be profitably grown each year. Rice is the staple diet, but villagers also eat noodles and other wheat-based foods.[6]

Besides food, many other aspects of local people's ways of life have been shaped both by climate and by cultural influences resulting from flows of people between northern and southern China. Take architecture as an example. In Ginkgo Village today, there are many single-storey old houses built or rebuilt in the 1980s according to a traditional design. They have tall walls and a high, open-gable roof, designed to keep the house cool and dry in summer by allowing plenty of air to circulate.[7] The roof is supported

---

6   Xinyang belongs to what American agricultural economist John Lossing Buck termed the 'Yangtze rice-wheat area'. John Lossing Buck, *Land Utilization in China: A Study of 16,786 Farms in 168 Localities, and 38,256 Farm Families in Twenty-Two Provinces in China, 1929–1933* (New York: Council on Economic and Cultural Affairs, 1956 [1937]), 27.
7   These houses are about 8 metres deep from front to back. The walls are 4 metres tall from the floor to the base of the roof. The height from the base of the roof to its ridge is another 2 metres or so.

by wooden 'dragon-gate' frames—so-called because they resemble a dragon gate: a traditional type of gateway with three portals. Dragon-gate frames—found throughout southern Henan—are a cross between the 'pillars and beams' (*tailiang*) roof frames typical of northern architecture and the 'pillars and transverse tie beams' (*chuandou*) of the south.[8]

The influence of population flows between north and south is apparent in the language, too. People in most of Xinyang speak a version of the Central Plains dialect of Mandarin (Zhongyuan Guanhua), which has been heavily influenced by another Mandarin dialect, called Jiang-Huai. In Guangshan and Xin County, they speak Jiang-Huai. More specifically, they speak a language belonging to the 'Huangxiao' subgroup (Huangxiao pian) of Jiang-Huai Mandarin.

Plate 1.2 Two dragon-gate roof frames
Photo: Li Wei, 2017.

8　Before the 1980s, only the houses of the wealthy had dragon-gate frames. Most villagers economised on wood by constructing simpler roof frames more closely resembling the pillar-and-beam type. The dragon-gate frames of the 1980s' houses were modelled on those of the elite before 1949. They were a symbol of increased prosperity. Even in the 1980s, though, some villagers couldn't afford dragon-gate roof frames. For more on southern Henan architecture, see Guo Ruimin, Zhang Chunxiang, and Li Shui, 豫南民居 [*Southern Henan Houses*] (Nanjing, China: Dongnan Daxue Chubanshe, 2011).

Linguists claim that today's Huangxiao subdialects were originally the languages of northerners who had settled in the Jiang-Huai region. They were then influenced by the speech of those immigrating from Jiangxi in the late fourteenth century, in what has come to be known as the 'Jiangxi fan'.[9]

We can see the impact of the Jiangxi fan in local historical records.[10] Ginkgo Village lineage genealogies show that most of the village's men are descended from families who left Jiangxi during the reign of the first Ming emperor, Zhu Yuanzhang (1368–98 CE). The migrants settled first in Macheng and Hong'an in northern Hubei. Then, in the early seventeenth century, at the end of the Ming Dynasty, their descendants moved northwards through the Dabie Mountains.

The original migrants to northern Hubei most likely left Jiangxi as part of a state-organised mass relocation program, whereas those who later moved to Guangshan did so of their own accord. But the choice of destination for the two groups was motivated by the same consideration: both moved into an area depopulated by violent warfare.

An eighteenth-century Guangshan County gazetteer[11] described southern Henan's devastation in the late Ming:

> Numerous families fled and of every ten homes, nine were empty … In Guangshan, battles raged for ten years between bandits and soldiers and by 1641, the situation was particularly calamitous and wretched. Everyone had fled and all the farmland was overgrown, for there was no one left to tend it.[12]

This was neither the first nor the last time the region experienced savage fighting. The frequency of violent warfare in this and other parts of Eyuwan can be explained by the strategic significance of the Dabie Mountains. On the one hand, the mountains straddle a trans-provincial border region, where state control has long been weak. On the other hand, they lie at the centre of the Han Chinese empire. For centuries, passes through the mountains provided passage for all manner of rulers and rebels aspiring to

---

9   W. South Coblin, 'Migration History and Dialect Development in the Lower Yangtze Watershed', *Bulletin of the School of Oriental and African Studies* 65, no. 3 (2002): 529–43, at 539, doi.org/10.1017/s0041977x02000320.

10   See Liu Shusha, '明代豫东南地区人口流动与社会变迁 – 以汝宁府为中心 [Population Flows and Social Change in South-Eastern Henan in the Ming Dynasty: A Study Focused on Runing Prefecture]' (Master's diss., Guangxi University for Nationalities, Nanning City, 2017).

11   Gazetteers are local-level historical records.

12   *Guangshan County Gazetteer* for 1730, cited in Liu Shusha, 'Population Flows and Social Change', 27.

control northern and southern China. With their steep, forested slopes, the mountains also provided strategic vantage points and gave refuge both to fighters and to those fleeing them.

Civil war and revolution, 1927–1949

Today, Eyuwan is best known for its role in the Chinese Civil War of 1927–49. During this period, violent warfare raged between local bandits, community self-defence groups, regional warlords, followers of the Nationalist and Communist parties and, from the late 1930s, Japanese invaders.

In the early 1930s, the Communist Party consolidated its bases in Eyuwan into the Eyuwan Soviet, with Xin County at its heart. The town of Xinji ('New Market'), which later became Xin County City, was established as the seat of government for the Eyuwan Soviet in November 1931.

At its height in 1931–32, the Eyuwan Soviet had a population of about 3.5 million. At that time, it was the second most important of the Communist Party's bases, after the Jiangxi Soviet.[13] In later years, however, Eyuwan and its population were torn asunder by brutal fighting between the Nationalists and Communists, coming on top of earthquakes, drought, famine, epidemics and purges within the Communist Red Army.

Between 1930 and 1934, the Nationalists launched five encirclement campaigns against the Eyuwan and Jiangxi soviets, aimed at exterminating the Communists. The first three campaigns were unsuccessful, but they devastated the regions. As the local county gazetteer put it, Xin became a county of 'deserted districts, valleys of corpses, and widow villages'.[14]

With the fourth encirclement campaign of 1933, the Nationalists succeeded in wresting control of Xinji. They then created Xin County, or rather Jingfu, as they called it. By this time, the population of the Eyuwan Soviet had plummeted by 80 per cent to 700,000 people. The slaughter continued. Reports later claimed that between 1932 and 1934, the Nationalists killed 200,000 people in Eyuwan.[15] Thousands more fled when their villages were razed. Others starved, were forcibly recruited into the Nationalist army or sold as wives or slaves.

---

13   Ibid., 240.
14   Ibid., 244.
15   Gregor Benton, *Mountain Fires: The Red Army's Three-Year War in South China, 1934–1938* (Berkeley, CA: University of California Press, 1992), 314.

With the fifth encirclement in 1934, the Nationalists routed Communist forces. Most of the Communist cadres[16] and Red Army soldiers broke out of the encirclement and joined the Long March to Yan'an. In Eyuwan, they left behind only a couple of Party cadres and 1,300 troops.[17] The fighting in Eyuwan died down briefly and then flared again from 1937, when both Communists and Nationalists fought the Japanese.

At the beginning of the 1930s, Xin County's population numbered fewer than 100,000 people. By the late 1940s, 55,000 of its 'heroic sons and daughters' had 'sacrificed their precious lives for China's revolution'.[18]

In 1947, Communist troops, led by Liu Bocheng and Deng Xiaoping, took control of Jingfu and established their own seat of government in Xinji. They retained the town's name but changed the name of the county to Xin—literally, 'New County'. As Liu explained, the name echoed that of Xinji and signalled the beginnings of a bright new life under the Chinese Communist Party (CCP).[19]

But the violence did not end. Ginkgo Villagers use 'Liberation' to describe October 1949. That's when the CCP's chairman Mao Zedong announced the establishment of the People's Republic of China. But even after this historic moment, locals continued to suffer brutality and deprivation. What's more, as in other former revolutionary base areas, Xin County's environment and economy took decades to recover from the ravages of war.

Politics and economy, 1920s – 1970s

Land and class, 1920s – 1950s

Across south-eastern Henan in the 1920s, 89 per cent of households farmed or were without a stable occupation.[20] Of these, almost 60 per cent had no more than a few mu of land. Some of these 60 per cent were sharecroppers

---

16   In the Chinese context, the term 'cadre' (*ganbu*) refers to anyone in a position of authority.

17   Odoric Y.K. Wou, *Mobilizing the Masses: Building Revolution in Henan* (Stanford, CA: Stanford University Press, 1994), 160–61, doi.org/10.1515/9780804766821.

18   Xin County Gazetteer Compilation Committee, *Xin County Gazetteer 1986–2005*, 245.

19   Ibid., 243.

20   The next two paragraphs draw on Hou Zhiying, 大别山风云录 [*A Record of the Tempests in the Dabie Mountains*] (Zhengzhou, China: Henan People's Publishing House, 1990), 4–6. The figures come from Republican government data, cited in this work. For further discussion, see Wou, *Mobilizing the Masses*, 99–106.

or tenants paying fixed rent to a local landowner. More than half of what they produced went on rent. These households lived in thatched-roof mud huts or mudbrick houses with tiled roofs. They made a living by farming 10–15 mu (0.7–1 hectare) of mostly rented land, selling home-woven cotton cloth in local market towns like Red River and Xinji, peddling and working as short-term or long-term labourers for their landlord. Many others owned no land and couldn't afford to rent. They worked as itinerant labourers, prostitutes or mercenaries, or begged, thieved or sold family members. These unfortunates had nothing more to live in than makeshift shacks of sticks and straw.

For most people, life was a constant struggle for survival and reproduction. Traditionally in China, a man's inability to marry and support a family signified the lowest depths of destitution and shame. In south-eastern Henan in the 1920s, every hamlet had at least three men who couldn't afford or couldn't find a wife. In some hamlets, one-third of adult men were bachelors or 'bare sticks' (*guanggun*), as they're known in Chinese.

Through the 1930s and 1940s in some parts of the Eyuwan Soviet, including Xin County, Communist cadres took land from the wealthy and distributed it to the poor. But this process of land reform didn't occur in the villages of Red River. There, land reform was completed in 1950.

About 250 households lived in Ginkgo Village at this time. Of these, 21 were classified as 'landlords'. Each owned several tens of mu of farmland. Most were in Bitter Hollow and were headed by men surnamed Wang. Altogether, Bitter Hollow's Wang landlords owned about 3,000 mu (200 hectares). Another seven relatively land-rich households in Ginkgo Village were deemed 'rich peasants'. Seventeen households who owned enough land to sustain themselves (about 10 mu or 0.7 hectare) were classified as 'middle peasants'. The remaining 205 households (82 per cent of the total) were deemed landless 'poor peasants'.[21]

In the process of land reform, cadres confiscated land, buildings, farm tools, clothes and other property from those classified as landlords and rich peasants and shared it among the poor peasant households. Each person was assigned 1 mu (667 square metres) of farmland.

---

21   These figures are based on information from current and former village cadres.

Cadres also organised public 'speak bitterness' meetings at which poor peasants were encouraged to vent their anger and bitterness at the exploitation they had suffered at the hands of wealthy landowners. A few landlords fled. Among those who remained, those considered most evil were shot and killed. Others were jailed. Their families were taunted and abused during speak bitterness meetings.

With land reform completed, cadres urged villagers across China into mutual aid groups and, from 1953, cooperatives. By the end of 1957, all village households across Red River belonged to 'higher-level' cooperatives, in which most land, water buffaloes (for ploughing) and farm tools were collectively owned.

The Great Leap Forward and the Great Famine, 1958–1961

In 1958, Chairman Mao launched a campaign to speed up collectivisation and to achieve a 'Great Leap Forward' in industrialisation and progress towards communism. At the heart of this campaign were efforts to extract from the countryside as much as possible in the way of grain, cotton, steel and other resources to siphon into industrialisation. CCP leaders in Henan, especially Xinyang, led the charge.[22]

Xinyang's Suiping County established China's first commune, in April 1958.[23] The rest of the country quickly followed suit. By 1959, 24,000 communes had been set up across China, each including between 2,000 and 20,000 households, grouped into production teams and brigades.[24] All farmland and domestic animals were brought under collective control and private production and marketing were banned.

Red River was merged with an adjacent township to form Red River Commune in August 1958. Within this commune, Ginkgo Village and its slightly smaller neighbour, Deng Inn Village, were brought together into one brigade. Within the brigade, hamlets became production teams.

---

22   See Yang, *Tombstone*, 23–86; and Jean-Luc Domenach, *The Origins of the Great Leap Forward: The Case of One Chinese Province*, trans. A.M. Berrett (Boulder, CO: Westview Press, 1995).

23   Yang, *Tombstone*, 163–66.

24   Klaus Mühlhahn, *Making China Modern: From the Great Qing to Xi Jinping* (Cambridge, MA: Belknap Press of Harvard University Press, 2019), 440, doi.org/10.4159/9780674916067.

The leaders of Xinyang's newly established communes soon began reporting extraordinarily bountiful grain harvests. This set off waves of wild exaggeration and deception, with increasingly unreal harvests reported across China and larger and larger grain quotas sent to the state.

Model communes in Henan also pioneered collective institutions like kindergartens and canteens. The aim was to relieve women of their domestic duties so they could take on more farming work for the commune. Red River Commune ran a kindergarten between the autumn of 1958 and the autumn of 1960. In the autumn of 1958, each production team also set up a canteen providing free meals. By early 1960, though, the canteens were serving nothing but thin soup made with water, a few leaves of wild greens and a bit of pumpkin. By the end of 1960, all had closed.

Another Henan innovation was the militarisation of labour management. Villagers were disciplined like soldiers and divided into a hierarchy of units under the command of the commune leader. This person had the power to appoint tens of thousands of labourers to fight 'battles' on a huge scale. One such battle was to complete water conservation and irrigation projects.

Xinyang suffers both droughts and floods. Through the 1950s, it experienced major drought most years and heavy, flooding rains in 1954 and 1956. By 1955–56, cooperative leaders had been pushing villagers to build reservoirs and large-scale irrigation canals as rapidly as possible. During the Great Leap Forward, the pressure was stepped up even further. But many of the large reservoirs and canals were constructed in such haste and had so many design flaws, they had to be abandoned or demolished and rebuilt in later years.[25] This waste came at a terrible cost: so much labour was pulled into these projects that there wasn't enough to complete farming tasks, so grain yields declined. Grain shortages led to hunger and exhaustion among the construction workers as well as their families. Yet, cadres forced starving workers to continue with backbreaking toil. Thousands starved to death.

---

25 Xinyang Prefecture Local Histories and Gazetteers Compilation Committee, 信阳地区志 [*Xinyang Prefecture Gazetteer*] (Beijing: Sanlian Shudian Chubanshe, 1992), 163–64; Domenach, *The Origins of the Great Leap Forward*, 43–44; Yang, *Tombstone*, 71–73. An official document from 1958 claimed that 191 reservoirs were built around the county that year. It also included a plan to build 10 medium-sized reservoirs and 400 small reservoirs across the county in 1959 (Xin County People's Committee, '关于今冬明春大力开展兴修农田水利和水土保持工作的方案 [A Plan for the Major Development of Farmland Water and Soil Conservancy Construction and Maintenance Work this Winter and Next Spring]', Unpublished document, Xin County Archives, 1958). However, a later county gazetteer claims that only two medium-sized and 124 small reservoirs were built between 1950 and 1985 (Xin County Gazetteer Compilation Committee, *Xin County Gazetteer 1986–2005*, 297).

Xinyang also led the way with the steel-smelting campaign that Widower Yang mentioned. Across Xinyang through the course of 1958, 30 per cent of the labour force was dragooned into steel-smelting.[26] But again, the effort was wasted: the village furnaces produced only high-carbon pig iron, which was of little value to industry.

More than 50 years later, memories of the Great Leap Forward still cast a dark shadow over Ginkgo Villagers. They didn't use the phrase 'Great Leap Forward'. Instead, some called it 'The time of eating from one big pot' (*chi da guo fan shiqi*)—a reference to the canteens. Others referred to the years between late 1958 and late 1961 as the 'three years of great famine' (*san nian da jihuang* or *san da huang* for short). In this book, I refer to this period as 'the Great Famine'.

Here's how Widower Yang explained the famine suffered in Ginkgo Village: in September 1958, so much of people's time went into smelting steel, the rice harvest was neglected. Most of the grain rotted in the fields. In the spring of 1959, heavy rains led cadres—fearful of flooding—to drain village ponds. When drought hit, just as the rice grains were forming, there was no water for the rice plants, so they yellowed and died. Once more, the harvest was meagre. But when the commune sent an inspection team, brigade cadres tricked them. They padded the rice bins with a thick layer of stalks and leaves before pouring in the grain. What the inspectors saw were full bins of rice. In fact, they were less than half-full. Then, because local cadres had exaggerated the harvest yield and both they and their superiors were keen to impress the higher-ups with their revolutionary zeal, most of the rice was handed to the state. Almost nothing was left for villagers to eat.

Nationally, between 15 and 40 million people—mostly villagers—died unnatural deaths during the Great Famine.[27] Xinyang was 'the epicenter of the disaster',[28] but across the prefecture, the impact of the famine was uneven. Guangshan was among the worst-hit counties.[29] Widower Yang claimed that one-third of Guangshan's population starved to death. The *Guangshan County Gazetteer* shows that the county's natural population growth rate between 1950 and 1958 averaged 2 per cent. But between 1958

---

26 Yang, *Tombstone*, 28.
27 Felix Wemheuer, *A Social History of Maoist China: Conflict and Change, 1949–1976* (Cambridge, UK: Cambridge University Press, 2019), 121–22, doi.org/10.1017/9781316421826. Most villager deaths were due to starvation, but millions were also killed for pilfering grain and other 'crimes'.
28 Yang, *Tombstone*, 23–86.
29 Ibid., 44.

and 1959, it declined to −5 per cent and the following year to −27 per cent.[30] By the end of 1960, the county's population was lower than it had been in 1935.[31]

Far fewer starved to death in Xin County. Some Ginkgo Villagers claimed no deaths in their production team; others counted one or two. Widower Yang estimated that 0.6 to 0.7 per cent of Xin County's population died of starvation. That amounts to between 1,176 and 1,372 people across the county, or an average of six or seven in each of the county's present-day villages.[32]

Ginkgo Villagers gave a few reasons for the difference between the two counties. Widower Yang said that Xin County villagers were given a state grain subsidy. From 200 grams of hulled rice per day per person at the beginning of the 1959–60 winter, the subsidy was increased to 350 grams in early 1960, and 400 grams from spring until after the autumn harvest that year. Guangshan villagers didn't get this because their leaders lied about harvest yields. They said villagers had so much grain they didn't need a subsidy.

A more common explanation had to do with topography. Guangshan has more flat arable land than Xin County. From the Maoist state's perspective, this made the former more valuable, because higher grain quotas could be appropriated from its communal fields. But with no private land or other source of food to make up for grain shortages, villagers starved in huge numbers. Much more of Xin County's territory was forested mountains unsuitable for large-scale grain growing. That proved a lifesaver for desperate villagers. Even after the destruction of trees, they could go deep into the mountains to collect edible leafy greens and berries and dig up the starchy roots of the kudzu vine. To be sure, these sources of food also were exhausted and villagers suffered extreme hunger, malnutrition and oedema. But relatively few starved to death.

---

30 Guangshan County Histories and Gazetteers Compilation Committee, 光山县志 [*Guangshan County Gazetteer*] (Zhengzhou, China: Zhongzhou Guji Chubanshe, 1991), 468.

31 Guangshan's population numbered 389,977 in 1935, 503,440 in 1958 and 358,956 in 1960 (Guangshan County Histories and Gazetteers Compilation Committee, *Guangshan County Gazetteer*, 466–67). For other estimates of the number of deaths due to the Great Famine across Xinyang, see Yang, *Tombstone*, 23–86.

32 I have been unable to find any population statistics for the period 1959–61 for Xin County. I've calculated the number of deaths during the Great Famine as a proportion of the 1958 population of 195,981 (Xin County Gazetteer Compilation Committee, *Xin County Gazetteer 1986–2005*, 83). There are 194 villages in Xin County today.

The collective political economy, 1960s – 1970s

In the early 1960s, central leaders finally acknowledged the failures of Great Leap Forward policies. After this, state grain quotas were reduced and there was a relaxation of the ban on private farming and marketing activities. Production teams allocated small private plots to each household, which villagers used to grow their own vegetables and cotton.

Red River Commune was found to be too large and unwieldy, so the neighbouring township was hived off into a separate commune. Within the now-reduced Red River Commune, Ginkgo hamlet and Deng Inn continued to function as a single brigade. Production teams remained as before but their leaders now took a greater role in governance. From the early 1960s until the end of the 1970s, they made decisions about the distribution of collective labour tasks and how tasks were to be remunerated.

Each day, individuals were paid in 'work points' (*gongfen*). A range of methods were used to determine work points. Usually, though, they were based on whether you were male or female and the amount of time you spent in collective labour.

After the harvest, production team leaders deducted enough to cover agricultural taxes and other costs. Then, they divided the rest of the harvest among production team members. A certain percentage was distributed to each household according to the number of work points earned by its workers and the rest according to the number of mouths to feed. In the early 1960s, half was distributed according to work points and half according to the number of mouths. Later, in some production teams the ratio was 60:40, while it was 70:30 in others.

Widower Yang told us that, through the collective era, villagers in Ginkgo Hamlet received a nominal amount of between 200 and 250 kilograms of unhulled rice—the equivalent of roughly 160–200 kilograms of hulled rice—and 20–40 kilograms of unhulled wheat. But a portion of the grain was commonly substituted with sweet potatoes. Five kilograms of sweet potatoes counted for 1 kilogram of unhulled grain. Villagers generally received between 75 and 100 kilograms of sweet potatoes. Sometimes soybeans were given instead of grain, but each household received only enough soybeans to make 5–10 kilograms of *doufu* (soybean curd) each year.

Wealthier households received up to 10 kilograms of pork, but most others received none. Small amounts of sugar cane were given out, but only enough for a household to make between 0.5 and 1 kilogram of sugar each year. Villagers had to use their private plots to grow all other food or else they bought it. However, they received very little cash from collective labour. A few better-off households could earn up to 20 yuan (US$12) a year, but most couldn't earn enough work points to cover their food needs and were in debt to their production team.

Through the 1960s and 1970s, Maoist rhetoric held that everyone was equal but, in reality, rural citizens were severely disadvantaged compared with urbanites. And, in the countryside, villagers' material wellbeing varied from one region to another.

Even within production teams, the material wellbeing of differently positioned villagers was far from equal. First, brigade and commune cadres had salaries and privileged access to resources. This led to a crucial difference in food intake between them and others. The only Ginkgo Villagers who told Li Wei and me that people had enough to eat during the collective era were those who had been brigade-level cadres at the time. Having a bit of cash also meant that cadres had better clothing and footwear and their children were more likely to go to school.

Second, gender inequality was built into the work points system of remuneration. Rarely did women earn more than seven work points to a man's ten. Women and girls also took almost sole responsibility for unpaid domestic work, including sewing, spinning and weaving. And, on average, they were given much less schooling than their male peers.

Aside from gender, the most widespread inequality within production teams related to the size of families and their position in the life cycle. The wealthiest households were those with many able-bodied adults who could earn work points. The poorest were those burdened with numerous children too young to work in collective agriculture.[33]

The final significant source of inequality was class. Land reform in 1950 more or less eradicated old class divisions. But it was also the beginning of a new hierarchy, with landlord families and others deemed 'bad class

---

33   Huaiyin Li, *Village China under Socialism and Reform: A Micro-History, 1948–2008* (Stanford, CA: Stanford University Press, 2009), 208–28, doi.org/10.1515/9780804771078.

elements' at the bottom and poor peasants, especially those seen as serving the revolution, at the top. Through the 1950s and early 1960s, surviving members of former landlord families were assigned the most demanding and unrewarding tasks in collective agriculture. They were also required to do more unpaid labour than other villagers.

The Cultural Revolution, 1966–1976

Even greater persecution came with the Great Proletarian Cultural Revolution. This was another period of chaos and violence instigated by Mao Zedong. The chairman had been sidelined after the Great Leap Forward. Essentially, the Cultural Revolution sprang from his efforts to regain power by fomenting 'continuous revolution' and violent class struggle.[34]

In the mid 1960s, there were 30 households in Ginkgo Village labelled landlords or landlord descendants. Twenty-nine were Bitter Hollow households headed by men surnamed Wang. The thirtieth household lived in Ginkgo Hamlet and was headed by a man surnamed Yang. In 1966–67, cadres and activists publicly paraded members of these households in dunce's caps, subjected them to repeated verbal and physical abuse and stole or destroyed their property.[35]

By the end of the 1970s, the survivors of this persecution and violence cowered at the bottom of the social hierarchy. They were the most stigmatised and poorest of villagers, living in the worst conditions. In the mid 2010s, Li Wei and I learnt about seven 'bare sticks' in Bitter Hollow born between 1935 and 1965.

Local cadres also ordered the destruction of roadside shrines and lineage halls. The shrines—one for every hamlet—were destroyed in 1966 as part of a campaign to 'Destroy the Four Olds' (*Po Si Jiu*). Most were not rebuilt until the 2010s.

---

34 See Wemheuer, *A Social History of Maoist China*, 193–277.

35 Besides landlord descendants, many others labelled 'bad class elements' were persecuted. Across China, 22 to 30 million people were persecuted during the Cultural Revolution and one to two million were killed. Andrew Walder, 'Rebellion and Repression in China, 1966–1971', *Social Science History* 38, nos 3–4 (2014): 513–39, doi.org/10.1017/ssh.2015.23. I have no figures for Xin County or Ginkgo Village.

Plate 1.3 Roadside shrine and paddy field
Photo: Tamara Jacka, 2017.

The village had two lineage halls—one belonging to the Yang lineage in Ginkgo Hamlet and one to the Wang lineage in Bitter Hollow. Before Liberation, these had been used for ancestral worship. The inside of the Yang lineage hall was smashed in 1966. For its part, the larger Wang lineage hall—a compound rather than a single hall—was converted into a primary school in 1950. It continued to be used as such until 1977, when a new primary school was built in Poplar Hamlet. Its interior was destroyed then. Only the ruined shells of the Yang and Wang lineage halls remain today.

Aside from violence and destruction, rural China saw other transformations in the 1970s, including improvements in basic health care and education. Ginkgo Brigade bought its first tractor in 1976. Land continued to be cleared and more hillsides were terraced for collective grain planting. Ginkgo Brigade's production team leaders were urged by their superiors to plant two crops of rice each year rather than one, but they resisted the pressure, undertaking double cropping for only a few years.

Meanwhile, for four months in the winter of 1974–75, Red River Commune organised teams of thousands of villagers to replant hills and mountainsides denuded in 1958. They planted mainly China firs. Altogether, they cleared and then replanted about 5,000 mu (330 hectares) of mountainous land in a great belt around the commune.[36]

Tea-growing was another venture begun during the Cultural Revolution. In Ginkgo Brigade, tea bushes were first planted in 1967–69. Altogether, about 200 mu (13 hectares) of hillside land was cleared and planted with tea. Then, in 1974–75, a tea factory was built on the edge of Ginkgo Hamlet.

Through the second half of the 1970s, the factory employed about 50 villagers. Thirty women were hired to pick tea-leaves between March and May each year. One man from each production team was employed year-round to tend the tea bushes and process the leaves. The factory also employed all 20 of the 'educated youth' (zhiqing) sent to the brigade.[37] The 12 male educated youths worked alongside the village men. The female youths joined the men maintaining the tea bushes and helped the village women pick tea.

The tea factory sold its produce across south-eastern Henan and northern Hubei and became an important source of revenue for Ginkgo Brigade. Some of the profits were invested back into the tea factory and into other brigade enterprises set up in the 1970s. These included a grain grinding mill, a blacksmith, a noodle-maker and two carpenters.

Tea also benefited individual village households. This wasn't just through employment in the factory. In the second half of the 1970s, the mature tea bushes produced more leaves than the factory employees could pick, so the factory allowed other village women to pick tea and paid them 0.08–0.10 yuan (US$0.05–0.07) per kilogram of leaves. This became one of very few sources of cash for village households.

In the 1980s, the tea factory was privatised. From the 1990s, the business became less profitable and was scaled down. In subsequent decades, more than half the land planted with tea was bulldozed and built on. But even in the 2010s, tea-picking remained a source of income for village women.

---

36 Red River Township Gazetteer [pseud.], Unpublished draft, 2017.
37 The 'educated youth' were young urbanites sent to the countryside to 'learn from the peasants'. Those sent to Ginkgo Brigade were Xin County City residents aged in their twenties. They arrived in 1975–76. One woman married and remained in the village. The rest returned to the city in 1980–81.

From a twenty-first-century vantage point, it's hard to say how much villagers appreciated the tea factory and other improvements of the 1970s at the time. In hindsight, though, they paled in significance compared with what came after Chairman Mao's death in 1976 and the rise of the reformist 'post-Mao' state led by Deng Xiaoping.

Politics and economy, 1980s – 2010s[38]

De-collectivisation and the return to family farming

When Li Wei and I asked older Ginkgo Villagers about the biggest changes in their lives, most simply said, 'We didn't have enough to eat before. Now we can eat whatever we want.'

The major turning point in their eyes was *dangan* (literally, 'working on one's own'). This is a reference to de-collectivisation, the introduction of a 'household responsibility system' and, with it, a return to family farming.[39]

In the first half of the 1980s, most collective structures across rural China were disbanded. Governance was taken over by county and township governments and, at the village level, by village committees and Communist Party branches. Ginkgo Village was split from Deng Inn. By 2015, each village's government had been pared down to a Party secretary, a deputy Party secretary, who doubled as the village committee accountant, a village committee director and a women's director. Each hamlet (previously production team) had a leader, too, but this position was shorn of power.

Under the household responsibility system, individual households took responsibility for their own economic decisions, and private businesses and markets were permitted once more. Villages retained ownership of the land but divided it up for households to farm. In Ginkgo Village, farmland was distributed in the autumn of 1981 according to the number of mouths to feed in each household. Each year thereafter, hamlet heads made minor adjustments to allow for changes in household size due to births, deaths

---

38 The following discussion takes the reader up to the time of Li Wei's last research visit to Ginkgo Village in August 2019, before the Covid-19 pandemic. Aside from a few comments made in Chapter 9, the impact of the pandemic on village life is beyond the scope of this book.
39 For a general discussion of post-Mao rural reforms, see René Trappel, *China's Agrarian Transition: Peasants, Property, and Politics* (Lanham, MD: Lexington Books, 2016).

and marriages. Every three years, a more significant adjustment took place: the village committee took back all the land and divided it anew. The last adjustment took place in 1998.

With the return to family farming and marketisation, villagers worked hard to boost their incomes through farming. They continued to plant mostly rice, but also grew other crops and raised chickens, pigs and other animals, both for their own consumption and for sale.

To make way for more crops, villagers felled trees. This included giant Chinese tallow trees that had grown for centuries in the middle of fields. Back in 1958, these trees were the only ones not chopped down and burnt in the steel-smelting furnaces. They were spared because oil from their nuts was a source of collective revenue for the brigade. It was sold in the cooperative store for use as lamp oil. But in 1986, Ginkgo Village homes were connected to the electricity grid and the market for lamp oil dried up. The Chinese tallow trees were felled. By the time Li Wei and I visited Ginkgo Village, there were only a few spindly specimens growing in the hills.

Meanwhile, by 1993, the trees planted across Red River Commune in the mid 1970s had matured. Over the next two years, the Red River Township Government felled them all and sold the timber.[40]

However, other trees were planted. Through the 1990s, village leaders organised the planting of cash crops of chestnuts and China firs. They also had ginkgo trees planted along roads and paths, the seeds of which were sold for use in Chinese medicine. In the 2000s, the market for ginkgo seeds dried up, so many of the trees were cut down. The male trees were spared, but because their fruit smells bad, most of the female ones were removed.

In 1998, in Ginkgo Village's final major redistribution of land, hillsides planted with chestnuts and China firs were contracted to village households along with farmland. Village leaders handed out chestnut seedlings, too. Then, in 2001, the Returning Farmland to Forest (*Tuigeng Huanlin*) program was introduced and households were given a small state subsidy for each mu of land they planted with trees. Over the next several years, some villagers planted former paddy land with China firs.

*

---

40   Red River Township Gazetteer.

In the early years of the post-Mao reforms, the food intake of villagers across Xin County improved, and some earned enough money to rebuild their ageing houses. But their cash incomes remained severely constrained by taxation, low returns on agriculture and a lack of non-agricultural employment. In 1983, 82 per cent of the county's population lived below the official poverty line. The average annual disposable rural income across the county was 86 yuan (US$43) per person—just 28 per cent of the national rural average of 310 yuan (US$155).[41]

In 1986, the state designated Xin County a 'poor county' (*pinkun xian*) and began efforts at poverty alleviation. Tax relief, loans, and education and other subsidies were given to poor households. Funds were also provided for the construction of roads, clinics and other infrastructure. In Ginkgo Village, as mentioned, village homes received electricity in 1986. A new medical clinic was also established that year to replace the smaller, more basic one built in 1970.

But it wasn't until the year 2000 that Xin County officials finally felt able to declare that all county residents could meet their basic needs for food and clothing.[42] The big breakthrough didn't result from state funding; it came when villagers began leaving the land and the countryside for wage work.

Rural outmigration

In the post-Mao period, Xin County officials were early advocates of rural labour outmigration, promoting it as a route out of poverty.[43] In 1984, the county government established a recruitment agency that acted as an intermediary between employers and potential migrant labourers. But the agency found work for only a small quota of villagers each year.

---

41 Xin County Gazetteer Compilation Committee, *Xin County Gazetteer 1986–2005*, 251.
42 Ibid.
43 During the Maoist period, the state severely restricted rural outmigration, especially to the cities. Bans on rural-to-urban migration were enforced through a combination of central planning and a household registration system that prevented those without a local registration booklet from obtaining food and other necessities in the cities' state-run shops. Marketisation in the 1980s led to a breakdown in this system because rural migrants could now circumvent the household registration system and obtain goods on the market. For more on this, see Tamara Jacka, Andrew B. Kipnis, and Sally Sargeson, *Contemporary China: Society and Social Change* (New York: Cambridge University Press, 2013), 65–81, doi.org/10.1017/CBO9781139196178.

Ginkgo Village's quota was filled mostly with men recruited for unskilled construction work.[44] Very few women left the village as migrant labourers in the 1980s.

The picture quickly changed though. By the mid 1990s, a large proportion of both men and women were migrating out. Most went alone or with their spouse, leaving children in the care of grandparents.

Rather than being recruited by the government agency, would-be migrant labourers usually used their own contacts to find work. Most men ended up in the urban construction industry and women worked as agricultural labourers, factory workers and in the service sector. By 2015, 45 per cent of the labour force (360 people, 160 of them women) worked away from home, mostly in China's metropolises, for at least six months each year. Another 100 men and 30 women worked as seasonal labourers, returning home for the busiest agricultural season. On top of this, 306 people (38 per cent of the village labour force) worked overseas.

Xin County labourers began going overseas in significant numbers in the 1990s. At this stage, most had travel and work organised by the Jixing Overseas Labour Company, a new recruitment agency under the auspices of the Xin County Labour Bureau. The state imposed restrictive annual quotas on the number of workers recruited for overseas employment. By the late 1990s, Jixing was already receiving larger quotas than any other intermediary recruitment agency in Henan. Then, in 2000, the company was accredited by the Ministry of Commerce as the only county government intermediary in China with the official right to train and recruit workers for overseas employment.[45]

These unusual privileges most likely derived from the Xin County Government's connections with high-ranking cadres in the military and CCP who came from Xin County. Many of these powerful figures first distinguished themselves in the Eyuwan Soviet. They were so numerous that Xin County has adopted the nickname 'County of Generals' (*Jiangjun*

---

44   Ginkgo Village leaders said they filled the quota with the poorest men, most of whom were the descendants of landlords from Bitter Hollow. Other villagers denied this, saying that village leaders chose their own relatives. The quota probably included people from both groups.

45   Li Xiaoxuan, '成为 "洋工人": 河南省新县对外劳务输出机制研究 [Becoming an "Overseas Worker": Research into the Mechanisms for Exporting Labour in Xin County, Henan Province]' (Master's diss., China Agricultural University, Beijing, 2019), 16–17.

Xian).[46] In 1996, the CCP's powerful Central Commission for Discipline Inspection became the Xin County Government's partner organisation in poverty alleviation work. It's likely that members of the commission from Xin County were the ones who secured its privileges in overseas employment.[47]

Through the first two decades of the twenty-first century, a centre set up by Jixing put potential migrant labourers through a few months' training in etiquette, technical skills and discipline. The labourers were then sent to Japan and South Korea to work in agriculture, construction, manufacturing and processing. In the 2000s, Ginkgo Villagers competed for a place in this program because they could earn up to 10 times more working in Japan and South Korea than they could in China.

In the 2010s, however, the number of people recruited by Jixing declined, in part because migrant wages overseas became less attractive relative to domestic migrant wages. Villagers also found that, while overseas, they lost touch with their networks of contacts in China, so when they came home, they had trouble finding more work.

Another reason was related to the costs of using Jixing as an intermediary. Not only did the company charge a high service fee; villagers also had to forgo wages from domestic migrant work to do the Jixing training.[48] Other, cheaper channels for migration had by then emerged. Aside from there being numerous other private intermediary agencies, it was now relatively easy for villagers to get three-year tourist visas, including to countries like Australia, where higher wages were promised.

By 2015, just about everyone in Ginkgo Village between the ages of 18 and 40 had gone overseas to work. Most had gone only once or twice, for sojourns lasting no more than a few years. Li Wei and I met only two

---

46 Neighbouring Hong'an is another self-identified 'County of Generals'. Altogether, about 10 counties in China have adopted the nickname.
47 Li, 'Becoming an "Overseas Worker"', 16.
48 In the case of South Korea, there was an additional problem: South Korean employers recruited labourers only after they had undergone the training. They recruited only a small proportion of graduates, and recruitment could take months. So, those who undertook the training couldn't be certain that they would be able to recoup the costs of seeking overseas employment through Jixing. For more on this, see Li Xiaoxuan, '移民时代: "流动基础设施"内部不断演变, 出国务工容易了吗? [The Era of Migration: With Constant Developments in "Migration Infrastructure", Has Overseas Labour Migration Become Easier]?', 澎湃新闻 [The Paper], [Shanghai], 11 July 2020, www.thepaper.cn/news Detail_forward_8225916.

villagers with family members living overseas long term.[49] What's more, with each passing year, fewer people were going overseas, even for short periods. Most of those who did seek overseas employment went through private, often illegal, channels rather than via Jixing.

Transformations in village life after outmigration[50]

Mass outmigration led to a cascade of transformations within the village. Here, I will trace the most significant shifts, including those resulting from the contribution that migrant earnings made to villagers' incomes and those driven by the loss of labour power that outmigration entailed.[51]

Migrant earnings greatly boosted villagers' incomes. The average disposable per capita rural income across Xin County increased from 1,188 yuan (US$140) in 1995 to 2,905 yuan (US$360) in 2005. By 2015, it had reached 9,800 yuan (US$1,500)—86 per cent of the national rural average.[52] Newfound prosperity attracted would-be brides. In 2015, there were no 'bare sticks' among Ginkgo Village men aged between 30 and forty.

---

49   In this respect, overseas migration from Ginkgo Village and elsewhere in Xin County has been different to that experienced in villages in some parts of southern China, which have long histories of long-term migration overseas and strong international kinship connections. In the post-Mao period, these latter villages saw the emergence of new cosmopolitan subjectivities and transnational movements of money, people, ideas and cultural practices on a much greater scale than in Xin County. For discussion, see Frank N. Pieke, Pál Nyíri, Mette Thunø, and Antonella Ceccagno, *Transnational Chinese: Fujianese Migrants in Europe* (Stanford, CA: Stanford University Press, 2004); and Julie Y. Chu, *Cosmologies of Credit: Transnational Mobility and the Politics of Destination in China* (Durham, NC: Duke University Press, 2010), doi.org/10.1515/9780822393160.

50   The focus of this book, as of the fieldwork research on which it is based, is transformations within Ginkgo Village and in the lives of those resident in the village. I provide less information about transformations in the lives of villagers who live elsewhere. However, the experiences of a rural migrant worker overseas are discussed in Chapter 6 and the lives of migrant workers in Chinese cities are discussed in Chapters 6, 7 and 9. These accounts are based mainly on reports from people living in the village who had experience of migrant work and conversations with migrant workers returning to the village for the 2018 Lunar New Year.

51   In the following discussion, I do not distinguish between the effects of domestic and overseas migration. The only way in which the specifics of migrants' destinations significantly affected transformations in the village was in relation to the amount of money the migrants earned and remitted. But even in this regard, the difference in impact between domestic and overseas migration was slight. This is both because of the brevity and infrequency of most migrant sojourns overseas and because the gap between domestic and overseas migrant net earnings narrowed over time.

52   Xin County Gazetteer Compilation Committee, *Xin County Gazetteer 1986–2005*, 9–10; Xin County People's Government, 新县年鉴2016 [*Xin County Yearbook 2016*] (Zhengzhou, China: Zhongzhou Guji Chubanshe, 2016), 19; National Bureau of Statistics of China, 'China's Economy Realized a Moderate but Stable and Sound Growth in 2015' (Press release, Beijing, 19 January 2016), www.stats.gov.cn/english/PressRelease/201601/t20160119_1306072.html.

Bigger incomes also contributed to new desires and social expectations for consumption. There were huge increases in spending on children's education, housing, furniture, household appliances including televisions and washing machines and, later, cars, mobile phones, smartphones and televisions with broadband internet connection.[53]

Less predictably, perhaps, when combined with a relaxation of official attitudes towards religious and ritual practices, rising incomes fed increased spending on gift-giving and ritual events like weddings, funerals and New Year. Villagers also donated money for the rebuilding of roadside shrines.

At the same time, variations in villagers' abilities to lift their incomes through outmigration led to greater inequalities in income, consumption and living standards. At one end of the wealth spectrum, several men in Ginkgo Village who had been among the earliest cohort of migrant labourers in the 1980s and had continued both domestic and overseas migrant employment through the ensuing decades had accumulated capital and become successful entrepreneurs. By 2015, their individual annual disposable incomes amounted to between 1 and 3 million yuan (US$154,000–462,000). They had long since left Ginkgo Village, accompanied by their families. At the other extreme, a handful of poverty-stricken villagers had annual disposable incomes of no more than 3,000 yuan (US$460) per person. I will say more about their situations shortly.

Within the village, the extent of the gap between these two extremes in wealth was less obvious, for the simple reason that the wealthiest households had moved away. But new inequalities were still apparent, especially in relation to housing. Better-off households used migrant earnings to build large new houses in the village with amenities such as running water and flush toilets. Most of these houses were incomplete and many stood empty but others were occupied, mostly by middle-aged women and children left behind by their migrant menfolk. In contrast, poorer households, most of whom were elderly individuals and couples, lived alone in older, smaller and more dilapidated houses and were less likely to have toilets or running water.

Outmigration didn't just increase inequalities in income, consumption and living standards. It also transformed power relations between women and men. The impact was mixed: on the one hand, women's work away from

---

53   By 2015, 98 per cent of households had at least one mobile phone and 22.5 per cent had broadband internet connection.

home and the incomes they earned sometimes boosted their confidence and increased their bargaining power in household decision-making. On the other hand, the wages that married women could earn as migrant workers were generally lower than their husbands'. In part because of this, mothers were far more likely than their husbands to withdraw from migrant work to care for their children. These trends perpetuated wives' financial disadvantage and dependency on their husbands, which in turn undermined their bargaining power in the household.

New forms of intergenerational inequality emerged, too. Not only did many elderly parents live in old, substandard housing in the village with lower incomes than their adult children. Loneliness and lack of physical support and care were also serious concerns, especially for the frailest living alone in the more remote hamlets. A more widespread problem was the burden of work that older village residents felt compelled to take on.

This leads me to the second set of village transformations driven by outmigration, which stemmed from the loss of labour power in the village. They began with shifts in gender and intergenerational divisions of labour and heavy workloads for older people remaining in the village, especially mothers and grandmothers left with burdens of child care as well as farm work.

For many, the workload was unsustainable. So, in the 2010s, a large and increasing proportion of villagers gave up rice-growing and began buying the rice they ate. In some fields, they replaced their rice crops with China firs. Others they stopped irrigating, turning them over to less water and labour-intensive crops such as peanuts and canola. They subcontracted or gave away some paddy fields and simply abandoned others, especially inaccessible plots high in the hills and those in the valleys that were too small or too boggy for tractors.

This historic withdrawal from rice-growing spurred two further shifts: the merging of numerous small landholdings into large tracts, controlled by just two businessmen; and a decline in animal husbandry.[54]

The third major consequence of outmigration was a shift in marriage patterns, family living arrangements and residence patterns, and ties between kin. First, outmigration led to a small increase in interprovincial marriages.

---

54 These trends are explained in Chapters 4 and 9, respectively.

As mentioned, in 2015, there were 18 women from other provinces among the married women in Ginkgo Village. All 10 of the Han women had met their husbands while working as migrant labourers. Among the eight non-Han women, three had been trafficked and sold into marriage with poor Ginkgo Village men unable to afford the local bride price. The remaining five non-Han wives had met their husbands while working as migrant labourers.

Outmigration, increased incomes and mobility among young married couples led to bigger shifts in patterns of residence and living arrangements. Until the twenty-first century, most of Ginkgo Village's newly married couples lived with the husband's family at least until their first child was a year old and often much longer. At some stage, though, the family would divide its property between parents and sons (a process known as *fenjia*) and all but one son would set up separate households. Usually, though, sons moved their wives and children no further than a building adjacent to their parents' house. In the 2000s, families divided increasingly early and new couples lived at greater distances from the old family home.

Then, in the 2010s, two new trends emerged. First, a minority of villagers found secure, well-paying urban jobs or succeeded in business and moved permanently out of the village. They established a new home in the city where they worked and their spouse, children and in some cases ageing parents lived with them. Second, it became increasingly common for young mothers to withdraw from migrant labour to care for their children. Usually, they rented or bought an apartment in Red River Township or Xin County City. Some parents and parents-in-law remained in the village. Others moved with a daughter-in-law or divided their time between the village and their adult children's town residences.

Meanwhile, young people were losing interest in village property as well as in farming and living in the village. This contributed to a decline in the formal practice of family division.

Another reason for the decline of family division was younger women's need for childcare help from their mother-in-law. Not everyone had access to such help. Some mothers of small children had mothers-in-law who supported other family members but not them. In other cases, the mother-in-law had died or was too frail to care for young children. This problem led increasing numbers of young mothers to rely on their own mothers for support. In some instances, villagers entered living arrangements that were previously unheard of: parents lived with their daughter and son-in-law instead of their son and daughter-in-law.

Outmigration and the dispersal of villagers also led to some weakening of kinship ties. However, such ties continued to be important well into the twenty-first century. They were maintained through Lunar New Year rituals, weddings, funerals and other ritual get-togethers, through obligatory gift-giving and lending between kin, and via new technologies, including smartphones and social media.[55]

*

Aside from the return to family farming and the promotion of outmigration, two other shifts in state policy in the post-Mao period had a major role in transforming villagers' lives. Let's look at these in chronological order.

Birth planning

In 1979, even before the return to family farming, the state introduced the strict One-Child Policy.[56] This was met with strong resistance. In Xin County at the time, village women commonly gave birth to at least four children and, unlike in the past, most survived. Son preference and the need for at least one son to provide support for ageing parents and to carry on the male family line were felt especially keenly in these parts. Indeed, the need for sons and the stigma attached to being sonless remained strong in Ginkgo Village even in the 2010s. Above all else, it was this need for sons that fuelled villagers' resistance to the One-Child Policy.

County and township officials faced with sanctions for failing to meet birth reduction targets responded with brutality. They forced village women to abort, imposed harsh fines and confiscated property. For their part, some

---

55   Ownership of smartphones and the use of social media platforms, especially WeChat, became widespread among young and middle-aged Ginkgo Villagers from the mid 2000s. They were important for social networking and accessing information. For more on this topic, see Tom McDonald, *Social Media in Rural China: Social Networks and Moral Frameworks* (London: UCL Press, 2016), doi.org/ 10.2307/j.ctt1g69xx3.

56   For an annotated bibliography on China's One-Child Policy, see Martin K. Whyte, 'China's One Child Policy', in *Oxford Bibliographies in Childhood Studies* (Oxford, UK: Oxford University Press, 2019), doi.org/10.1093/OBO/9780199791231-0221.

villagers paid for the sex of their foetus to be tested and, if it was female, aborted it. Others killed or hid baby girls so they would have another chance to have a son.[57]

Most provinces, including Henan, loosened the birth planning rules at the beginning of the 1990s. From then on, after waiting four years and provided the annual collective birth target hadn't been exceeded, rural parents whose first child was a girl were permitted to try for a son.

The ban on a second birth after a son remained in place until 2016. From the mid 2000s, however, local officials became less coercive in enforcing this rule. Many Ginkgo Villagers limited themselves to one son in the 1990s, but, seeing the situation had eased, tried for another a decade later. A few couples were able to pull strings and escape the worst punishment, but many more paid dearly for their second child.

After 2016, things relaxed even further and some couples dared to try yet again. It was not until 2021 that the Three-Child Policy came into effect across China.

State investment in poverty alleviation, infrastructure and welfare

Another transformative shift in post-Mao state policy related to poverty alleviation and investment in village infrastructure and welfare. From the mid 2000s, concern about mounting rural–urban inequalities and rural disadvantage led the state to introduce a series of overlapping measures known as the Construction of a New Socialist Countryside (*Xin Nongcun Jianshe*) campaign, including poverty alleviation and improvements in villager welfare.

From Ginkgo Villagers' perspectives, the most important of these were the 2006 removal of agricultural taxes and the 2007 abolition of tuition fees for nine years of compulsory schooling.

---

57 One indication of the prevalence of such practices is an abnormally high male–female child sex ratio. According to 1982 and 1990 census data, Xin County's male–female sex ratio was 114.1:100 and 111.2:100, respectively (Xinyang Prefecture Local Histories and Gazetteers Compilation Committee, *Xinyang Prefecture Gazetteer*, 856–67). Ginkgo Village Director Zhou said that among those born in the village between 1989 and 2001, only 40 per cent were women. For further discussion, see Laurel Bossen, 'Reproduction and Real Property in Rural China: Three Decades of Development and Discrimination', in *Women, Gender and Rural Development in China*, eds Tamara Jacka and Sally Sargeson (Cheltenham, UK: Edward Elgar, 2011), 97–123, doi.org/10.4337/9780857933546.00014.

The state also introduced new welfare schemes. Two contribution schemes, rural cooperative medical insurance and a rural old-age pension, were launched nationwide in 2003 and 2009, respectively. New non-contributory welfare payments were also introduced. Before the twenty-first century, the most important such payment in rural China had been for *wubaohu* ('five-guarantee' households)—those needing care, who had no family to support them. Disaster relief was also sometimes given. Then, in 2007, the state boosted non-contributory welfare funding by extending its *dibao* ('minimum livelihood guarantee') scheme to disadvantaged rural, as well as urban, residents.[58]

By 2015, just over 90 per cent of Ginkgo Villagers were paying 90 yuan (US$14) each year to receive medical insurance. All 260 villagers over the age of 60 received a pension of 60 yuan (US$9) a month. Sixteen of these also received a special annual payment of 7,000 yuan (US$1,100), given to army veterans from Eyuwan Soviet days and their descendants. And four elderly men received an annual *wubaohu* payment of about 2,000 yuan (US$300). Two of these men were sent to live free of charge in Red River's elderly care home. The other two wanted to join them, but there were no places left. Another three people received a disaster relief payment at the end of 2014 of 300–800 yuan (US$40–120) in cash, plus 200 yuan (US$30) worth of cooking oil, rice and wheat flour. Ninety-one people received about 100 yuan (US$15) a month in *dibao*.

Through the late 2000s and 2010s, provincial and county governments also increased funding for rural infrastructure. Another new medical clinic was built in 2009 and the village government office buildings were renovated the following year. Ginkgo Village's roads were concreted between 2010 and 2013.

Village leaders also received funds for the Construction of a Beautiful Countryside (*Meili Xiangcun Jianshe*) program. In 2014, they spent these funds beautifying the hamlet of Twin Maidens Shrine and paving a square in Five Hills Hamlet. Then, in early 2015, the Red River Township Government installed concrete garbage tanks along the main road through Ginkgo Village. They employed a couple of older men to sweep the sides of the road and began a garbage collection service, with a truck coming once a week to empty the tanks.

---

58   Joe C.B. Leung and Yuebin Xu, *China's Social Welfare: The Third Turning Point* (Cambridge, UK: Polity Press, 2015). For discussion of rural *dibao*, see also Christof Lammer, 'Care Scales: *Dibao* Allowances, State and Family in China', *The China Quarterly* 254 (2023): 310–24, doi.org/10.1017/S0305741023000309.

Plate 1.4 Garbage collection, main road
Photo: Tamara Jacka, 2015.

In 2016, further state funds were provided for the repair of hamlet ponds and the laying of pipes to provide running water to houses along the main road and in a couple of hamlets in the hills.[59]

These projects were undertaken as part of a new poverty alleviation strategy introduced by Xi Jinping's leadership in 2013. With this new strategy came a doubling in the central government's budget devoted to poverty alleviation between 2012 and 2018[60] and a national goal of overcoming poverty by 2020. Xin County officials went one better: they embraced a commitment to lift the county out of poverty by 2017.

---

59   Most households across the village had already installed pipes to take water from mountain springs into their homes, but these sources often dried up during droughts.
60   Camille Boullenois, 'Poverty Alleviation in China: The Rise of State-Sponsored Corporate Paternalism', *China Perspectives* 3 (2020a): 47–56, at 47, doi.org/10.4000/chinaperspectives.10456.

Aside from infrastructural developments, household poverty alleviation was achieved in Ginkgo Village through a range of subsidies.[61] These included payments for emergency medical care and scholarships for secondary school and university students. In 2016–17, subsidies worth a total of 4,000 yuan (US$600) over two years were also given to households raising domestic livestock.

Another set of payments was for housing. By the 2000s, residents in White Cloud Hamlet and the upper reaches of Twin Maidens Shrine had been offered subsidies to move out of their old houses, buy land, and build and resettle into new housing closer to the centre of the village, where amenities were more accessible. Most had accepted the subsidies and abandoned their old houses. From 2014, more people living in decrepit old housing were offered subsidies to help them rebuild in the village or buy apartments in Red River.

At the beginning of 2014, Ginkgo Village was one of 73 villages in Xin County officially labelled 'poor'. Thirty-two per cent (146) of its households had a total gross annual income below the local poverty line of 2,736 yuan (US$437.80) per person. By the end of the year, all but two households had been officially lifted out of poverty. The first of the remaining poor households comprised a frail older couple and their mentally disabled unmarried daughter living in the upper reaches of Twin Maidens Shrine. The second was a household in White Cloud Hamlet comprising a physically disabled man and his ageing mother.

In 2017, the local poverty line was raised to 3,026 yuan (US$466). This added another household to the list of those still classified as poor. This one, in Stone Gully, comprised a recently widowed woman with two children in secondary school.

Speaking with Li Wei and me in August 2017, Accountant Wu was confident that the three remaining poor households could be relieved of their poverty by the end of the year, at least 'on paper'. But they would continue to live in miserable conditions.

---

61   The following is a description of only those subsidies considered most important by Ginkgo Villagers. For further discussion of the subsidies and other aspects of the targeted poverty alleviation campaign in Xin County, see Zhang Yangyang, Xinye Zheng, and Lunyu Xie, 'How Do Poverty Alleviation Coordinators Help the Impoverished in Rural China? Evidence from the Chinese Poor Population Tracking Dataset', *China Economic Review* 69 (2021): 101686, doi.org/10.1016/j.chieco.2021.101686. For a more general discussion, see Suyuan He and Weiye Wang, 'Social Resources Transfer Program Under China's Targeted Poverty Alleviation Strategy: Rural Social Structure and Local Politics', *Journal of Contemporary China* 32, no. 142 (2023): 686–703, doi.org/10.1080/10670564.2022.2109844.

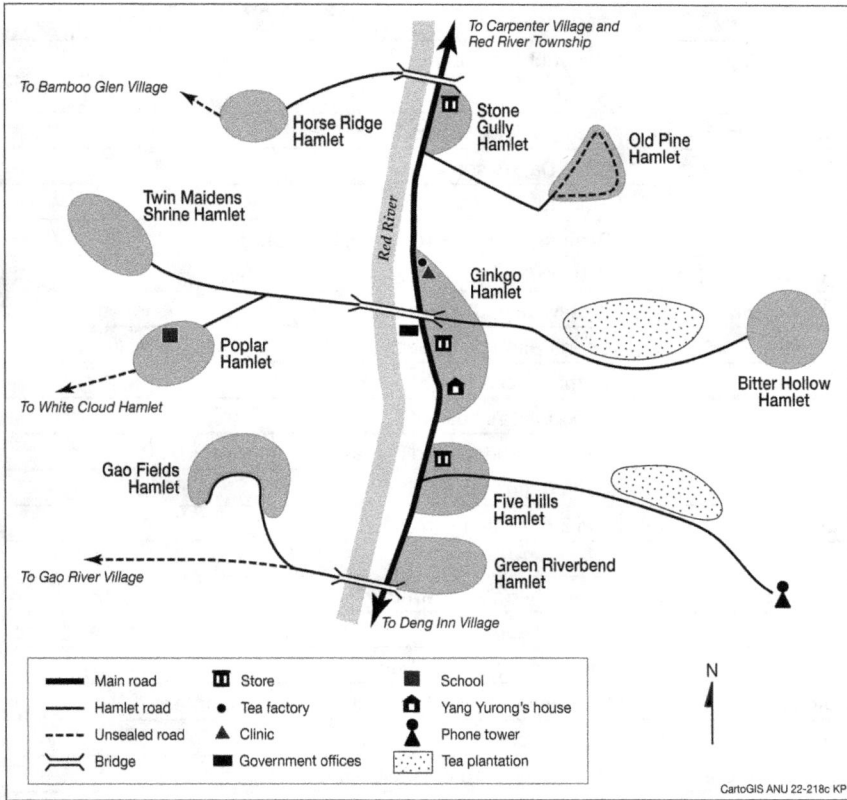

Map 1.1 Ginkgo Village, including only those hamlets named in the book
Source: CartoGIS ANU.

Table 1.1 Cast of characters

Name	Description
Accountant Wu	Ginkgo Village accountant
Aunty Gao	Lives in Ginkgo Hamlet; raises chickens (Chapters 7, 9, Epilogue)
Baobao	Huang Zhiwu's daughter (deceased)
Baoli	Yang Yurong's younger son
Cao Fuguo	Former village Party secretary (appropriates land, Chapter 4)
Chen Dajin	Protagonist, Chapter 6
Chen sisters	Gao Xiuhua's childhood friends
Deng Jinmei	Gao Xihua's mother
Director Zhou	Head of Ginkgo Village committee
Fang Wenli	Yang Yurong's friend with a pig farm (Chapter 9)

Name	Description
Gao Delong	Gao Xiuhua's father
Gao Deyi	Gao Xiuhua's uncle
Gao Xiuhua	Protagonist, Chapter 3
Guotao	Chen Dajin's son
Hu Xiaoming	Suicide victim (Chapter 5)
Huang Dajun	Businessman (appropriates land, Chapter 4)
Huang Zhengjun	Father of twins in village myth (Chapter 2)
Huang Zhiwu	Protagonist, Chapter 2
Huifen	Chen Dajin's daughter
Laoshi	Author/researcher
Li Changyin	Gao Xiuhua's husband
Li Wei	Laoshi's student and research assistant
Liang Anqin	Chen Dajin's wife
Little Dog	Tan Zimei's son
Marcus	Laoshi's brother
Meiling	Chen Dajin's sister-in-law
Misha	Laoshi's son
Mrs Cao	Yang Yurong's neighbour
Old Liu	Lives in Ginkgo Hamlet, raises ducks (Chapters 7, 9)
Old Wu	Zhang Hongren's neighbour
Party Secretary Guo	Head of Ginkgo Village Communist Party branch
Renkai	Yang Yurong's older son
Tan Zimei	Protagonist, Chapter 8
Tommy	Laoshi's brother (deceased)
Wang Shifu	Protagonist, Chapter 5
Wang Xinran	Zhang Hongren's friend
Widower Yang	Protagonist, vignette at start of Introduction
Widow Zhou	Deceased (funeral described in Chapter 5)
Women's Director Liu	Ginkgo Village women's director
Wu Jianfu	Yang Yurong's husband (Chapters 7, 9)
Wu Weiying	Gao Xiuhua's aunt
Xiaobing	Gao Xiuhua's grandson
Yang Yurong	Wu Jianfu's wife (Chapters 7, 9)
Ye Yuzhen	Huang Zhiwu's wife
Zhang Hongren	Protagonist, Chapter 4
Zhao Ling	Bandmaster's wife (Chapter 5)

2

Ghosts

Ginkgo Village is full of the ghosts of children and youths. They haunt rivers, roads and bridges. I don't believe in ghosts and villagers say they don't either. But they tell their stories.

Some of the stories are old; some are new. Some of the youngsters were treasured by their parents; some were not. Some died of illness; others came from hamlets torched by bandits, revolutionaries or soldiers. Some drowned in floods. Others were felled by starvation or disease. Baby girls were smothered at birth. Teenagers were raped and murdered. One young newlywed killed herself. One boy's corpse was found, its organs stolen.

Some ghosts have been given special offerings. They wander about the village, peaceful and unseen. Others have been neglected. These ghosts rage down the years, decades, centuries—ugly and vengeful. If you're not careful, there'll be one who will flay you with her bloody knife.[1]

I will tell you two stories about young people who died and became ghosts. The first is about twin girls, and the second is about a baby. The stories are separated by many decades: the baby was killed in 1959, while the twins died in the 1800s. The stories also feel different. The baby's story is an angry

---

1   In Chinese culture, the souls of family members who have died young without descendants are not accorded the same ritual treatment as those with descendants. They become ghosts, rather than ancestors. Ghosts are seen as unfortunate and potentially dangerous beings. However, if treated with respect and sympathy, they won't harm the living. I return to this topic in Chapter 5. See also Arthur P. Wolf, 'Gods, Ghosts, and Ancestors', in *Studies in Chinese Society*, ed. Arthur P. Wolf (Stanford, CA: Stanford University Press, 1978), 131–82, doi.org/10.1515/9781503620803-005; Stephan Feuchtwang, *Popular Religion in China: The Imperial Metaphor* (Richmond, UK: Curzon, 2001); Kipnis, *The Funeral of Mr Wang*.

splinter. That of the twins is a fairytale, smoothed by the passage of time. In my mind, though, the stories are connected because Li Wei and I heard them from the same person: an older man by the name of Huang Zhiwu.

He and his wife, Ye Yuzhen, live in Twin Maidens Shrine Hamlet, which village leaders recently did up with state funds for the Construction of a Beautiful Countryside program. Accountant Wu said they chose to spend the money in this hamlet because it was already beautiful. It has a square with a graceful ginkgo tree in the centre. The original tree was cut down in 1958, at the start of the Great Leap Forward, but it was replaced in the 1990s.

The square has been laid with swirls of rough grey paving stones to make it look traditional. Around the square, the houses have been whitewashed. To one side, a wall has been painted with propaganda pictures urging youngsters to uphold their filial duties and care for their elders. On another side, colourful metal exercise equipment has been installed for use by the hamlet's older residents. It stands unused.

Huang Zhiwu and Ye Yuzhen live at the end of the row of houses overlooking the ginkgo tree. Like all the other houses in the row, its front has been newly cleaned and whitewashed, but it remains dingy inside.

They make an odd couple. Ye Yuzhen sags like a dusty, bruised peach. When we meet her on the road, she just nods before shuffling on. When we visit their home, she usually avoids us.

Huang Zhiwu is stooped and thin. He has a worn black cap, stubbly chin and knobbly hands. When he speaks, I glimpse gaps and yellowed stumps.

He's a garrulous fellow, though he doesn't like our questions about everyday life.

'Why ask about such trivial things?' he says gruffly.

I tell him again: 'I want to write a book about Chinese villagers' lives. I won't give your real name or the name of the village. But I want to hear the story of your life. Then I'll tell other foreigners, so they'll understand. The book will be a bridge between people.'

Others seem to like that idea, but Huang Zhiwu accepts it only grudgingly. He knits his wiry eyebrows.

'I'll tell you about the Civil War,' he says. 'People should know about that.'

His uncle, he says proudly, fought in the Communist Red Army. 'He lost his life in the Fifth Encirclement, just before I was born.'

He likes to tell stories about his ancestors, too. On one of our visits, he brought out his genealogy for Li Wei and me to admire. 'There are 24 generations of us around here,' he said, pushing his shoulders back. 'I belong to the twenty-third.'

The genealogy is a heavy red brick of a book with long lists of men and a few women surnamed Huang who've excelled as scholars and bureaucrats. This volume was put together a few years ago. It's an updated, condensed version of one compiled in 1994 from records from the 1940s. They had to hide the old records after Liberation. No-one dared bring them out again until the 1990s.[2]

Li Wei scans the genealogy avidly and takes photos of several pages with her smartphone. I'm not so interested. It's full of pompous, flowery language I can't understand. Huang Zhiwu probably can't understand it either. Not that either of us will admit that.

*

On another visit, Huang Zhiwu took us to see the shrine after which Twin Maidens Shrine Hamlet is named. It sits on the outskirts of the hamlet, 20 minutes' walk further up the hill. The hill is steep and Huang Zhiwu is surprisingly nimble. He's only chest-high to me and Li Wei. Childhood undernourishment has left the oldest villagers with such small stature. I lumber along, feeling big and awkward in my baggy bushwalking gear. Li Wei trots beside me in her tight jeans, her long hair tied back. She looks so trim.

We stop near the top of the hill. Most of the houses up here have been abandoned. They stand reverential in the still air. The forest is crowding in: oriental oaks, China firs, bamboo and trailing kudzu vine. A strange scent encircles us—some flowering plant I suppose. The green tree canopy is singing with birds I can't identify.

2   Each of Ginkgo Village's five main lineage groups has compiled at least one genealogy since the 1990s. For more on genealogies, see Frank N. Pieke, 'The Genealogical Mentality in Modern China', *Journal of Asian Studies* 62, no. 1 (2003): 101–28, doi.org/10.2307/3096137.

The shrine is surrounded by tall weeds. As we step off the path towards it, clouds of insects rise. Li Wei bats at them as we push through, moaning in distress. I chuckle to myself. Both she and I have led comfortable urban lives, but even before I began doing fieldwork in rural China, I'd been exposed to more nature than Li Wei. She grew up in an apartment near the centre of the northern Chinese city of Shenyang. In contrast, from the age of five, I lived in a large suburban house in the Adelaide Hills in South Australia, surrounded by bushland. What's more, I spent my school holidays camping and bushwalking with my family. I'm more used than Li Wei to long weeds and creepy crawlies. Her parents wouldn't have dreamt of inflicting a rugged outdoor holiday on their daughter.

As we get closer, we see that the weeds have been cut and cleared away in front of the shrine's door. Ye Yuzhen did that. She and Huang Zhiwu come up here on the fifteenth day of every lunar month to clear the weeds, sweep inside and burn a few sticks of incense. At the Lunar New Year and on Ghost Day,[3] they burn spirit-money and set off firecrackers in a cleared space outside. Other residents of Twin Maidens Shrine go to the hamlet's second shrine, down by the road that leads to the centre of Ginkgo Village. At New Year, some have their adult sons drive them all the way to the giant temple at the top of Mount Phoenix, resplendent with its new gold Buddha. But Ye Yuzhen and Huang Zhiwu come here and here alone.

It doesn't look like a shrine: it's just a grey mudbrick and stone house with a roof of broken tiles. There's carved stonework above the doorway. It's badly eroded, but we can just make out three small figures in decorated gowns. On either side of the old wooden door and above the stonework, Huang Zhiwu has stuck red strips of paper featuring *duilian* (rhyming couplets). On each wing of the door, he's pasted images of bug-eyed door gods in martial get-up, brandishing halberds. The door is bolted with a heavy padlock, but Huang Zhiwu has the key.

---

3   Ghost Day, also known as the Ghost Festival or Hungry Ghost Festival, occurs on the fifteenth day of the seventh month of the lunar calendar. On this day, villagers pay their respects and seek to absolve the suffering of family members who have died, including ghosts as well as ancestors. This day is different from Tomb-Sweeping Day (held on the fifteenth day after the spring equinox), the Double Ninth Festival (the ninth day of the ninth lunar month) and the Lantern Festival (the fifteenth day of the first lunar month). On these last days, only ancestors are paid homage.

'This shrine was built during the reign of the Daoguang Emperor,'[4] he tells us as we make our way inside. A faint trace of sandalwood drifts on the air. The shrine has one large main room and a smaller side room. At the back of the main room, there once stood an altar with a wooden tablet for Guanyin.[5] It was smashed by the the people's militia in 1966, at the start of the Cultural Revolution. In the 1980s, the shrine was turned into a distillery. You can still see a couple of concrete troughs and some strange-looking equipment in the side room. The distillery went bust after only a year. Then, for a while, a mentally ill man camped inside. But he's long since disappeared.

A leggy table now stands in place of the altar. Huang Zhiwu put it there. On its wrinkled top, he and Ye Yuzhen stick their incense in a little bowl of sand. They bow to Guanyin, though her tablet has gone. High above, the beams of the dragon-gate roof frame are black and draped with spider webs.

*

As you've probably guessed by now, the twin maidens after whom the shrine and hamlet are named are the young twins whose story I want to tell. Huang Zhiwu recounted it at New Year 2018. Li Wei and I felt we knew him quite well by then. The three of us sat in the heating-room (*kaohuo de wuzi*)[6] at the side of his house, warming ourselves around the woodstove. It wasn't the first time Li Wei and I had heard the story, but I'll tell you Huang Zhiwu's version because I like it best.

In fact, the twin maidens were only girls, just entering their teenage years. Their father, Huang Zhengjun, was the fourth son of a well-off landowner, who had made his money through farming and trade. They lived in a large courtyard home, near where Huang Zhiwu lives now, a short distance from the ginkgo tree. In time, Huang Zhengjun married and had four sons as well as twin daughters.

Huang Zhengjun's father was an evil tyrant and so were his older brothers. But Huang Zhengjun was a gentle, cultured soul. He had two great loves. He loved to escape from the troubles of this world and walk into the mountains. There, he'd write poems about raindrops on bamboo and the whisper of a breeze on his face. Or he'd climb higher, perch on

---

4   The Qing Dynasty's Daoguang Emperor reigned from 1820 to 1850.
5   Guanyin, the Goddess of Mercy, is China's female-gendered Bodhisattva Avalokiteśvara.
6   Literally, a 'room for warming oneself by a fire'.

a rock and listen for the cry of the golden eagle. He also loved his twin daughters to a degree that others found strange. He watched them as they sat embroidering cloth shoes for their dowries.

They were willowy girls, full of mischief. Their mother had bound their feet as tight as she could manage, but they were not to be tamed. They twittered and skipped; they danced and played. You couldn't see their pain. They laughed and sang through their courtyard home, weaving through the inner sleeping quarters and colonnades and around the plum trees in the central courtyard. They even pulled open the heavy doors at the front and ran out. Their uncles and brothers fumed; their mother bowed her head in shame. But their father did nothing to stop them.

One spring night, after everyone else had retired, the girls crept outside and down the hill. The air was crisp and clear. A full moon beamed its liquid light on the ginkgo tree, and they saw that it was flowering. They stopped in wonder, for they'd never seen a ginkgo's flowers before. They didn't stay out long. But it was long enough.

The next day they sat meekly at their embroidery. They both looked pale. Each girl stitched a spray of white ginkgo flowers onto the tiny shoe in her lap. They retired early. The following morning, a servant found them curled in each other's arms and went to shake them awake. They were cold and lifeless.

When he learnt about his daughters' passing, Huang Zhengjun wailed and tore his hair. Then he slid into a dark silence. His sons and brothers were left to ensure the girls' corpses were disposed of properly. Being young and childless, they couldn't be buried in the family grave plot. After several days, Huang Zhengjun roused himself. The family, he said, must pay for a shrine to be built as a memorial for the two girls. At first, his brothers baulked at this. The family was not so wealthy that they could afford such a thing, they protested. But after a while, they relented. Perhaps, they thought, a shrine would appease the girls' ghosts, so they wouldn't wreak havoc on the rest of the family. This was not how Huang Zhengjun thought about it; he didn't believe in ghosts. But it was a traditional thing to do that others understood.

Meanwhile, rumours flew about how the girls had died. Some said they'd been struck down by a terrible disease; others that they'd been poisoned. But the explanation that stuck and was handed down from one generation to another was that they died because they saw the flowers of the ginkgo tree. It was said that the ginkgo flowers only very rarely and no-one who sees the flowers survives to tell the tale.

*

The other villagers who told us this story mostly laughed it off. They didn't believe this stuff about ginkgo flowers any more than Li Wei and I did.[7] But when we asked Huang Zhiwu if he really thought the twins had died from seeing the flowers, he merely smiled. Perhaps that's why I love his version of the story best—that, and his lilting storyteller voice, so different from his everyday one.

Huang Zhiwu didn't recount the story quite as I've told it here, but I haven't changed much. If the tale is a tree, I've given it more leaves. I wanted you to have more of a feeling for the times and the place and the people. Huang Zhiwu said the father was gentle and cultured, but I added his two loves. I imagine him as a model Chinese gentleman-scholar.[8] He's like my own dad, too: a quiet, decent man. My dad died many years ago and I miss him.

And the twins? Huang Zhiwu said nothing about their characters, so their delightfulness is entirely made up. I'm not sure where the girls came from. I feel as though they danced their way into the story all by themselves. They could have come either from a Chinese story or from the fairytales read to me during my European–Anglo-Australian childhood. They seem to have wafted in from some lost age of innocence. I wonder about that.

I wonder, too, at my desire to repeat this fantasy. Chinese village life in the 1800s was riven by injustice. In real life, the girls' father probably exploited those who worked for him, including his wife. And maybe he loved his daughters dearly or maybe he didn't. Perhaps he abused them. What if the girls didn't die from seeing the ginkgo flowers or from disease? What if they hanged themselves from the ginkgo tree, having been raped repeatedly by their father, grandfather, uncles or brothers?

---

7   Ginkgo trees don't bear flowers. The 'flowers' the girls embroidered were probably the cones produced by the male ginkgo tree. These are pale green and covered with pollen balls that, once ripened and open, are white.

8   The name I have given him, Zhengjun, means 'upright gentleman'.

And what about the girls' mother? She must also have had bound feet and been in agony as she went about her tasks and tried to keep her daughters in check. What did she feel when the girls died? Did she feel guilty and even more grief-stricken than her husband? Or just relieved?

I am a feminist. So, where did the impulse come from to shape this story as a charming tale and not a thing of pain and horror? I thought these were peaceful ghosts, but perhaps they're not.

***

The second story is about the death of Huang Zhiwu's own daughter. The old man told Li Wei and me what happened the first time we met him, long before we heard the story of the twin maidens.

It was late May 2015, towards the end of our first visit to Ginkgo Village. One night, the village leaders took us to a banquet, plied us with liquor and kept us up late. So, we were feeling hungover and sorry for ourselves. We stayed inside the next morning, typing up our fieldnotes. But, by the afternoon, we'd tired. My hands ached from so much typing.

We decided to go to Twin Maidens Shrine Hamlet as we hadn't yet interviewed anyone there. It's a fair walk from Yang Yurong's place: north along the main road, across the river just past the government office buildings, down another road through a flat expanse of fields and up the hill on the other side. My head was pounding. We paused in the hamlet square to catch our breath and admire the ginkgo's delicate fan-shaped leaves. I peeled my heavy daypack off my shoulders and took my water bottle out for a swig.

Huang Zhiwu sat on a stool just outside his front door wearing a loose blue cotton jacket and flip-flops, his grey trousers rolled halfway up his ropey calves. As we came up the hill, he stood to greet us. We explained who we were and what we were doing and he invited us in for a cup of tea. I don't know where Ye Yuzhen was that afternoon; she didn't appear.

Even with the door open, the front room was dim and cool and slightly sour smelling. It felt hollow. On the back wall was the family altar: a battered old wooden cabinet with bits of spent candles on top. Above it hung Huang Zhiwu's ancestral scroll. The newer scrolls bought in town have three or five panels of cheery pictures and gold lettering and they're either laminated or behind glass. They're hard to photograph because their surface reflects the light. But this one was just a single piece of dull, dark-red paper, three columns of handwritten black calligraphy stumbling down it.

I struggled to read the handwriting while waiting for Huang Zhiwu. He'd gone out the back to make tea.

'What does the central column say?' I asked Li Wei.

'*Zuzong zhaomu shenwei*,' she read out: 'A scroll to show reverence to the ancestors.'

'Huh. Same as all the others.'

Li Wei nodded.

To one side of the family altar was an ancient bicycle and a sack of rice sat next to the door leading to the back of the house. Li Wei nudged me: several empty liquor bottles leaned on the top and to the side of the rice sack. I remember that now because it's the only village house in which we saw signs of heavy drinking outside the New Year period.

Huang Zhiwu came back with three mugs, which he put on a small square table in the middle of the room. We sat on low wooden stools around it. There was no other furniture. I had to put my daypack on the dirty concrete floor.

Once settled with our notebooks in our laps, Li Wei and I began asking Huang Zhiwu simple questions about himself and his family. We learned that he was born in 1936 and Ye Yuzhen in 1938. They were married in 1956. They have a son, four daughters and seven grandchildren.

For the better part of an hour, we talked about all the children and grandchildren. Huang Zhiwu was getting restless. I, too, felt uncomfortable and was finding it hard to keep track of who was who.

I reached forward for my tea and tried to change the topic: 'Grandpa, can you tell us about the early years of your marriage? What was your life like then?'

He looked away. 'It was the time of the Great Famine.'

'Your son was born just beforehand, right?' I quickly scanned my notes.

'Yes, in 1957. The others were all born afterwards.'

'Did your wife give birth to any other children? Were there any who didn't survive to adulthood?'

For a moment, Huang Zhiwu just stared at me, his gnarled hands gripping his knees. 'We had another daughter,' he said finally. 'She died aged two months. December 1959. We were working on the reservoir out beyond Red River. There was no-one else to care for the baby, so my old woman had it with her while she worked. One day, she left it swaddled in a corner of the sleeping shack. Another woman went in there to rest. She saw a bundle on the ground and sat on it. She killed it.'

*

I'm ashamed to admit that Li Wei and I recorded only the bare facts of this account in our fieldnotes. Neither of us wrote anything about either Huang Zhiwu's expression while he was recounting the story or our own emotions on hearing it. And now I can't remember. I honestly don't know whether I was blindsided by the banal horror of the story or so tired and hungover that I couldn't take it in. The winter of 1959–60 was the height of the Great Famine, in which tens of millions of people across China starved to death. Perhaps I was so intent on hearing one story that I scarcely noticed another, different one.

Nor did we learn more about the baby's death later. Neither Li Wei nor I ever brought it up again with either Huang Zhiwu or Ye Yuzhen. I wish I could say we made a considered decision not to probe any further on such a sensitive issue. But that's not what happened. Fear comes closer to the truth. And not knowing how to ask. And thinking we should look for the typical, not waste time on one individual family's unique tragedy. And we ought to be able to imagine what it must have been like; we didn't need to ask.

But in the years since Li Wei and I last talked with the couple, this story has haunted me. The more I try to block it out, the more it boomerangs back. My mind snags on trivial details. Did Ye Yuzhen put her baby to the breast before lying her down? Was her daughter sleeping when she was sat on? How long was it before she died? Did the woman who sat on her realise she'd killed a baby? What was the baby swaddled in: Was it a jacket or a blanket or just a rag full of holes? Was it thick or thin? What colour was it? Did Ye Yuzhen weave the cloth herself? Did she bury her baby in it or did she keep it?

Of all the ghosts in Ginkgo Village, this baby's is the one that troubles me most. I'm not sure why. Is it because I understand the tragedy of her death and the grief of her parents? Or is it because I don't understand and never will?

I don't know the baby's name or even whether she had been given a name before she died. I'll call her Baobao. It means 'darling' or 'baby'. I don't know exactly how Baobao died—whether she was crushed or suffocated. And I don't know how her parents felt about her death when it happened and how they feel about it all these years later.

I don't even know whether Huang Zhiwu told us the truth. Perhaps Baobao wasn't sat on. What if she starved to death? Or Ye Yuzhen had nothing to feed the baby and she just faded away. Or what if Ye Yuzhen suffocated Baobao herself? Or Huang Zhiwu did. And what happened to Baobao's body afterwards? It's unlikely she was given a funeral. Probably, they didn't even take her body back to the village; they just scratched a shallow grave somewhere and went back to work. Perhaps a fellow villager came afterwards, dug up the corpse and ate it.

When Li Wei and I asked villagers about the Great Famine, our few questions were commonly met with silence. But many responded in bitter detail when we asked about reservoir construction. From the late 1950s right through the 1960s and 1970s, most of Ginkgo Village's able-bodied adults worked on the reservoirs each autumn and winter, which was the slack farming season. They joined huge brigade-wide and commune-wide teams of village labourers.

Some women with young children and no-one else to care for them were sent to build reservoirs nearby. They were trucked out before daybreak, then brought home at night to care for their families. But other mothers, like Ye Yuzhen, were sent to work many miles from home. They lived onsite for two or three months at a time, their babies with them.

At night, women and men slept separately, crammed into shacks made of bamboo and straw. Fifty bodies in each one, not including babies. They were cold. No-one dared light a fire in case the shack caught alight. And they were starving, especially in December 1959. Ye Yuzhen and Huang Zhiwu would have had no more than watery soup to keep themselves alive.

During the day, they worked long, hard hours digging and shovelling, cracking rocks, lifting them with bleeding hands and aching backs, and carting them in barrows and wooden tubs suspended from shoulder poles.[9] Villagers can sketch this scene and I can picture it. I can see hunched

---

9   This description is based on Ginkgo Villagers' accounts. For another description, see Hershatter, *The Gender of Memory*, 240–41.

stick figures crawling over torturous hillsides of sliding rubble. I can see suppurating wounds and hollowed eyes. I can imagine—or try to imagine—toiling in the fearsome cold, day after day, with only fantasies of food. I can see a tiny, silent scrap of a baby buried in swaddling; a starving villager beyond exhaustion slumping. I can make out the outline of these things. I can see their thin shadows, even if I can't truly feel and comprehend them.

But I run into serious trouble when I try to imagine how Huang Zhiwu and Ye Yuzhen felt about Baobao's death.

***

I used to have two brothers: Tommy, who was 18 months younger than me, and Marcus, who was four years younger. When I was 19, Tommy was killed. Like Baobao's, it was a stupid, accidental death. It, too, happened in winter. One morning, he was running late for school, so instead of him walking to the train station, Dad drove him on his way to work. Tommy jumped out of the car and ran across the tracks and a train smashed into him. In front of Dad's eyes, the train screamed to a halt.

Seven months after Tommy's death, Dad suffered a near-fatal heart attack, a stroke and brain damage. He lay comatose for three weeks in a clean-smelling hospital ward. I held his hand and raged at the pink carnations by his bedside. I held on tight and willed him to pull through.

But there was nothing I could do for Mum. She was broken and unhinged. Walled up inside of my own grief and fear, I couldn't reach out or help her. She screamed and screamed at Marcus and me. Especially me.

'You care for no-one but yourself!' she screamed. 'You show no understanding!' On and on and on she screamed. I was alone and falling then, no solid earth in sight.

Finally, Dad came out of hospital, partially recovered from his brain damage and severely depressed. Mum decided we should salvage our summer holidays and go to the coast. It was February 1985, just before my twentieth birthday. Trapped in a shack in the burning heat, the air was a blade. I suffered panic attacks.

On the beach it was easier. One afternoon, Mum and I came out of the water and sat together on our beach towels. We had matching towels: hers with red stripes, mine with blue. The sun beat down.

'Where's the suntan lotion?' I asked, scrabbling around for it.

'Here.' Mum thrust it at me.

I took the bottle and squirted the lotion onto my arms and legs. I smeared it on my white thighs and throat; over my shoulders and around, where my bathers had left my back bare. I breathed in its cloying coconut smell. 'It's stinky stuff,' I said and laughed.

Behind her sunglasses, Mum stayed silent.

I chattered on.

Then she turned to me and said, 'I cannot be your mother anymore.'

I looked down at my towel. I'd got sand on it. I struggled to brush it off with my sticky fingers.

*

Did Baobao's death break her family the way my brother's death broke mine? I don't know. I've never had a baby die, let alone killed one. I can't imagine it. Or I can. My mind draws near like a moth to a flame, but then reels away; refuses to let me feel it.

But perhaps I have it all wrong. Sometimes, I'm relieved to think that, but at other times, it feels even worse.

What if her parents didn't care about Baobao's death? It was just a girl, after all, and they already had a son. In a time of such hunger and strain, perhaps the baby's death brought a measure of relief. Or maybe Ye Yuzhen was grief stricken but Huang Zhiwu was not. Or perhaps Ye Yuzhen was so exhausted, she was beyond caring. What if her life had already been so dulled by tragedy, she couldn't feel anything anymore?

***

The second time Li Wei and I went to visit Huang Zhiwu, Ye Yuzhen was also home. She made tea and sat with us, hot-water thermos by her side. After we'd all been chatting for a while, I asked her to tell us about her childhood and youth.

There was silence. She stood to refill our mugs with more hot water.

'Aiya, we were so pitiful,' Huang Zhiwu finally sighed.

'Don't talk about it!' his wife glared at him. She remained standing.

He kept going: 'I could write a book about our lives. I only went to school for three years, but I taught myself to write. The *duilian* we put around the door at New Year—I write them myself. I even wrote that ancestral scroll.' He swivelled and pointed to it.

Turning back, he folded a leg and clasped his hands around one knee. 'If I wrote a book about my life, it'd make you weep,' he said.

Li Wei and I stared at him, then at his wife.

'Don't talk about it,' she said again and marched off through the door behind us.

'We both come from poor families,' Huang Zhiwu continued. 'I was the only son, with four older sisters. My family was so pitiful. We ate wormwood to survive.'[10]

He wiped a hand over his face and twisted around again to see whether Ye Yuzhen was coming back. She wasn't.

'My old woman has suffered even more than me,' he murmured: 'She grew up in Carpenter Village, just north of here. Her mother died when she was three, just after giving birth to my wife's little sister. She went out to work and bled to death in the middle of a field. Then my wife's second older brother killed himself. He was a cripple. After their mother died, he knew there'd be no-one to care for him, so he threw himself in the river. My wife's father died when she was twelve. The oldest brother married not long after. He was good to his two sisters, but his wife wasn't.'

After all that, the birth of her first child, a boy, must have been a benediction for Ye Yuzhen. But how painful was the loss of her second? Was it an awful blow or just a chill draught under the door compared with what she'd already suffered?

And what about what happened later? Ye Yuzhen's oldest brother and his wife were unable to have children. So, after the birth of their son, Ye Yuzhen and Huang Zhiwu agreed to let the couple adopt their next child if it was

---

10 Wormwood is a bitter herb with a long history of medicinal use in Asia and Europe. When eaten in large quantities, it's poisonous.

a boy. After Baobao's birth and death, the agreement still stood. Three years later, Ye Yuzhen gave birth to a second son and he was handed over. Surely that hurt.

Then her oldest brother was killed. Again, it was an accidental death. It happened towards the end of 1966, when he was thirty-two. The Cultural Revolution was in full swing. Ginkgo Village's Red Flag faction of rebels and the East is Redders from Carpenter Village were at war. One day, there was a brawl between the two gangs. Mostly, they were bashing each other with sticks, but some had guns. One East is Red teenager waved his rifle and it went off. Ye Yuzhen's brother was standing on the sidelines and the bullet hit him in the head.

What happens to a person when their baby's death is merely a single tragedy in a whole chain of them—a chain that stretches on and on and on?

* * *

I like to imagine that Baobao's death is what takes her parents to the Twin Maidens Shrine. And maybe that's why Huang Zhiwu told Li Wei and me the story of the twin maidens. I imagine that if my baby died, the beauty of such a shrine and such a story might be a comfort. At least eventually, in my old age. So maybe that's what they are for Ye Yuzhen and Huang Zhiwu. I like to think that.

But I'm probably wrong. After all, what would I know?

Who cares anyway? One baby's death and the loss of one unfortunate couple sit on one side of the scales. The other side is weighed low by the Great Famine, inflicted by Chinese leaders on their own people. The worst famine in human history, some say.[11]

And yet, it is Baobao's ghost that haunts me. She haunts and taunts and threatens me. She yells at me to speak and renders me mute. Sometimes she's a baby, staring at me with her mother's dull eyes. Sometimes she's a dying teenager and I'm her dying twin. Some nights, her deathly voice is at my ear: 'If my story doesn't matter,' she breathes, 'then neither does

---

11 Yang, *Tombstone*, ix. The validity of this claim is discussed in Wemheuer, *A Social History of Maoist China*, 147–52.

yours.' Or she has me up against a wall, a knife at my throat. She grabs my hair and slams my head back. 'Don't you dare back out of this,' she hisses. 'Tell my story. Tell it.'

Other nights, she screams across the room: 'That's *my* story; you have no right to tell it. You know nothing. Nothing, nothing, nothing.'

Sometimes there's a pile of rags and we're both being smothered. Other times, we're trudging along a railway line, mile after mile. The heat bears down or there's a bitter wind. The tracks blur and slide. Baobao's way up ahead but something makes her turn. She plods back, squats down beside me. 'What is it now?' she sighs. She waits, gets fed up, stands. 'Pull yourself together,' she says finally. Marches off again and leaves me stranded.

*

All of us have ghosts, though you may not call them that. Some will be at peace eventually. Some never will. Some ghosts smile, inconsolable; some rage. Some are brutal, deaf and mute.

We all have ghosts, though each one is different. Huang Zhiwu and Ye Yuzhen, Li Wei, me and you—we all have ghosts, though each one speaks a different language.

Is translation possible? Some days I think it is. There's just a ditch between us that we can jump. Some days the gap is larger, but we'll build a bridge. Some days I talk with Baobao's ghost. I can tell her story and her parents'—have you see in them my story, too, and yours.

But some days, some nights, I can't. Some nights I don't believe in ghosts. Only this unfathomable distance between us. A chasm I can't see how to bridge. Some nights there's nothing I can do but stand at the edge and close my eyes. Listen to my questions sinking; wait for the silence winging back. What form does it take? What scent, what colour, what taste?

3

Weaving lives

The other night, I dreamt about Gao Xiuhua. Or perhaps it was my grandma, before she died. A sparrow-like woman with chirpy eyes. She's in her courtyard, watering the pot plants with a green plastic watering can. There are aloe vera and gardenias and something else with dark, fleshy leaves. A toddler clings to the woman's thin trousered leg and stares at me. Is it Gao Xiuhua's grandson, Xiaobing? Or is it one of my younger brothers? Or my son, Misha?

Then I'm with the old woman in her front room. She's making a gown for me. She's climbed onto her wooden stool and I'm standing facing her. Right up close. There's a clean, sharp smell, like tiger balm.

She tells me to stretch out my arms so she can pin the cloth around my chest. She winds it around my body and turns me like a top, spinning me round and round till the whole room swims. Then she stops and holds me with her slim, strong hands.

She's so small, I can see over the top of her soft grey hair. I'm staring at the glossy red poster of Xi Jinping and his opera-singing wife stuck on the wall above the couch. Beyond my left arm, the family altar is in shadow. My right arm stretches towards the open door and the pot plants outside. Sunlight pours in.

The fabric she has wound around me is a fine white cotton, threaded through with filaments of gold. She's woven it herself. It's a cloth of delicate, heartbreaking beauty, glowing in the warm light.

***

Gao Xiuhua was born in the hamlet of Green Riverbend in 1944. Hers was a traumatic childhood, twisted out of shape by what her mother, Deng Jinmei, had suffered during the Civil War years.

Deng Jinmei came from Guangshan to the north, where she was married and had two sons before Xiuhua was born. The family had nothing to eat, so Deng Jinmei went out to beg. She was on the road for weeks, shuffling on bound feet from one poor hamlet to the next, through Red River Township and all the way through Ginkgo Village until she came to Green Riverbend.

There, a man named Gao Delong took her in. His parents had died and his older sister had married and left the family. Gao Delong had only one other sibling alive—a younger brother, named Deyi, who was almost blind. The brothers lived together in a thatch-roofed hut, crouched close to the bend in the quiet green stream from which Green Riverbend gets its name.

Apart from their family altar, the brothers' only furniture consisted of two wooden beds and a stool. But they also had a wooden spinning wheel and loom once used by their mother and sister that had long stood idle. After Deng Jinmei joined the family, their comforting whirring and clacketing could be heard once more.

The couple didn't have a wedding. But, as well as spinning and weaving, Deng Jinmei cooked for Gao Delong and his brother, mended their clothes and bore Gao Delong a child. To his dismay, it was only a girl. They named her Xiuhua.

Gao Xiuhua wiped away tears with the back of her hand as she told Li Wei and me about her mother. When Xiuhua was 18 months old, her mother left her and went back to Guangshan. During the Great Famine, she starved to death.

Back in Green Riverbend, Xiuhua's father and uncle struggled mightily with a baby and no woman in the house. Then, when Xiuhua was eight, her father found a new wife: an older widow in White Cloud Hamlet. He went to live with her there. His new wife already had three children and refused to take Xiuhua. So, the girl stayed behind in Green Riverbend with her uncle. By this time, Gao Deyi had married. His wife, Wu Weiying, was another widow. The family lived in a new house, built next to the old one. It was a little bigger than the old hut, but just as bare. Still, they had the spinning wheel and loom.

Wu Weiying was unable to have children, but with her first husband she had adopted a boy, named Xianjiao. She was raising a child bride for the boy, too.[1] Her name was Beibei. Both children were three years older than Xiuhua.

After his marriage, Xiuhua's father retained control over 2 mu (1,300 square metres) of land in Green Riverbend assigned to him and his daughter by the new communist government as part of its land reform. Wu Weiying wanted to grow cotton on Xiuhua's portion, but Gao Delong wouldn't let her. Unable to get her way, Wu Weiying kicked Xiuhua out of the house.

The girl made her way to the dirt track leading to Deng Inn Village, just south of Ginkgo Village. For more than a month, she scrounged food in Deng Inn. At night, she slept under the bridge at the junction between Deng Inn and Ginkgo Village. One evening, the head of an inspection team from Red River Township saw her there. She was a peaky, dishevelled little stick. Her filthy, faded blue cotton *changpao* (robe)[2] was full of holes and far too short in the arms. The man felt sorry for her and reported her plight to Red River's Party chief. He agreed that the girl's situation was too pitiful for words. He forced Gao Delong to return 1 mu (670 square metres) of land to Xiuhua and told Wu Weiying to take the girl back. Grudgingly, she did so. Xiuhua stayed with the family until she married at the age of twenty.

*

From the moment Xiuhua rejoined the family, her aunt put her to work sweeping the floor, washing clothes, feeding the chickens and helping Beibei with the spinning. Beibei also fetched water from the well, collected firewood, did most of the cooking and mended clothes each evening. Neither girl ever went to school. Wu Weiying's son, Xianjiao, started school at the

---

1   Child brides usually came from families too poor to raise them. Others adopted them to avoid the usual bride price (*caili*)—the gifts of goods and cash that a groom's family is expected to pay the family of the bride before a wedding. A child bride could also be more easily trained by her mother-in-law than an adult woman and could provide her marital family with labour for a longer period. The betrothal or marriage of minors was banned under China's Marriage Law of 1934 and again in the Marriage Law of 1950. However, child marriages remained common in Ginkgo Village in the 1950s.
2   Before the Chinese Communist Party came to power in 1949, village children wore *changpao*, men wore *changpao* or jackets and trousers, and women wore side-buttoned jackets and trousers. In the 1950s in Ginkgo Village, adults wore jackets and trousers, while children continued to wear *changpao*. From the 1960s, both adults and children, male and female, wore jackets and trousers.

age of 10 and continued for another three years. He never did domestic chores. When I asked Gao Xiuhua how she felt about this, she shrugged. 'That's just how it was,' she said.

In 1956, when Xiuhua turned 12, she was tasked with taking two of the newly formed cooperative's water buffaloes out to pasture each day. Sometimes, she took them down to Red River. While they ate the lush grass at the river's edge, she would sit in the shade under the bridge—the same bridge under which she had camped after her aunt kicked her out. She would play with the willow switch meant for keeping the buffaloes in check, drawing pictures in the cool dirt and thinking of her mother. She had no memories of her, but her father had said her mother was skilful with her hands. To decorate their mud hut, she'd made intricate papercuts of flowers and chickens.

The same year, Wu Weiying taught Beibei to weave and put her to work stitching cloth shoes. Xiuhua had to take over her sister's job of mending clothes in the evening. Sitting inside in the half-dark was nowhere near as nice as being out by the river, she told Li Wei and me. They didn't have electricity or even kerosene lamps back then. Instead, they used oil lamps. The oil was pressed from the nut of the Chinese tallow tree and sold in the cooperative store next to the bridge in Green Riverbend. It burned well but cast only a weak light.[3] She didn't mind mending; it gave her a challenge to work at, she said.

In those days, cotton was in short supply because the state had collectivised most of the land and was buying up almost the entire collective cotton crop. To compensate, villagers received cloth ration coupons with which they could buy machine-woven cotton cloth at the cooperative store. But the rations were meagre: 3 square metres per person each year. That was barely enough to keep a family clothed, let alone to make the quilts and clothes needed for betrothal gifts, dowries and bride-price payments. What's more, both rationed cloth and non-rationed cotton thread and wadding (for winter jackets and quilts) were awfully expensive.

So, like everyone else, Xiuhua's family had very few clothes and each item— each child's only *changpao* and each adult's one or two thin jackets and one or two pairs of trousers—had to be worn until they were threadbare and

---

3   'Kerosene lamps' didn't come in until the late 1960s. In fact, they used diesel, not kerosene. Even in the 1970s, oil lamps continued to be used because Chinese tallow tree oil was cheaper than diesel.

patched many times over. Xiuhua's mending was vital and she had to be clever about it. She had to sew layer upon layer of patches, one on top of the other. And each time, she had to use as small a patch as possible and sew with tiny stitches. Her aunt and sister would get mad if she used up too much cloth or thread.

She chuckled, recalling those times. At lunchtime, she said, she and her friends would squat on the riverbank and compete over who had the most patches. She would win occasionally, but only when a Chen girl wasn't there. The two Chen sisters shared just one *changpao* between them, so you only ever saw one girl at a time; the other one had to stay inside. Xiuhua's *changpao* was no match for the Chen sisters'—theirs was nothing but holes and patches.

*

When Xiuhua was 17, Wu Weiying taught her to weave and stitch cloth shoes, which she had to do as well as the mending. Wu Weiying had made sure to arrange Xiuhua's betrothal soon after she joined the family. Now the girl needed clothes, cloth shoes and insoles for her dowry. She also had to learn the weaving and needlework skills expected of a wife.

To make cloth shoes, Xiuhua sewed cloth uppers onto soles made of several layers of stiffened cotton. She made each layer with pieces of waste cloth stuck together with flour paste. Sometimes she added bamboo leaves to make up for the lack of cloth. After they'd been left in the sun to dry and stiffen, each layer was sewn together with lines of tiny, dense stitching. It was tedious, time-consuming work. Her slim fingers quickly became calloused.

She made insoles in the same way, but with just one layer of stiffened cotton. Mostly, she stitched her insoles with plain white thread. It took her two days to make one pair. But when it came to the insoles for her dowry, she put in extra time and effort. She stitched them all over with a white geometric pattern. Then she used a few coloured threads to embroider a delicate flower in the centre of each one. She imagined her mother would be proud of her handiwork. For her dowry, she made five pairs of embroidered insoles and her aunt made another five plain pairs.

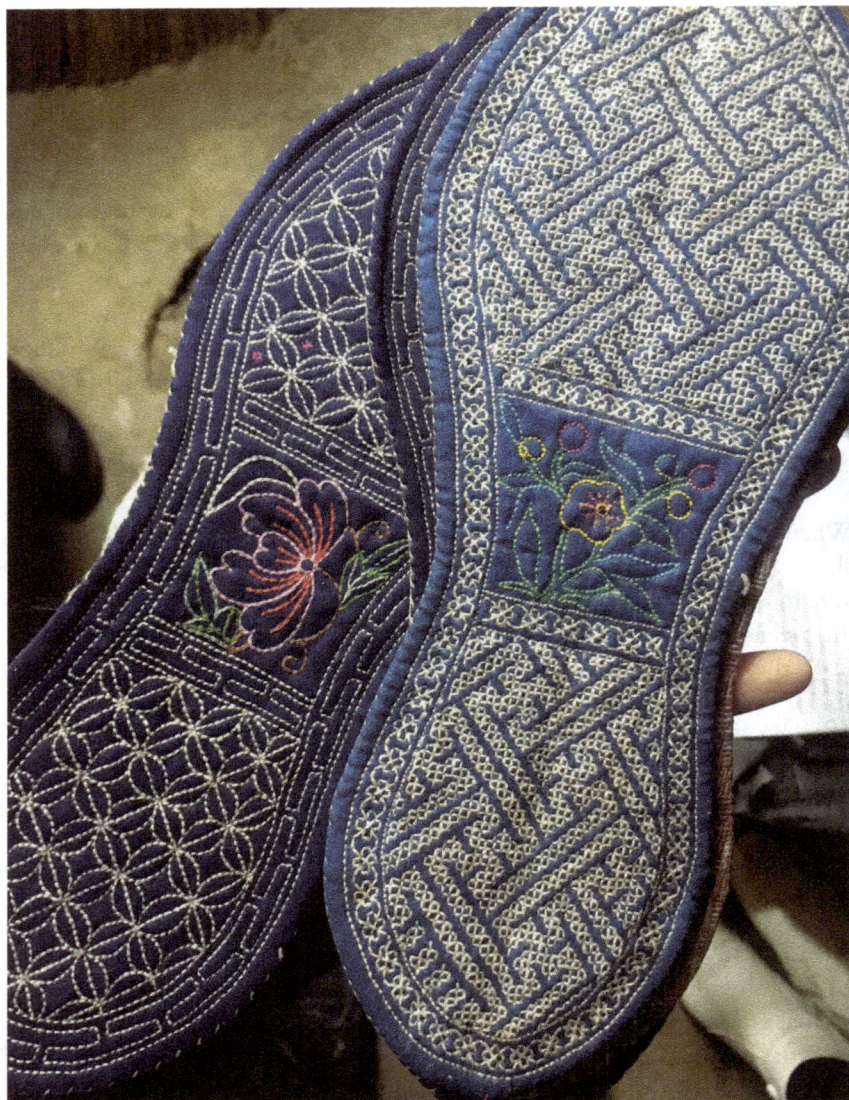

Plate 3.1 Embroidered insoles from the Maoist era
Photo: Li Wei, 2019.

But it was weaving that Xiuhua loved best. As an eight-year-old, she would stand by her aunt's side as she wove, watching the cloth growing, weft by weft, with each sweep of the shuttle. She wanted to try it for herself, but her aunt shooed her away. 'You're too small,' she said. 'Wait till you're older.'[4]

When her turn at the loom finally came, she learned quickly and soon became more skilled than her aunt and sister. She was proud of that.

At the time, the state was trying to prevent women from spinning and weaving so they would use less cotton and have more time for collective work. In 1960, the central government issued a 'directive to immediately end the hand-spinning and hand-weaving of cotton'. But bought cloth was too expensive and the cloth rations too miserly, so the directive was ignored.[5] Ginkgo Villagers' rations had dwindled by then to just 1 square metre per person each year. That wasn't even enough for one set of jacket and trousers. But, from the early 1960s, villagers could grow a bit of their own cotton on their private plot. Some also planted cotton on land they cleared in secret, deep in the hills. More than half the cotton they grew went into stuffing the quilts and padded jackets they made for dowries and wedding gifts. The rest they spun and wove into cloth, which they dyed and hand-sewed into clothes and bedding.[6]

---

4   Most girls in Gao Xiuhua's generation learnt to spin at the age of eight to 10 years but didn't learn to weave until they were between 15 and 17 years old. In part, this was because weaving was skilled work, considered too difficult for younger girls. In part, it was because looms were too big for smaller girls to manage. Spinning could be done by a small girl sitting on a stool. Spinning wheels were about 1 metre in diameter. The looms, though, were bigger and more awkward. They were about 1.8 metres tall, 2 metres deep and about 1.2 metres wide. To weave, a woman sat on a bench and operated the loom with a wooden foot pedal.

5   Jacob Eyferth, 'Women's Work and the Politics of Homespun in Socialist China, 1949–1980', *International Review of Social History* 57, no. 3 (2012): 365–91, at 379, doi.org/10.1017/S0020859012 000521.

6   Ginkgo Villagers' cotton rations gradually increased through the 1960s. In the 1970s, they reached 4 square metres per person each year. Jacob Eyferth claims that, in addition to cloth rations, production team leaders across the country distributed 1 kilogram of raw cotton per person per year to village families during the Maoist period (Eyferth, 'Women's Work', 377). My research suggests, however, that much less than this was given out in Xin County. One internal Communist Party document notes that after a poor harvest in 1963, production teams retained only enough of the collective cotton harvest to distribute a per capita average of 75 grams (Xin County, Henan, County Committee, '关于缺衣群众用布的请示报告 [A Report and Request for Instructions Regarding the Use of Cloth Among the Masses Lacking Clothes]', Unpublished document (Xin County Archives, 1964). A former Ginkgo Village cadre stated firmly that, across the village, cotton was distributed only once every few years and only to the very poorest. In most years, most families received none.

Wu Weiying taught Xiuhua and Beibei how to dye their woven cloth. To make blue dye they put the leaves of an indigo plant in a vat of water and left them to ferment. After taking out the leaf residue, they added lime to the water, which produced a blue precipitate that formed the dye. Black dye came from the tannin in the leaves of the Huaxiang tree (*Platycarya strobilacea*). They collected the leaves and boiled them to extract the black pigment. To dye cloth, they first boiled it in the black pigment. Then, they took it out to the paddy fields and covered it with mud. After five or six hours, they washed the mud off and boiled the cloth in the black pigment again to produce an even colour.

'What a lengthy process!' I said when Gao Xiuhua told Li Wei and me. She grinned and nodded.

For the last three years before Xiuhua married and left home, almost all the clothes that Wu Weiying sewed for her family were made from cloth that Xiuhua or Beibei wove and dyed themselves. So, too, were most of the items that Wu Weiying, Beibei and Xiuhua made for Xiuhua's dowry.

As far as dowries went in the 1960s, Xiuhua's wasn't bad. It included 10 pairs of cloth shoes that she and Beibei made, five pairs of embroidered insoles that she made and another five pairs of plain ones that Wu Weiying stitched. She also had two quilts, one cotton-padded jacket, one pair of trousers and two summer jackets that Wu Weiying made for her. Only the cotton-padded jacket was made from bought, rather than handwoven, cloth.

It was a similar story in her fiancé's home. Li Changyin was a few years older than Xiuhua. He had one younger sister and a younger brother. In preparation for Changyin's marriage, his mother and sister wove cloth and sewed three jackets and three pairs of trousers, which they gave to Xiuhua as betrothal gifts. They also gave her seven pairs of homemade cloth shoes. The clothes that Xiuhua and Changyin wore on their wedding day were homemade, too. Xiuhua wore an ordinary blue cotton-padded jacket and blue trousers. Changyin wore a black jacket and trousers. Both sets of clothes were sewn by Changyin's mother from cloth his sister wove.

I was surprised that Gao Xiuhua didn't wear red on her wedding day, but she said very few women did in those days. The reason was not, as I had thought, fear of being denounced as 'feudal' or 'bourgeois'. It was simply that the traditional red was unaffordable. You could buy red cloth in Ginkgo Brigade's cooperative store and special red and other coloured dyes in the

Red River Commune cooperative store or from a passing peddler. But few families had the money to buy enough red cloth or dye for a whole jacket, even for a wedding.

'What about your wedding shoes?' Li Wei asked. 'Did you just wear ordinary homemade cloth shoes?'

'Yes, Li Changyin's sister made his, and I made mine. His were black and mine were green. I bought the green cloth in Red River. I still remember the cost: 1.35 yuan per metre.'[7] She straightened her back and her eyes twinkled.

'Why green?' Li Wei asked in surprise.

Gao Xiuhua gave a shrug. 'That's the custom in these parts. Even today it's the same. Nowadays women wear traditional red wedding dresses and Western-style white dresses, too. But they still wear green shoes.[8] Only nowadays they're high-heeled. I don't know how they walk in those things—it's like having bound feet!'[9]

Gao Xiuhua smiled when Li Wei and I asked her questions about her wedding clothes. But when I asked how she felt on her wedding day, her head sank. She was sad because she had no mother and next to nothing to take into her marriage. Normally, a bride would be given at least one quilt for her new family from each of her maternal uncles. But because her mother had died, she didn't get any.

***

After their marriage, Gao Xiuhua and Li Changyin lived with his family in Five Hills Hamlet. Their house was up the hill from the main road.

Li Wei and I first met the couple on a warm Saturday afternoon in May 2015. The village schoolkids were home for the weekend and were helping their parents and grandparents harvest the canola. Walking along the road, we saw whole families out in the fields. They'd already cut the canola stalks

---

7   Gao Xiuhua married in 1964. At that time, 1.35 yuan was equivalent to US$0.55.
8   The custom of green bridal shoes is specific to this locality. Neither Gao Xiuhua nor anyone else could explain it. It may derive from the fact that the colour green or azure (*qing*) symbolises health, prosperity, fertility, harmony and growth in Chinese culture.
9   Unlike her mother, Gao Xiuhua didn't have bound feet. The practice of foot-binding was more or less universal among village women in southern Henan until the early 1930s, but it quickly died out after that. For more on foot-binding and its demise, see Laurel Bossen and Hill Gates, *Bound Feet, Young Hands: Tracking the Demise of Footbinding in Village China* (Stanford, CA: Stanford University Press, 2017), doi.org/10.2307/j.ctvqsdshq.

and left them to dry. Now they were beating them and shaking the seeds onto plastic sheets. They sifted the tiny black seeds onto flat wicker baskets and raked up the remaining straw to use as stove-fuel. The children were horsing around and the air was full of laughter.

Gao Xiuhua's neighbours had locked up and gone out, but the gate to her place was open. We peeked into her courtyard and saw that it was crowded with pot plants. There were Buddha's palm plants with big, heart-shaped leaves, aloe vera, delicate pink peonies and white gardenias.

'Is anyone there?' we called. No sound. We were assailed by the gardenias' sweet fragrance as we ventured in. A little boy with a shaved head and green split pants[10] came toddling out through the half-open front door. When he saw us, he stopped abruptly and turned back, falling over the wooden lintel. A few seconds passed before he started whimpering. By that time, Li Changyin had come to the door and creaked its double wings wide. He picked up the crying child and came out to greet us. Gao Xiuhua's thin, stooped frame then slowly emerged from the shadows of the house.

Li Changyin was wary of Li Wei and me. But Gao Xiuhua had heard there were two outsiders in the village and was curious to meet us. She beckoned us into the front room and made us sit on the couch to one side, under a poster of President Xi Jinping and his wife. The couch was soft and saggy, draped with a piece of blue and white checked cloth. Li Wei and I drew our notebooks and pens from our daypacks and waited while Gao Xiuhua bustled about. She switched on a light overhead and, against our protests, shuffled to the other side of the room to make tea. A hot-water thermos stood on the ground next to a squat round table, neatly arranged with a cannister of tea-leaves and two mugs. She pinched a few tea-leaves into the mugs for Li Wei and me, before calling for her husband to carry the table and thermos over to the couch. The thermos looked new. It was bright red with a shiny metal cap and a clean cork stopper.

Gao Xiuhua was neat and bright, too. She wore black slacks and a smart orange and yellow floral blouse, gold earrings and a gold bracelet. She was dressed up because that morning she had taken the bus to Red River

---

10   Split pants are trousers that are open at the crotch to allow for urination. They're worn by young children from the age of a few months.

Township to visit one of her daughters-in-law. She apologised for not coming out sooner. She had been resting. She suffered from a debilitating heart condition and her outing had exhausted her.

Li Changyin sat apart from us on a wooden stool, the toddler on his lap. The boy, it turned out, was his 15-month-old grandson, Xiaobing. I fished in my daypack and leant forward to give him a small toy koala. He curled into his grandfather's chest, so I gave the gift to the old man. The pair stayed with us for a while, listening to the to-and-fro of our conversation with Gao Xiuhua. But then Xiaobing got fidgety, so Li Changyin took him out to the courtyard.

*

We chatted with Gao Xiuhua about her adult children and their families. She had four sons and a daughter. The oldest was born in 1965—the same year as me—and the youngest 12 years later.

'Are they all married?' I asked.

'Yes, of course—they all have children of their own! My third son has one and the others have two. I have five children and nine grandchildren. I even have two great-grandchildren!' She paused and bent to rub a knee. Perhaps she suffered from arthritis.

'I had too many children. We had no way of stopping births in those days.' She looked out to her husband. He was squatting with Xiaobing, helping him to pee.

I scribbled in my notebook: 'No contraception!', and underlined it.[11]

'Laoshi,' Gao Xiuhua said, 'how many children do you have?'

'Only one: a son.'

'One is good.' She smiled.

Just then, she was distracted by her husband carrying Xiaobing inside. Li Changyin sat the boy down on the floor next to his wife and went out again. This time he hoisted a straw broom over his shoulder.

---

11   Contraception didn't become available to Ginkgo Villagers until the early 1980s, when the One-Child Policy was introduced. Through the 1980s, contraception took the form of tubal ligations and abortions. Intra-uterine devices (IUDs)—the only other contraception used in the village—were introduced in the 1990s.

Gao Xiuhua watched him go. 'He's been given the job of sweeping the main road,' she explained. 'It's a good job for an old man—not too demanding. Usually, he goes out in the morning. He's only doing it now because I went out earlier. He stayed to look after Xiaobing.'

I don't think he enjoyed his job. Li Wei and I would sometimes see him idling by his motorised three-wheeled cart, the broom sticking out the back. We would sing out a greeting from the other side of the road, but he'd turn away, take up the broom and start sweeping again in a desultory fashion. Maybe he thought the job was beneath him. Sweeping was women's work.

I watched his receding figure. 'How much is your husband paid?' I asked Gao Xiuhua.

'Just 8,000 yuan[12] a year. My medical costs alone come to more than that!' She sighed and brushed at her slacks.

'But you both get the elderly pension, don't you? That must make a difference?'

Gao Xiuhua frowned. 'Of course, we're extremely grateful for it,' she said. 'But it's very little. Even if I didn't have such high medical expenses, it wouldn't be enough. It's the same for everyone. It doesn't matter how old and frail we are, we have to keep working, just to make ends meet.'[13]

I returned her to the topic of children and grandchildren. It turned out she had been the main carer for each of her sons' children when they were toddlers.

'From the moment they began wearing split pants, it was me who cared for them. In the 1990s, I cared for five at once!' She said this with great energy, but I couldn't tell whether she was proud of her role as a grandmother or upset at the burden of care she'd had to shoulder.

---

12   US$1,200.

13   Commentators on China's ageing population crisis often highlight a lack of care for frail elderly people, especially in rural areas. My own and others' research suggests, though, that a far more prevalent and serious problem is overwork among older villagers with adult migrant worker children, who, in addition to caring for grandchildren, must keep working 'till they drop' to grow their own food and earn an income to cover their grandchildren's costs as well as their own. See Lihua Pang, Alan de Brauw, and Scott Rozelle, 'Working Until You Drop: The Elderly of Rural China', *The China Journal* 52 (2004): 73–94, doi.org/10.2307/4127885; and Tamara Jacka, 'Left-Behind and Vulnerable? Conceptualising Development and Older Women's Agency in Rural China', *Asian Studies Review* 38, no. 2 (2014): 186–204, doi.org/10.1080/10357823.2014.891566.

Her oldest son's wife deserted him, Gao Xiuhua told us. That's why she raised his two daughters. 'Their mother rang up once,' she said. 'The girls were teenagers by then. Their mother wanted to see them, but they refused to even speak with her on the phone. What a nerve—to abandon your children, then ring up out of the blue, all those years later!'

Had we known about her own mother abandoning her as a child, we might have better appreciated the bitterness in her voice as she said this. But she didn't tell us that story until later.

'What about the other three?' I asked, looking up from my notebook. 'Why were you looking after them?'

'They were my second and third sons' kids. We didn't have a choice. Both sons and their wives were migrant workers, living in Shenzhen. They couldn't keep their children there—they couldn't afford it. It's been the same with our youngest son: he and his wife work in Beijing.'

'This little fellow,' she added, patting Xiaobing's soft bristly head, 'is their second child.'

The plan was for Gao Xiuhua to raise the boy until he reached school age. His mother would then give up her job and take him to live in Xin County City, so he could go to school there. His 12-year-old brother was already in boarding school in the city. He came home to his grandparents for one weekend each month.

*

I mused about the extraordinary amount of child care done by village women of Gao Xiuhua's generation. In the second half of the 1990s, I was in my early thirties, struggling with one demanding child. Gao Xiuhua would have been in her fifties, responsible for five small grandchildren, having already raised five children of her own. And even now, at the age of 71, she was caring for a toddler.[14]

---

14   Mass rural outmigration has resulted in heavy childcare burdens for non-migrant grandmothers. For further discussion, see Yunxiang Yan, 'Intergenerational Intimacy and Descending Familism in Rural North China', *American Anthropologist* 118, no. 2 (2016): 244–57, doi.org/10.1111/aman.12527; Tamara Jacka, 'Translocal Family Reproduction and Agrarian Change in China: A New Analytical Framework', *Journal of Peasant Studies* 45, no. 7 (2018): 1341–59, doi.org/10.1080/03066150.2017. 1314267; Gonçalo Santos, *Chinese Village Life Today: Building Families in an Age of Transition* (Seattle: University of Washington Press, 2021), 128–51; and Erin Thomason, 'United in Suffering', in *Chinese Families Upside Down: Intergenerational Dynamics and Neo-Familism in the Early 21st Century*, ed. Yunxiang Yan (Leiden: Brill, 2021), 76–102, doi.org/10.1163/9789004450233_005.

'How do you feel about having to care for so many grandchildren?' I asked. 'That must have been a heavy burden for you!'

Gao Xiuhua shrugged: 'We had no choice. Someone had to look after them.' She bent down to Xiaobing, who was playing with the toy koala on the floor. 'It's okay. See how quiet this one is? It was harder when there were five of them all at once. But I've had my rewards.'

'See my jewellery?' she grinned, holding out her arm so we could look at her gold bracelet. 'This comes from my oldest granddaughter. And these come from her sister.' She fingered her earrings.[15] 'She also bought this blouse for me. Most of the clothes my husband and I own come from our daughter. But some are things our granddaughters bought. They're closer to me than to their mothers!'

I leant forward to admire her jewellery and blouse. 'What about your grandsons? Do they give you clothes, too?'

'No, but they give us money at New Year.'

Li Wei reached for her tea. 'Granny, have your sons always given you money to look after their children?'

'All except the third son did. The youngest gives us 2,000 yuan[16] a year for this little one.' Gao Xiuhua smiled and patted Xiaobing's head again. She sat up and looked out to the courtyard. There were midges dancing in the afternoon light.

'Does that cover Xiaobing's costs?' Li Wei asked in a worried voice.

'More or less. He doesn't need milk powder anymore, and we grow most of our own food; we don't need to buy much.'

'What about your third son? How much money did he give you for his two children?'

'He couldn't give us anything. His wages were too low and he couldn't always find work. What could we do? We had to cover his kids' costs ourselves.' She sagged in her chair and her head drooped.

---

15 Gold jewellery was proudly displayed by middle-aged and older women as a mark of prosperity and the filiality of their children and grandchildren. It was most often bought by those who had earned relatively high wages as migrant labourers overseas.

16 US$300.

I looked out to the courtyard and tried to change the topic. 'You have so many lovely flowers!'

Gao Xiuhua straightened and her eyes lit up. 'They're easy to grow,' she said modestly.

Li Wei looked up from her notebook and smiled.

I flipped through my notes. 'Aunty, apart from clothes, does your daughter give you money?'

Gao Xiuhua shook her head. 'No, sons give money, not daughters. But some people have daughters who give money, too. Daughters are often more filial than sons …' Her voice trailed off.

'How much money do your sons give you altogether?'

She sagged again. 'Our third son still doesn't earn much, but he gives us 2,000 yuan each year.'

'And the others?'

'We get 1,000 yuan[17] from the oldest. Two thousand from the youngest, for Xiaobing. But the second son gives us nothing.' She frowned.

'Why is that?' I asked.

Li Wei shifted uneasily on the couch.

'The third brother didn't give us anything for looking after his children. So now, his brothers think he should be the one to support us in our old age.' Gao Xiuhua looked down. 'The oldest still gives us money. He's very filial. But the second refuses. It's because of his wife. She won't let him give us anything.'

She looked up again. 'We manage,' she said.

***

It was during our second visit, one damp morning several days later, that Li Wei and I learnt about Gao Xiuhua's difficult childhood. She also told us about the early years of her marriage. For most of the first four years, she and Li Changyin lived in a household of eight, including Li Changyin's

---

17   US$160.

parents and younger brother and sister, as well as their own first two sons. They didn't divide the family until after Li Changyin's sister had married and left home and his brother had married and had a child. Gao Xiuhua and Li Changyin moved out then, but they only went to the opposite side of the yard. There, they built a new two-roomed house with a kitchen tacked onto the side.

Her mother-in-law refused to help with Gao Xiuhua's babies. 'She didn't lift a finger,' Gao Xiuhua said miserably. 'Even just after I gave birth, she said I had to go out and earn work points. And I still had to do the cooking and washing.'

'Did you rest for a month after childbirth?'[18] Li Wei asked, tilting her head.

Gao Xiuhua shook her head. 'My first son was born in the middle of winter. It was so hard having no-one to help. I had to get up in the dark to wash clothes in the river. I had to break the ice on the water.' She frowned and picked at the sleeve of her white shirt. 'By the time I'd finished, there'd be a bit of light in the sky and other women would be coming out. They'd see someone climbing up the riverbank with a baby on her back and they'd know it was me. They all knew I had a no-good mother-in-law.'

Just then, Li Changyin came in, leading Xiaobing by the hand. Li Wei and I had seen them on our way here. Xiaobing had been sitting in the tray of the three-wheeler, while his grandfather swept and emptied rubbish into one of the concrete garbage tanks. It had started drizzling, so he'd knocked off early.

Xiaobing tottered to his grandmother's side and she bent down to him. Li Changyin pulled up a stool and sat down next to his wife. We kept talking about the early years of their marriage, but Gao Xiuhua said nothing more about her mother-in-law.

'Did you give birth to your children in hospital?' I asked her.

She gave a brief shake of her head. 'They were all born at home.'[19]

'Did you have a midwife?'

---

18 Across rural China, women were, and still are, expected to rest for one month after childbirth (*zuo yuezi*). Doing anything but light chores indoors during this month of rest is a mark of desperate hardship.
19 Hospital births didn't become common among Ginkgo Villagers until the 1990s. For more on the history of birthing practices in China, see Santos, *Chinese Village Life Today*, 98–127.

'No, we couldn't afford it. When our third son was born, I was all on my own. My sister-in-law had married out by then and we'd split the family. My mother-in-law didn't come to help.'

'He was away,' she added tersely, waving in her husband's direction. 'Gone for three days.'

Li Changyin butted in. 'We had nothing to eat, so I'd walked to Macheng. I bought live fish fry and carried them back. I earned a lot of money selling them. It made a huge difference, you know: it meant we could buy enough grain to get us through the winter.'[20]

Gao Xiuhua made a humph sound.

He ignored her: 'I was the breadwinner. She never earned more than seven work points a day, so I had to work extra hard. I did a lot of overtime.'

That was too much for Gao Xiuhua. 'What?!' she cried. '*You* did a lot of overtime? What was I doing, looking after the children? I was doing overtime every single day!' Her eyes blazed.

We all laughed awkwardly, but Gao Xiuhua continued to complain. Eventually, she pushed Xiaobing to her husband and got up to make tea.

'We were truly pitiful,' Li Changyin mumbled, his head down. 'It was no life for a human.'

Li Wei and I didn't know what to say. I wrote down that phrase, 'It was no life for a human.' But my mind was on his wife's outburst. It was rare for village women to denounce their double burden so vehemently, especially in front of their husbands. I wanted Gao Xiuhua to say more. So, after she sat down again, I asked whether she thought life during the collective era was harder for men or for women.

'Women!' she snapped. 'All he had to do in the morning was pull up his trousers and go to work. I had to get up before him to make breakfast and look after the children. And then I went to work for the collective as well.'

---

20 Gao Xiuhua and Li Changyin's third son was born in 1968. At that time, production teams only occasionally allowed individuals to engage in private trade, on condition they hand over part of their earnings to the production team in exchange for work points. Li Changyin made a profit of 30 yuan (US$12) selling fry—more cash than most could earn in a year. With it, he bought 50 kilograms of rice and 50 kilograms of wheat. In addition, he gave 2 yuan (US$0.80) to the production team in return for three days' worth of work points.

'And in the evening?'

'When the sun went down, he just fell into bed. I had to stay up for hours, spinning and weaving and making cloth shoes.' She wiped a weary hand over her face.

***

Li Wei and I made our third visit to Gao Xiuhua's home on another overcast morning two weeks later. Walking down the road, we saw that villagers were burning off the canola stubble. In the distance, small figures in straw hats were silhouetted against the flames. I struggled with my Australian anxiety about bushfires.

We were shocked to find Gao Xiuhua ill and weak. She had been lying on the couch before we arrived and, as we came in, she sat up slowly. She looked haggard and her eyes were dulled. She reminded me of my grandma, lying in hospital at the end of her life. I grew afraid.

Li Changyin made Li Wei and me sit on stools, so Gao Xiuhua could stay on the couch. He hovered around and wouldn't let his wife get up to make tea. I don't know where Xiaobing was.

I had a long list of questions but didn't ask any of them. Li Wei and I kept our notebooks shut and we all just chatted quietly. Then, Li Changyin said the village doctor would come over shortly, so we'd better leave. We nodded and started getting up.

But Gao Xiuhua waved us down again. She wanted to talk. 'You go,' she said, shaking her husband off. 'I'm fine.'

Li Changyin frowned at his wife and threw a dark look at me and Li Wei, before stomping off in disgust.

'Would you like tea?' Gao Xiuhua asked again, leaning forward.

'No, sit down,' we cried, 'there's no need!'

'It's no trouble,' she insisted, levering herself up.

'Well, I don't want tea, but I wouldn't mind some hot water,' I said finally. I reached down to the water bottle in my daypack on the floor.

'I'll get it,' Li Wei said hurriedly, as Gao Xiuhua struggled to stand up. 'Granny, you sit.'

Li Wei fetched the thermos from the other side of the room. While she poured hot water into my water bottle, Gao Xiuhua started talking in a thin, harried voice. 'I know I'm dying,' she said. 'The doctor told us I need surgery. But I can't get it done here: I must go to a specialist hospital in Beijing. That's impossible—we can't afford it.' She sighed weakly. 'There's nothing to be done.'[21]

'Doesn't your son live in Beijing?' Li Wei asked. 'Why don't you stay with him and get him to pay for your surgery?'

'No, no, I couldn't. They don't have money either. And I don't want to tell him about my troubles; I don't want him to worry.'

'Oh, you should tell him!' I cried out. 'How will he feel if you die and you haven't even told him you're sick?' I gripped the edge of my chair. 'You need to tell him. Ask him for help!'

'No, I couldn't do that,' she murmured again, disconcerted. 'It's better if I just slip away.'

The room filled with a tense silence.

'Must you go to Beijing?' Li Wei said, fiddling with her pen. 'Can't they do the operation in Xin County City?'

Gao Xiuhua shook her head and there was silence once more. She picked at the blue and white checked couch cover and then smoothed it. Finally, she looked up and said, 'I'm not afraid of dying. Perhaps it would be better that way. My medical costs are so high!'

Her hands twisted in her lap. 'I'm just a burden,' she continued. 'It was okay until a fortnight ago, but now I have no energy. I can't even water my pot plants.' She picked at the couch cover again, radiating distress.

I got up and sat next to her. As gently as I could, I put my hand on hers and held it there for a moment. She seemed to calm down, but then jerked her hand away.

---

21   Despite medical insurance and subsidies, the high cost of medical care remains a major cause of household poverty in rural China.

'I worry about my old man,' she said abruptly. 'How's he going to manage when I'm gone? His health is poor, too. Lately, he's had to manage all the farm work by himself. He's really struggling. And what about Xiaobing? What will happen to him?'

She turned her head and I saw Li Changyin at the door with the village doctor. How much had they heard?

We watched as the doctor set up the infusion for Gao Xiuhua. Apparently, she had been having regular infusions at home for some time. A metal pole stood in a corner near the family altar. Li Changyin fetched it and placed it next to the couch. The doctor suspended a bag of liquid from the top, with a tube travelling down to Gao Xiuhua's thin hand, resting on her knee. He flicked the bag to get it dripping and we all watched the level of the liquid drop steadily.

Li Wei and I stayed only a little longer. Before leaving, I bent down to Gao Xiuhua and quickly pressed some banknotes into her hand. 'Please go to Beijing,' I whispered. She protested weakly.

***

Li Wei and I made another visit to Gao Xiuhua's home on a bright afternoon in March the next year. The canola was in flower, with swathes of brilliant yellow shimmering on both sides of the main road. We set out for Five Hills with trepidation, fearing that Gao Xiuhua might have passed away since we'd last seen her.

But she was shuffling around her courtyard when we arrived, the green plastic watering can in one hand. She welcomed us in a chirpy voice. Quickly putting the watering can down, she came forward, clasping my hands in hers and reaching out to Li Wei. A curious smell hung about her. Tiger balm perhaps. Li Changyin was out but Xiaobing was with her. He walked more confidently now.

We made our way towards the house, pausing as Gao Xiuhua watered the Buddha's palm plants and the gardenias, with their lustrous green leaves. She had gone to the specialist hospital in Beijing, she said, but the doctor told her she was too frail to have the operation. So, after she came home, she bought some Chinese medicine. It was expensive, but it seemed to really help, she said, straightening up and beaming at us both in turn. 'I'm so much better than before. I might even be able to help with the canola harvest this year.' She took Xiaobing's hand and ushered us inside.

*

That afternoon, Gao Xiuhua moved the round table to the couch again and went out to the kitchen. She made two trips and loaded up the table with bowls of sunflower seeds and sweets as well as mugs of fragrant tea. When Xiaobing reached for a sweet, she pulled him away and sat down with him on the hard chair, motioning for Li Wei and me to take the couch. I felt Xiaobing's weight on her frail knees and frowned. Li Wei gave him a biscuit to stop his tears. He sat, nibbling, staring at me and Li Wei as we talked.

We had a long list of questions about the clothes villagers wore in the 1960s and 1970s, and the work of making them. Gao Xiuhua responded patiently, amusement tickling the corners of her mouth.

In the first several years of her marriage, she said proudly, she wove almost all the cloth her family needed for their clothes and bedding. But she paid to have it dyed and sewn. By that time, the late 1960s, most women had given up dyeing their cloth themselves. Instead, they took it to one of a handful of dye stores in Ginkgo Village, where they dyed it blue or black— the only colours available. Some older women still sewed clothes by hand, but younger women paid a tailor. Most production teams had a tailor.

In Gao Xiuhua's marital family, they owned more clothes than when she was a girl. The adults had three or four sets of jackets and trousers, which she replaced every few years. The children had new clothes made each Lunar New Year—one set for summer and one for winter. Getting them was a special occasion, marked by its own ritual. It was called 'waiting up for a cotton-padded jacket' (shou mian'ao). Gao Xiuhua's eyes sparkled as she told us. Children were supposed to stay up all night on New Year's Eve and receive the new clothes first thing in the morning. They didn't really stay up all night, she said, but they got up early. They were too excited to sleep past dawn.

I thought of Christmas in Australia: my brothers and I getting up in the half-dark, squatting at the Christmas tree to secretly examine the carefully wrapped presents underneath. The tradition has continued with Misha. Both of us love the ritual of giving and receiving presents, even if they are just small tokens: a book or a bar of soap for me; a book or a pair of socks for Misha.

'Did children get underwear and socks at New Year, too?' I asked.

Gao Xiuhua laughed. 'Children didn't wear underwear in those days!'

Li Wei raised her eyebrows and I, too, was startled. We had forgotten to include underwear in our list of questions about clothing. 'Did adults wear underwear and socks?' I asked now. 'And hats?'

Adults wore cotton underpants, it turned out, but owned only one or two pairs each. And only cadres wore socks. There was a man in Ginkgo Hamlet with a machine for knitting cotton socks, but ordinary villagers couldn't afford them. In the cooler months, women sometimes wore black or coloured headscarves and men wore cloth caps. In summer, everyone wore a straw hat.

'You could tell the cadres by their straw hats,' Gao Xiuhua said with a grin. 'Ours were grey and black with age but the cadres got new yellow ones each summer.'

Xiaobing was squirming in her lap. She helped the boy slide down and shepherded him to the round table with the sweets, bending and whispering something in his ear. He reached for a fistful and looked up at her. She nodded and nudged him towards me. He stepped forward and deposited four brightly wrapped sweets in my lap before returning quickly to the safety of his grandmother's encircling arms.

'Oh, thank you.' I gave him a grin.

'And me?' Li Wei said. He stared with his fingers in his mouth and turned away. I handed Li Wei two of my sweets.

Gao Xiuhua took Xiaobing out to the courtyard. I stood up from the saggy couch to stretch my back. Li Wei wrote notes. When Gao Xiuhua came inside again, Li Wei looked up: 'Granny, apart from hats, was there anything else different about what cadres wore?'

'Let me see. Shoes—their shoes were better.' She sat down.

'In wet weather, some brigade leaders had their cloth shoes waterproofed with tung oil. Others wore wooden platform shoes with hemp uppers. But they'd only wear them on special occasions, like banquets. Even then, they'd only put their tung-oiled shoes on just before entering the house where the banquet was held. They took them off again when they left.'

We all laughed.

She went on to explain that cloth shoes would be ruined within a week if they got wet. So, apart from cadres, most men went barefoot in the rain or when working in the paddy fields. In dry weather or if they had to walk long distances over rough ground, they wore grass sandals. Men made these themselves, from wheat or rice leaves. They were much easier to make than cloth shoes, but lasted only a few days. Cloth shoes lasted two or three months if you looked after them.

'What about women: what did *you* wear in wet weather?' I asked.

'And did you ever wear grass sandals?' Li Wei chimed in.

'It wasn't proper for a woman to show her naked feet. So, we went barefoot in the paddy fields but otherwise, we always wore cloth shoes. Only men wore grass sandals; we didn't.'

'And children?'

'They went barefoot in the village. If they went to secondary school in Red River, they wore cloth shoes.'

I bent to write some notes.

'Eat your sweets!' Gao Xiuhua commanded. Before we could object, she grabbed another two handfuls and dumped one on my notebook and the other in Li Wei's lap.

I unwrapped one hard lozenge and stuck it in my mouth. It was sickly sweet. 'When did villagers start buying leather shoes?' I asked.

Gao Xiuhua had to think about it. After the reforms of the 1980s, she said, men occasionally bought synthetic leather shoes for special occasions, like weddings. In the 1990s, migrant labourers bought shoes in the city, but again, they were synthetic, not leather. 'I kept making cloth shoes for my family,' she said. 'But I didn't make the soles. I bought plastic ones.'

'See, these have plastic soles.' She stretched out a dainty foot.

I became self-conscious about my own clodhoppers and tried to pull them in closer to the edge of the couch.

'What about clothes?' Li Wei asked. 'When did you start buying clothes instead of having them made?'

'You could buy clothes in the coop store at the end of the 1970s, but they weren't any good. There were private clothes stores in Red River in the 1980s, but we didn't start buying most of our clothes till the 1990s. There wasn't much variety before then. Anyway, they were too expensive.'

She again pressed me and Li Wei to eat our sweets. I still had the first one bulging my cheek.

'Did you teach your daughter to spin and weave when she was young?' I asked.

She shook her head. 'She didn't have time—she was going to school. In any case, I did all the weaving we needed.'

'Did she sew cloth shoes?'

'No, but she embroidered insoles. Still does. She does the embroidery on a piece of cloth, then sticks it onto ready-made cloth insoles and stitches them with a sewing machine.'

I pricked up my ears. 'When did she get a sewing machine?'

'In 1991. When she got married, she bought it with her bride-price money. By then, all the new brides were getting sewing machines when they married.' Gao Xiuhua chuckled.

'What else did they get?' I asked, leaning forward.

'Oh, so much more than when I married! We gave my daughter a wardrobe full of new tailor-made clothes and three quilts. And the groom's family gave her money for the "three things that turn and one that makes a sound": a bicycle, a sewing machine, wristwatch and a radio. That was the standard in those days.' She laughed.

'Nowadays, brides expect even more,' she added. 'They don't want a sewing machine; they want an apartment! Some even want a car as well. That's on top of cash: 70,000 yuan[22] or more—a year's wages for a migrant labourer. The wedding costs a fortune, too!' She shook her head disapprovingly.

---

22   US$10,000.

My mind was still on the sewing machine. I recalled my grandma's sewing machine and the clothes she made. Neither my mum nor I ever learnt to sew, but long after Grandma's death, her sewing machine remains in a sacred corner in Mum's house.

'Does your daughter sew clothes?' I asked Gao Xiuhua.

'No, no-one does; they buy everything. My oldest granddaughter spends a fortune on clothes. She buys them online.'

'My son's the same,' I said, and we laughed together.

***

Li Wei and I returned to Gao Xiuhua's house a few days later with several more questions about her spinning, weaving and needlework. Arriving just after lunch, we found her and Xiaobing in the courtyard again. Once more, she came forward and I breathed in that curious sharp smell. Li Changyin was inside, napping. After a while, he emerged looking cross and crumpled. He wandered out, Xiaobing in tow.

That day, we learnt that, as a newlywed, Gao Xiuhua was unusual in undertaking all the spinning and weaving in her marital family. Most other newly married women shared the burden with their mother-in-law and sisters-in-law. And some bought cloth, rather than weaving it.

Xiuhua did less needlework than other women, though. This wasn't just because she had clothes made by a tailor, rather than sewing them herself. She also spent less time making cloth shoes and insoles than others. Her mother-in-law and sister-in-law did most of that work.

The Maoist state didn't recognise women's handcraft textile production as real work, yet it was crucial to families' survival and took up a great deal of time. Gao Xiuhua told us she produced about 60 square metres of cloth a year.[23] For each square metre, she had to do about a day and a half of spinning and one-third of a day of weaving. In other words, she spent the equivalent of almost 110 days a year—nine days a month—spinning and weaving. This was on top of raising five children and participating

---

23   Some women told us of others who engaged in the illegal practice of selling cloth and/or cloth coupons in exchange for money, grain or cotton. It's possible that Gao Xiuhua did this, but she didn't admit to it. She said the cloth she wove was entirely for her family's consumption.

in collective farm labour. For their part, her mother-in-law and sister-in-law each spent about eight days a month stitching cloth shoes and insoles. Between them, they made 40 pairs of shoes and 16 pairs of insoles each year.

On rainy days, both Gao Xiuhua and her sister-in-law stayed inside the whole day, spinning, weaving, mending clothes and stitching shoes and insoles. And they worked late into most nights. 'We got so tired,' she laughed. 'Sometimes, sitting at the spinning wheel, my eyes would close and I'd fall sideways off my stool.'

'But I liked weaving,' she continued, wistfully. 'And my sister-in-law and I were close. We talked and we helped each other. It was harder after she married and left home. I had to make my own cloth shoes then, as well as do the spinning and weaving.' She paused and looked out to the courtyard. There was a sparrow hopping around out there.

'In winter,' she continued, 'I sat in bed, wrapped in a quilt, and stitched by the light of a kerosene lamp. I worked well past midnight. It was so cold and dark …' Her voice trailed off.[24]

'Aunty,' I said, trying to call her back to the present. 'Can you show us some cloth you wove? Did you keep any?'

She smiled. 'I wove that cloth you're sitting on.' She gestured at the couch cover.

'Really? It's so soft!'

'I have more. Come, I'll show you.'

We followed her through the house. Her cloth shoes shuffled on the concrete floor. 'This was once our sons' bedroom,' she said as she led us into a dark room and around the bed to a wooden wardrobe. There were a few jackets hanging inside and a large black plastic bag on a shelf above. 'Laoshi,' she said, putting a gentle hand on my arm, 'you're nice and tall: lift that down for me, please.'

The bag contained a pile of cloth, neatly folded. 'These are sheets I wove,' Gao Xiuhua said, handing the top one to me. It was a fine, closely woven white cotton, with pink lines running through it. It smelt musty.

---

24   For more on rural women's spinning, weaving and needlework during the collective era, see Eyferth, 'Women's Work'.

Gao Xiuhua's eyes sparkled as I admired the fabric and Li Wei badgered her with questions. I wondered what my mum and grandma would have thought of Gao Xiuhua's woven sheets, and my thoughts meandered.

In the 1960s and 1970s, when Gao Xiuhua was burdened with child care and domestic work, so was my mum. She washed and ironed all our sheets every week. She would be doing the ironing when my brothers and I came home from school. I remember the sound of the jets of steam as she lifted the electric iron and put it down again. On Saturdays, my parents had friends over for afternoon tea and on Sundays we had lunch at Grandma's house. She would cook a roast and afterwards Dad would fall asleep in his favourite armchair. Standing in Gao Xiuhua's house with her sheet in my hands, thoughts about women's work contended with nostalgia about my childhood.

In my teens, I could have dismissed Mum as a boring suburban housewife and Grandma as nothing more than a kindly old lady. But I knew there was more to it than that. I had their stories. They were both great storytellers.

Grandma was born in Latvia in 1910, more than three decades before Gao Xiuhua. In the 1930s, she was an urbane young woman living in the Ukrainian capital of Kyiv. She was a skilled draughtswoman, married to a high-up member of the Soviet Communist Party. But in 1937, when her daughter (my mum) was 18 months old, her husband was sent to Siberia. She never saw him again.

In 1941, the Nazis invaded and she was forced to flee with her young daughter. For a while, mother and child were kept safe in a *kolkhoz* (collective farm) at the foot of the Caucasus Mountains. I have a photograph of them standing in a field of sunflowers. My grandma is shading her eyes with one slim hand. My mum—a wild little kid with short blond hair—is grinning at the camera. The photograph is black and white, but I can imagine the yellow of the sunflowers. I can feel the sun blazing. After that, they were in a German labour camp and then a series of displaced persons' camps in Germany and Italy.

In 1949, when Mao Zedong stood on a podium and announced China's liberation, my mum and grandma were on a ship sailing to Australia. By 1952, when Gao Xiuhua was camping under the bridge in Green Riverbend, they had moved out of the transit camp and settled in Albury, a country town in New South Wales.

As a young woman, Grandma didn't spin or weave; she didn't even learn to sew until after she came to Australia. But in Albury, she worked in a clothes factory. When I was a girl, she made skirts for me. I had to stand on a chair while she adjusted a hem, taking pins from a tin by her side. I didn't like either the process or the skirts themselves. But Grandma told funny stories and her laughter was infectious.

And my mum? She went to university, discovered philosophy and Russian poetry and became a translator. As a stay-at-home mother, she must have felt as stifled as any other Australian housewife. But she yearned to belong somewhere. Having a house and family, friends to invite to afternoon tea and clean white sheets to be ironed must have felt like an achievement.

Now, as I sit writing, I try to sharpen my focus on the life histories of each of these women: my grandma, my mum and Gao Xiuhua. I try to understand what sewing skirts for me must have meant to Grandma, what ironing sheets must have meant to Mum and what showing us her handwoven cloth must have meant to Gao Xiuhua.

At the same time, I marvel at how a simple handwoven sheet can be so redolent of meaning. And I wonder at all the different stories that you and I carry into our lives, into every moment we experience, every object we hold in our hands, every sentence we hear or read on a page.

*

'I don't weave anymore,' Gao Xiuhua was saying to Li Wei. 'I wove the couch cover and these sheets 10 years ago, but I gave up weaving after that. No-one wants homemade cloth nowadays.'

'Do you still have your loom and spinning wheel?' I asked.

'No, I broke them up and burnt them as stove-fuel.'

Li Wei and I were crestfallen. Later, we hunted high and low and eventually found an intact spinning wheel and loom in a nearby museum. We never saw any in Ginkgo Village, though. Some had been chopped up and burned. Others were dismantled and stored in pieces in the roof cavities of people's houses, along with other junk.

'You can have that, if you like,' Gao Xiuhua said, gesturing at the sheet still in my hands. I demurred, but she pushed it back.

'Take it; it's worthless. No-one else will want it.' She gave me a sad smile.

Plate 3.2 Loom in local museum
Photo: Tamara Jacka, 2017.

Plate 3.3 Spinning wheel in local museum
Photo: Tamara Jacka, 2017.

***

In August 2017, Li Wei and I visited Ginkgo Village again. Everywhere was green and teeming with life. One evening, we saw Gao Xiuhua and Xiaobing down by the Five Hills Hamlet square. They were watching a dance group of about 20 middle-aged women, who were dancing to lively Chinese pop music playing on a portable CD player and booming out of speakers placed on the ground. Other women stood on the sidelines chatting. They had brought their young children and grandchildren and the air was filled with boisterousness. The bigger boys and girls chased each other, weaving around the square. But Xiaobing stood watching the dancers, transfixed. He moved a little closer and began to imitate them. Chubby arms akimbo, he turned from side to side, stepping with his knees held high. He called out to his grandmother and she chuckled and clapped.

The following year, Li Wei and I spent the New Year holiday in Ginkgo Village. On our second morning, we set out early. Yang Yurong was clearing away the breakfast dishes. As we knelt by the door, pulling on our shoes, she called out: 'Where are you off to?' She liked to keep tabs on where we were going.

'Five Hills Hamlet!' we responded cheerily. We were eager to see Gao Xiuhua. I had a brooch to give her. It was just a small thing—a gum leaf made of fine gold wire. I also had a little pack of coloured pencils for Xiaobing.

Li Wei had her hand on the door handle, but Yang Yurong called us again: 'Wait a minute.' She set a pile of bowls back on the dining table and walked over, wiping her hands on her apron. 'If it's Gao Xiuhua you're going to see, you won't find her. She passed away a few weeks ago.'

Li Wei and I exchanged horrified looks. 'What happened? She was getting better!' I cried.

Yang Yurong shrugged her shoulders: 'Heart failure.' She turned back.

I stood paralysed, one glove on, one off. Li Wei's hand fell to her side.

4

The good earth[1]

The hamlet of Gao Fields curves like a sickle blade around a basin of paddy fields. The curve is formed by a road that rings the hillslopes rising gently from the fields. It's a long, slow road, lined with trees and houses.

Zhang Hongren's house squats halfway along the curve, looking out to the road and the paddy fields beyond. She's a solid nugget of a woman with a helmet of salt-and-pepper hair, cut short like mine. Until recently, she was the head of a rice-transplanting team. She established the team in 1995 and led it until 2013. Even in 2015, at the age of 60, she remained a member. There were eight other members: six women and two men. Most were in their fifties. The youngest was the new leader, aged forty.

'Rice transplanting is tiring work,' Zhang Hongren said. 'Today's youngsters aren't strong enough; they don't want to do it.'

In fact, rice transplanting isn't just tiring; it's also men's work. Or so Li Wei and I thought. We were excited to learn about a woman leading a mainly female rice-transplanting team. We wanted to hear her story.

---

1   Apologies to Nobel Prize–winning American author Pearl S. Buck, whose novel *The Good Earth* (New York: Washington Square Press, 1931) describes a farmer's life in pre-revolutionary China. In this tale, I challenge Buck's portrayal of farmers as men. I illustrate women's significant role in farming before 1949 and their growing dominance of agriculture in the Maoist and post-Mao periods. For more about Chinese women's farm work through the twentieth century, see Tamara Jacka, *Women's Work in Rural China: Change and Continuity in an Era of Reform* (Cambridge, UK: Cambridge University Press, 1997), 120–62, doi.org/10.1017/CBO9780511518157; Laurel Bossen, *Chinese Women and Rural Development: Sixty Years of Change in Lu Village, Yunnan* (Lanham, MD: Rowman & Littlefield, 2002), 85–150; and Hershatter, *The Gender of Memory*.

But in May 2015, it was hard to catch her. At the beginning of the month, villagers everywhere were busy planting peanuts. Later, they harvested the canola. We could be confident of finding Zhang Hongren home at only two times of the day. The first was when it was raining (most people preferred not to work in the rain). The second was in the early afternoon rest period. After lunch, the oldest villagers commonly napped, while others sat around chatting.

*

When we went to Gao Fields after lunch, we rarely found Zhang Hongren alone. She would be in her front room, surrounded by neighbours around a small wooden tea table with a plate of sunflower seeds, looking out the door and idly gossiping. Most were middle-aged and older women, but sometimes there would also be a few younger women and an older man or two. As we approached, the group would shuffle about and make room for us to sit.

Zhang Hongren didn't talk much. She was forever labouring off her stool to take a straw broom from a corner. She would wander around sweeping while her friends chewed sunflower seeds and chatted contentedly. We would ask Zhang Hongren a question and she'd give only curt responses. But the others would chime in. One woman, Wang Xinran, often spoke for her. She was six years younger than Zhang Hongren and more educated. In fact, Zhang Hongren never went to school, while Wang Xinran graduated from senior secondary school.

She made light of her schooling. 'It was when the Gang of Four were stirring up revolution,'[2] she said with a laugh. 'We had hardly any classes. Most of the time we were doing collective labour. It was like that all the way through. We didn't learn anything.'

---

2   The Gang of Four was an ultra-leftist group of CCP officials led by Mao Zedong's wife, Jiang Qing. They wielded enormous power across China in the later years of the Cultural Revolution.

All the same, her education seemed to have given her an unusual boldness when speaking with strangers like me and Li Wei. It made her different not just from Zhang Hongren, but also from most other women born before 1965.[3]

One time, Li Wei and I sat next to Zhang Hongren, with Wang Xinran on her other side. I asked Zhang Hongren whether she had ever worked away from home as a migrant labourer.

She said, 'Not long term but …'

Wang Xinran interrupted: 'She was one of the first! She got others to go, too—20 of them, mostly women. They went to a place on the edge of Beijing for two months, doing farm work—weeding and transplanting rice.'

'When was that? Did you go, too?' I leant forward to address Wang Xinran.

She shook her head. 'I was no good at transplanting. Anyway, my father-in-law wouldn't have let me go. It was 1988. Hardly anyone was going out then; it was before all the young women took up factory jobs down south.'

I sat back on my stool. 'Were you all married?' I asked Zhang Hongren.

'Yes, and we all had kids. Elder sisters Xu and Gao here—they went, too.' She waved at two frumpy-looking women sitting opposite and they grinned.

Wang Xinran reached for a handful of sunflower seeds.

'Nowadays,' she said, as Li Wei and I sat scribbling notes, 'all the young people leave home for work, but it was different then. Unmarried girls didn't go out. Everyone thought it wasn't safe; it wasn't proper.'

'Did your husband go, too?' I asked Zhang Hongren. 'Did he organise you all?'

'*She* was the leader!' Wang Xinran cried. 'Her husband stayed home and looked after their kids.'

---

3   Data provided by Ginkgo Village leaders in 2015 show that among villagers born before 1946, none had finished primary school. Among those born between 1946 and 1965, only four women, including Zhang Hongren, had not finished primary school. Wang Xinran was the only person to have graduated from senior secondary school. Secondary school attendance rates increased in the 1970s. Consequently, in the cohort born between 1966 and 1985, 31 per cent of men and 33 per cent of women graduated from senior secondary school or technical college. In the youngest cohort of adults, born between 1986 and 1997, roughly 95 per cent of both women and men had graduated from senior secondary school or technical college. Of these, 10 per cent of each gender were university graduates.

Li Wei and I sat back, startled; it was the first time we had heard of a man staying home while his wife went out to work, rather than the other way around.

'How old were your kids?' Li Wei asked Zhang Hongren.

'Eight and two. Our son was in school. My husband carried our daughter on his back while ploughing the paddy fields.'

'Isn't your husband a doctor?' I asked. Zhang Hongren had told us that when the first Ginkgo Village clinic was built in 1970, her husband had been the doctor. Later, he moved to another village clinic on the other side of Red River Township.

'Yes, but he did farm work, too.'

A rickety old man—Old Wu, the others called him—cleared his throat and spat on the floor. 'Women should stay home,' he muttered.

The women ignored him.

'How did you get the job in Beijing?' I asked Zhang Hongren.

'My older sister's brother-in-law was working there; he heard about it.' She paused, hands on her thighs, knees and feet splayed.

She sits like a bloke, I thought to myself.

'We took the bus to Xinyang and the train from there—our first time on a train. Before that, we'd never been further than Red River.'

Old Wu snorted: 'Got lost, I bet.'

Li Wei and I were taken back by his rudeness. But Zhang Hongren just smiled at the old man, like he was a little boy pouting. Wang Xinran and the others ignored him and went on chatting about their work experiences. None of the women older than Zhang Hongren had ever worked outside Xin County. But when they were in their fifties, many had been employed locally as farm labourers. They helped with the grain harvests in Ginkgo Village and nearby. Three had also been in Zhang Hongren's rice-transplanting team.

The younger women had all been migrant workers in the past. Wang Xinran had joined her husband in Beijing for a few years in the late 1990s. Another woman in her forties had worked in sweatshops in Shenzhen and Guangzhou both before and after she married.

Typing up my fieldnotes that evening, I reflected on what Old Wu had said. It looked like he was just trying to take Zhang Hongren down a peg or two. But he had a point: in those early days, it would have taken real daring for a woman to leave her husband and children at home and lead a team of other women out to work. Especially an illiterate woman like Zhang Hongren, who had never travelled before.

***

The first chance Li Wei and I had to talk with Zhang Hongren by herself was one warm, drizzly morning halfway through May. Walking along the sickle-blade curve, we breathed in the smell of rich, moist earth and green trees dripping in the rain. Coming off the road to her house, we had to pick our way around the puddles.

We began with straightforward questions about Zhang Hongren's family. She was born in 1955 in Horse Ridge Hamlet, at the other end of Ginkgo Village. She was the third-born child. Her older sister was born in 1948 and her older brother in 1950. Her younger brother and sister were born on either side of the Great Leap Forward.

While Zhang Hongren poured tea, we asked a few questions about her children, who were now grown up. Then we circled back to her own childhood and youth.

I asked about her earliest memories. At first, she said she couldn't remember anything. She plodded to a cabinet at the side of the room and came back with a plastic bag of sunflower seeds. Li Wei and I waited in silence while she added some to the plate on the tea table. The room filled with the rushing sound of rain.

'I remember when I was in kindergarten,' she said, sitting down. 'In Red River.'

Li Wei tilted her head. 'When was that?' she asked gently.

'During the Great Famine.' She sat down. 'Early 1959 it must have been. I'd just turned four. It was a live-in kindergarten for orphans and children from destitute families.' She rubbed at her grey slacks with both hands. 'My parents did collective labour and my sister looked after my baby brother. My mother took me to the kindergarten so I wouldn't starve to death.'

I stared unseeing out the door. A four-year-old girl, too young to work—the dispensable one. The kindergarten was a mercy, I realised.

I leant forward: 'When was the kindergarten set up? How many children did it have?'

'1958. There were four other kids from Horse Ridge Hamlet. Don't know how many altogether.' She folded her arms and sat in silence for a moment, watching Li Wei and me writing notes.

Then she got up and walked over to the doorway. She stood there, looking out at the rain.

'Elder Sister, did they feed you in the kindergarten?' I asked.

She turned back. 'Just a bit of soup.' Slowly, she lowered herself onto her stool. 'After a few days, they told my mother to come and take me home again. I was so malnourished, they feared I'd die there. But after another week I went back. I was left there for two years.'

'Can you tell us a bit more about the kindergarten? What were conditions like there?'

'I don't remember much. We slept on the floor.'

'What sort of building was it?' Li Wei prompted, reaching for her tea.

Zhang Hongren looked down, silent. 'There was a yard with a wall,' she finally mumbled.

I waited a few moments and then asked, 'Can you remember being in the yard? Were there a lot of children playing?'

Zhang Hongren frowned. 'I don't remember. There must have been a lot of us ...' She lifted her head and stared outside. 'But we were too weak to play.'

*

We fell silent and watched the rain. It was petering out. I tried to think of a way to change the topic, but Zhang Hongren started speaking again in a soft voice.

'There was a tree,' she said. 'A huge poplar on the other side of the wall.'

That gave me a jolt. I, too, recalled a tall poplar from my early childhood. My family lived in a thin-walled box of a place on the Adelaide Plains in those days. I remember being alone in a hot, bare yard. A single poplar grew out the front—a sentinel at the end of the driveway, reaching up to the stark blue sky. She twinkled and shimmered her white-backed leaves. She winked and whispered to me.

Mum was busy with my baby brother, Tommy. Dad worked long hours at the university. He was the director of a research institute. Then, just after Marcus was born, Dad was diagnosed with thyroid cancer and very nearly died. That was the first of a series of hospitalisations. He suffered a heart attack when I was nine and a second heart attack, followed by triple-bypass surgery, when I was twelve. I was 19 when he had his third heart attack and stroke, seven months after Tommy was killed. Dad died of lung cancer when I was twenty-seven.

My mind hangs onto the twinkly tree. Not the hollow yard or the hard glare of the vast sky. Or what lay beyond.

Why did Zhang Hongren remember the poplar outside her kindergarten? What did the tree mean to her? I didn't know how to ask.

But perhaps I didn't need to. In my mind's eye it was winter. I saw the tree shorn of leaves, skeletal branches stark against the white sky. It wasn't hard to imagine the desolation then.

*

Li Wei was frowning at her notebook. She tucked a strand of hair behind her ear. 'Aunty,' she said, looking up, 'what year did you say you started kindergarten?'

'1959.'

'Hadn't they cut down all the trees by then? Weren't they used to fuel the steel-smelting furnaces?'

I stared at Zhang Hongren.

She shrugged and looked away. 'Perhaps that's why I remember it—because all the others had gone.'

***

A week later, Li Wei and I once more sat on stools in Zhang Hongren's front room, looking out at the sniffling rain. We were perched opposite Zhang Hongren, the tea table between us. Another plate of sunflower seeds sat on one side.

That morning, we asked Zhang Hongren about farm work during the collective era. She hunched forward, elbows on her knees. She started working in collective labour in 1971, she told us. She was sixteen.

At first, her main task was to cut wild grass, which was then placed on the fields as green fertiliser.[4] Zhang Hongren and her teammates cut so much they bared the hillsides. With each passing month and year, they had to hike further and further into the mountains.

Zhang Hongren was quick and strong. In one day, she could cut 150 kilograms of grass: two heavy bundles, spiked onto each end of a long pole, in the morning shift and another two in the afternoon. Every day, she earned seven work points for her family. Her teammates earned no more than six.

I imagine her out there: a sinewy teenager with scraggly plaits. It's getting late; the sun is sinking behind the mountains. The other girls joke and tease each other. They're hurrying to fit their bundles of grass to the ends of their poles, lift them onto their shoulders and start the journey home. But Zhang Hongren is still off in the distance, cutting grass with her sickle. She's already cut more than anyone else.

Li Wei was busy asking more questions: 'How many work points did your parents earn?'

'My father and older brother earnt 10 a day—the same as all the other men. Elder Sister earnt seven. Women hardly ever earnt more than that.'

'And your mother?'

---

4   Chemical fertiliser wasn't used in Ginkgo Village until the 1980s.

'Six. She couldn't do as many hours as us; she had to knock off early to prepare our meals.'

*

Just then, Wang Xinran came splashing over. 'Oh, you've come again,' she said when she saw me and Li Wei. She folded her umbrella and plonked herself on a stool next to Zhang Hongren, still in her rubber boots. 'What are you talking about?' she said, brushing a wave of damp hair from her face.

'The collective era.' Zhang Hongren got up and fetched a thermos flask, a box of tea-leaves and mugs from a cabinet at the side of the room.

Wang Xinran picked up the box of tea and sniffed inside. 'Is this local?' she asked and shook the box a little.

'Of course,' Zhang Hongren said brusquely.

Wang Xinran looked at Li Wei and me. 'Did you know she's one of the best tea pickers in …'

'Nonsense!' Zhang Hongren interrupted. 'My fingers are too thick. I can't pick the smaller shoots.' She pushed a mug of tea towards me. 'Your host, Yang Yurong—she's more skilful. She just flies along, picking those tiny leaves.'

'Elder Sister Zhang,' I said, looking up, 'when did you start doing other tasks, aside from cutting grass?'

She lowered herself onto her stool. 'Aged 17, I was doing everything, even transplanting rice. Aged 19, they made me the women's head of the production team. I did that for five years. Then I married and came here to Gao Fields.'

'And after that? Were you the women's head for Gao Fields as well?'

'No.'

'What did you do as the team's women's head? The same things as the women's director does now?'

She frowned. 'The women's director just looks after women's problems: reproductive health, quarrels between mothers- and daughters-in-law—that sort of thing.'[5]

'So, what was your role?'

'I organised the women to get our tasks done. And I took the lead.'

Wang Xinran interrupted: 'They would've chosen her 'cos she was the strongest, most hardworking woman in the team—so she'd set an example for the others.'

Zhang Hongren straightened up.

'Was that true?' Li Wei asked.

She shrugged coyly.

I looked up from my notebook. 'Was that a paid position?'

She shook her head. 'The team leader was paid extra work points, but I wasn't. He decided who should do what each day. I just organised the women to carry out his orders.'

'How did you feel about that?

She looked directly at me. 'It wasn't fair. The team leader did less work than the rest of us, but he got more work points.'

'Nothing was fair in those days,' Wang Xinran butted in. 'Men got 10 work points a day; women got six or seven. How is that fair?'

'Did you complain?' I turned from one to the other.

Wang Xinran scuffed at the floor with her boot.

'Huh!' Zhang Hongren folded her arms. 'No-one dared! Cadres had much more power in those days.'

---

5   The village women's director is one of four village leaders in Ginkgo Village. She is a representative of the state's All China Women's Federation. For further discussion, see Jacka, *Women's Work in Rural China*, 84–100.

'But it wasn't always like that,' she added. 'For some things—rice transplanting and reaping grain—you were paid for the number of mu you finished. I was fast. Transplanting rice seedlings, I could easily earn 10 work points a day.'

'Really?' Wang Xinran cocked her head.

Zhang Hongren grinned.

'Were there other tasks paid by the area you finished?' I asked.

'You said cutting grass was paid according to the amount you cut, right?' Li Wei said. She turned aside to sneeze. She must have caught a cold. I fished out a small pack of tissues from my daypack and handed it to her.

'That was when I was sixteen,' Zhang Hongren said. 'But by the time I was 18, cutting grass and laying it in the fields was a single task. You had to complete a certain area before they'd give you your seven work points for the day.'

'It was like that in Bamboo Glen, too,' Wang Xinran said, rubbing her nose. 'When I cut grass, I was always the slowest. I often had to work into the night to finish.'

Zhang Hongren gave a brief chuckle. She got up and fetched her broom to sweep the sunflower seed husks from around our feet. Wang Xinran stood, too, and wandered to the doorway.

*

'Elder Sister Zhang,' I said after a pause, 'has it always been women who do the rice transplanting?'

Wang Xinran interrupted. 'Women had bound feet, so they only did light farm work, like weeding.'

A flicker of impatience crossed Zhang Hongren's face. 'Some did other tasks, too. My mother transplanted rice when she was young. She told me about it.' She plodded back to her stool and propped the broom against the tea table.

'Did she have bound feet?'

She shook her head. 'She was born in 1932. Foot-binding was dying out by then. Her older sister's feet were bound and so were hers when she was three. But her bindings were released when she turned five or so. Her feet were small, but they weren't the real 3-inch "lotus feet".'

Wang Xinran returned to her stool. 'They still would've been deformed,' she said. 'She must've been in pain.'

Zhang Hongren nodded.

Li Wei and I screwed up our faces thinking about it. I arched my back, which I'd damaged giving birth to my son. All these years later, it still gave me trouble. I couldn't imagine how much pain I would be in if I had to bend down transplanting rice all day—even without deformed feet.

'Men usually did the transplanting in those days,' Zhang Hongren continued. 'But my mother's father died when she was a child. She only had one older brother and one older sister. She and her brother did most of the farm work.'

'Was your mother still transplanting rice when you were a kid?' I asked.

'No.' Zhang Hongren folded her arms. 'In the 1950s and 1960s, the men did it. It was only later that young women like me took over. In the 1970s, we usually had a couple of men help carry the seedlings from one paddy field to another, but otherwise it was women.'

'The same as now.'

'Yes, but now we only plant one crop each year. For a few years in the 1970s, we planted two. We transplanted the first crop in early spring, when the water was still cold. Our legs and feet turned to ice. We didn't have boots in those days.'

'And the second crop?'

Zhang Hongren leant forward and clasped her hands: 'In the sixth lunar month.[6] It was so hot! We'd have sweat pouring off us the whole day. It wasn't worth it; the yield from a double crop wasn't much more than from a single crop.'

---

6   That is, July–August.

'What about ploughing? Before 1949, did your mother do the ploughing as well as the rice transplanting?'

Wang Xinran interrupted again, less strident this time. 'Men plough, women weave,' she murmured.[7]

Zhang Hongren frowned at her hands. 'They probably didn't have a plough or water buffalo; they were too poor.' She looked up. 'They probably just used a hoe to break up the soil.'

I turned to Wang Xinran: 'What about your mother's family: did they have a plough and water buffalo?'

'Maybe not,' she said and spat out a seed husk. 'But they might have borrowed one.'

*

I reached down to my daypack, where I had several sheets of questions stapled together. I pulled them out and began flipping through. 'Can you tell us a bit more about the gender division of labour in the collective era?' I asked.

Zhang Hongren and Wang Xinran exchanged puzzled looks.

I tried again. 'Apart from transplanting rice, what tasks did women do and what did men do?'

'Men and women worked together,' Zhang Hongren said.

'Yes, but—'

'Men did the heavy work; women did the light work,' Wang Xinran said shortly. 'Like weeding—that's always been women's work.'

'Who did the planting of the grain crops: women or men?'

'Both.'

Zhang Hongren shifted on her stool. 'The men's team ploughed and harrowed the soil; the women's team scattered the seed.'

---

7   'Men plough, women weave' (*nan geng nü zhi*) is a traditional Chinese saying reflecting norms about women's and men's work.

Plate 4.1 Harrowing with a water buffalo
Photo: Tamara Jacka, 2018.

'Did you have tractors?'

'No, not until the 1980s. The men used a water buffalo to plough and harrow.'

'A few still do,' Wang Xinran said. 'But most hire a man with a tractor.'

I could feel Zhang Hongren watching me as I scribbled this down and consulted my list of questions.

I looked up at her. 'Apart from rice, did women transplant other crops, like wheat and sorghum?'

'Yes, but not sweet potatoes. Men transplanted them.'

'Why was that?'

'For the seedlings to grow strong, you must transplant them while it's raining.'

Li Wei and I looked sideways at each other. 'Couldn't women work in the rain?' Li Wei asked.

'We stayed inside when it rained,' Wang Xinran said. 'We made use of the rainy weather to stitch shoes and weave.'

'It's not like nowadays,' Zhang Hongren added. 'We never rested.' She levered herself off her stool and reached for her broom again.

'You still never rest!' Wang Xinran laughed.

Zhang Hongren wacked her leg with the broom. 'Move,' she grunted.

Wang Xinran laughed again and did as she was told.

'Hey, Little Li, how old are you?' she said suddenly, looking at Li Wei.

'Twenty-four.'

'Oh! You look younger. How come you're still a student?'

'I'm a research student. Laoshi is my supervisor.'

'You must be very clever,' Zhang Hongren murmured, sitting down again.

Wang Xinran turned to me with a grin: 'Is she a good student?'

'Very good,' I said and smiled at Li Wei.

She blushed and bent her head. Wang Xinran considered her for a moment.

*

I looked at the list of questions in my lap and turned a page.

Wang Xinran came over to me. She peered upside down at my list. 'What are all these questions for?' she said.

'I want to write a book.'

'Oh right, you told us that. Tell us again, what's it about?'

'Village life—to show foreigners what it's like. And I want to write about how things have changed in the village; how it's developed over time.'

'I remember now,' she said, sitting back on her stool. 'Keep going.' She waved at my list. 'What else do you want to ask?'

I struggled to pick up the thread again.

Li Wei turned to Zhang Hongren. 'What else did you grow for the collective, aside from grain and sweet potatoes?'

'Soybeans, cotton, peanuts, canola.'

'Did women plant them?'

Zhang Hongren nodded.

Wang Xinran butted in again. 'It was the same with everything: men prepared the soil and women did the planting.'

'Those crops didn't need transplanting,' Zhang Hongren added.

'Did women harvest those crops as well as plant them?'

'We picked the soybeans, but we worked with the men on the cotton harvest. We cut the cotton bolls and picked the cotton out. The men carried the bolls back to the village.'

'What about the canola and peanuts? Oh, and the sweet potatoes: who harvested them?'

'Women mostly. But men helped pull up the peanuts.'

'And the grain: who harvested the rice and other grain?'

'Women reaped and tied the grain up in bundles. Both women and men carried the—'

'How did you carry them?' I interrupted. 'In baskets?'

Zhang Hongren shook her head. 'The same way we carried grass: stuck on each end of a pole.'

'Those poles were really long,' Wang Xinran chimed in, stretching her arms wide to demonstrate. 'As tall as us if you stood them on end.'

'Almost as tall as you two!' Zhang Hongren said to me and Li Wei.

We all laughed.

*

I looked again at my sheet of questions, but I needn't have bothered. Zhang Hongren continued by herself: 'Women threshed the grain. The men did the hulling in a stone grinding-mill.'

Wang Xinran shifted restlessly and started talking in dialect to Zhang Hongren.

I checked my list of questions again.

'How many more of those do you have?' Wang Xinran burst out.

That flustered me. 'Not many,' I mumbled and lifted my head.

Zhang Hongren was waiting expectantly.

'Which farming tasks were only done by men, never by women?'

'The ploughing and harrowing,' Wang Xinran said roughly. She turned and saw that the rain had stopped. The sun had broken through the clouds and steam was rising off the puddles in the yard.

A woman with black trousers tucked into rubber boots and carrying a floral umbrella came up the road. She had a bulging plastic bag in one hand; perhaps she'd been shopping. She looked tired.

'Old Chen,' Wang Xinran called out. She jumped up. 'Goin' home? Wait for me.' She grabbed her umbrella and hurried out.

*

I breathed more easily after she left. 'Do you mind if I ask a couple more questions?' I asked Zhang Hongren, scanning through my list once more.

'Go ahead.' She smiled.

'Who did the watering and who applied liquid fertiliser? You carried it in wooden tubs, right? That would have been very heavy work. Did women do it or was it always the men?'

'Both men and women carried the fertiliser; both spread it out.'

'And the watering?'

'We usually didn't need to carry water. We let water flow from an uphill pond or a spring down into the paddy fields. And we used water wheels. The big kind was pedal-powered. They took four people to pedal—mostly men worked those. The smaller ones were hand-cranked by two people. Both women and men could work them.'

A peal of music rang out and Li Wei pulled her phone from her jeans pocket. I bent to retrieve my own phone from my daypack to check the time: midday.

'It's Yang Yurong,' Li Wei said in English. 'She wants to know when we'll be back. She's made lunch already.'

'Yes, we better go; it's later than I realised.' I hastily returned my phone, shut my notebook and reached forward for one last sip of tea. Li Wei tapped out a reply to Yang Yurong and I told Zhang Hongren we were leaving; we had already taken up too much of her time.

***

One morning a few days later, we set out for Gao Fields once more. The sky, like grey felt, was snivelling yet again. My umbrella was too small. By the time we got to Zhang Hongren's place, my daypack and the bottom of my jeans and shoes were soaked. Li Wei was still sniffing.

We had set out extra early in the hope of finding Zhang Hongren alone. We were in luck: she was by herself in the back of the house.

I wanted to talk about the Cultural Revolution.

'Were you ever a Red Guard [*Hong Weibing*]?' I asked Zhang Hongren.

She said she was, but after a while it emerged that we'd misunderstood each other. Her nephew was a Red Guard, but she wasn't. She was one of the *jigan minbing*: the core people's militia.[8]

'There was glory attached to being a Red Guard,' she said with a laugh. 'But not to the core militia. The Red Guards didn't have to work, and some went on a train to Beijing to see Chairman Mao. We never went anywhere.'

---

8   For more about the people's militia, see Harvey W. Nelsen, *The Chinese Military System: An Organizational Study of the Chinese People's Liberation Army*, 2nd edn (Boulder, CO: Westview Press, 1981), 170–90.

She got up to make tea for us. While she poured, she explained that the Red Guards were secondary school students. And there were Little Red Guards, who were primary school kids.

'Tell us about the core people's militia,' I said, as she sat again. I reached for my tea. 'When did you join?'

'I was 18—1973.'

'The year before you became the women's head of the production team, right?'

'Yes. I did both till I got married. Apart from bad class elements, nearly everyone was in the common people's militia [*putong minbing*]. But there were only 17 in the brigade's core militia. We were chosen for our strength and courage.'

'How many women were there?'

'Seven, all unmarried. They didn't take married women.'

Li Wei turned aside to sneeze. 'What did you do in the core militia?' she asked.

'We got training. Once a year, the brigade's company commander took us up into the mountains for a few days. He taught us how to crawl forward on our stomachs with our guns. We had rifles. He showed us how to load the rifles and shoot targets.' She fell silent and looked out the door.

'Did you ever put your training to use?' I asked.

She nodded. 'In the evenings, our platoon leader would call a meeting for all the core militia in our production team. Then we'd go out on patrol. We were on the lookout for thieves and troublemakers.'

'How often did you go out?'

'Every night for the first year or so. Much less after that.'

I put my tea back on the table. 'What sort of troublemakers were you scouting for?'

Zhang Hongren knitted her eyebrows. 'Bad class elements, counterrevolutionaries. There was fighting. If the counterrevolutionaries were causing trouble, the company commander blew his whistle and we all came running.'

'Did you have rifles on patrol?'

'Yes, but a lot of them didn't work. Mostly we just used wooden poles—the ones for carrying bundles of grass. Some had sharp points on the ends. Others had metal blades.' She straightened up and brushed at her shirt.

*

I paused, trying to imagine the young Zhang Hongren as a fighter, trying to make the shift in my brain from carrying-pole to weapon, from young woman to core farmer to core militia.

Li Wei had her head down. She was fidgeting with a tissue. Perhaps she didn't like me asking about the Cultural Revolution. It was a sensitive topic. Some villagers got upset about us digging up painful memories of abuse and violence. In Bitter Hollow, one older man from a landlord family was in tears about the Red Guards. They had burst into his home, beaten his family and smashed their furniture. We quickly changed the topic so as not to cause further distress.

More commonly, villagers we talked with had not been the victims of Cultural Revolution violence. They were more likely to have stood mute in the face of brutality. Or else they were the perpetrators. They had probably hurled abuse and punched and kicked people, including those with whom they still lived side by side today. They would get an uneasy, guilty look and evade our questions. We didn't press them.

So far, though, Zhang Hongren seemed relaxed.

I pushed on: 'What was it like being in the core militia?'

She folded her arms across her chest. 'The training was fun. We were given work points for it. It meant we didn't have to work for a few days.'

'Seven points for the women, 10 for the men?'

'Uh huh.' She looked out at the drizzle.

I followed her gaze. 'There must have been a *bit* of glory, being chosen for the core militia?'

She gave me a brief, uncertain smile, then pushed herself up and went to fetch the thermos to replenish our tea.

*

I also got up and stood in the doorway for a moment, watching the rain blur the fields in the distance. I tried to recall myself at the age at which Zhang Hongren was serving in the core militia.

When Tommy died, I was midway through the second year of an undergraduate degree in Chinese studies at The Australian National University in Canberra. After my dad had his stroke and heart attack and my mum said she couldn't be my mother anymore, I went back to my studies. I became fascinated with the Cultural Revolution. Who would I have been in those turbulent times: victim or rebel?

Hunched over my books, hour after hour, I was a smear of misery and self-loathing—an unloved bad class element to be paraded and beaten to a pulp. Tommy had been the black sheep in the family—the rebellious, creative one. He sucked up everyone's attention, good and bad. Marcus and I were the dregs left behind.

But in the dead of night, some spark in me wanted out. I became the girl in the Cultural Revolution poster I had taped to my wall: stubby plaits, bold black eyebrows, ruddy cheeks. I'm wearing a khaki army jacket with a red and gold Mao badge, a rifle cradled in my right arm. On my left arm is a people's militia armband. In my left hand, I'm grasping the selected works of Mao Zedong, tied with a fat pink ribbon. I hold my head up and my eyes are fierce. I gaze out, mirroring a woman with a huge red flag and a lamp held high. We're standing together, gazing out to the new day breaking on the horizon.

I still have that poster. On one side it says: 'To be an upright person, this is who you must be.' Along the bottom is written: 'Carry the revolution through to the end.'[9]

Standing in Zhang Hongren's doorway all those decades later, I thought about how the poster masks violence. Or does it? Perhaps I just didn't let myself feel it back then. Or perhaps I did.

---

9   The poster 'Iron Girls', designed by Shan Lianxiao in 1968, is based on a Cultural Revolution model opera called *The Red Lantern* (*Hong Deng Ji*). It can be seen on Wikimedia Commons at: commons. wikimedia.org/wiki/File:Iron_Girls_3.jpg.

Now that gun, that pink ribbon, made me nauseated. The times had changed and so had I. Now I was a mother with a son, who was 18—the age at which my beloved, rebellious brother was killed. Now the violence of the Cultural Revolution slammed into me.

And yet, I recalled my younger self, yearning to be somewhere else. I'd wanted to be nowhere; I'd wanted to not be. Or else I'd wanted to be that woman in the people's militia. I'd wanted that hope, that righteousness and common purpose. I'd dreamed of soaring out of my tiny dorm room, my tiny self. I'd be a fighter jet and roar across the dawn. I could see Zhang Hongren in the core militia and feel the liberation of it.

*

Li Wei didn't share my sentiments. She was born in 1991, 15 years after Mao Zedong died. Her parents, she knew, had suffered during the Cultural Revolution. Her mother was sent down to the countryside after graduating from junior secondary school. Along with her classmates, she spent a few years in the early 1970s working on a commune to the north of Shenyang. Occasionally, she felt nostalgic about the bonds that had developed between the sent-down youth. But the bitterly harsh conditions were what she recalled the most.

Li Wei's father, who was several years older than her mother, had been an army officer in the early 1970s. Posted south, he led a brutal crackdown against rebels and was thereafter dogged by grotesque nightmares. Li Wei's mother had told her that much, but no more. 'My parents don't talk about the past any more than Ginkgo Villagers,' she said.

Nor had she learnt much about the Cultural Revolution at school. From her textbooks, the media and everyone around her, she absorbed the post-Mao state's judgement of Chairman Mao's policy decisions at the time as mistaken. There had never been anything to make her question that judgement or want to probe further.

'Was it the people's militia who smashed the shrines and lineage halls and beat up the landlord families?' she asked Zhang Hongren, after she and I sat down again.

Zhang Hongren pulled at her sleeves. It was a warm, muggy day. Li Wei and I were wearing T-shirts, but Zhang Hongren wore a long-sleeved red and brown checked shirt, with the collar buttoned up.

'Most of that happened before I joined,' she said after a pause.

'Were the core militia violent?' I asked softly. 'Did you kill people?'

Zhang Hongren hung her head. I could barely hear her response above the pounding rain.

'I didn't kill anyone,' she mumbled. 'We were only doing what we were told. They were bad times.'[10]

We fell silent.

***

In the last week of May, when Li Wei and I trekked up to Gao Fields, the sky was still grey, but it wasn't raining. We were hoping to ask Zhang Hongren about men's and women's farm work during the post-Mao period, but she wasn't home. Neither were her nearest neighbours. It was not long after lunch, but all their doors were shut and locked. We plodded a little further and found Old Wu, sitting outside his open doorway, smoking.

'They're out in the fields,' he said. 'Zhang Hongren is transplanting rice.'

Li Wei and I stood there, uncertain.

'Come in,' the old man said, standing and crushing his cigarette butt with his cloth shoe. He picked up his stool. 'Want tea?'

'No thanks, we'll just sit for a while if that's okay.'

His front room was cooler than outside. I asked to sit on the musty brown couch and Li Wei sat next to me. Old Wu eased himself onto his stool close by.

We learnt that he was 82 and a widower, living alone. He had five adult children, including two sons: one in Xin County City and one in Wuhan. We asked why he didn't live with one of his sons. He said he visited the younger one in Wuhan once, but he didn't like it: 'I'm too old. Can't manage the stairs—they live on the fifth floor. And their food is too hard for me to chew. It's better here in the village; more peaceful.'

---

10   Contrary to popular perceptions, most Cultural Revolution killings and persecutions were not perpetrated by Red Guards in 1966–67. Most casualties occurred in mid to late 1968 and were inflicted by state agents, including the people's militia, who were tasked with 'restoring order' (Walder, 'Rebellion and Repression').

'Uncle Wu,' I said, 'what's that growing in the fields below the road down there?' I pointed out the door. 'All I can see are green dots.'

'Huh. That land's been transferred to Cao Fuguo. He's planted it with a new type of "super rice" [*chaoji dao*]. He's trying a new planting method. You let the seeds grow sprouts about an inch long. Then you plough and harrow the earth and just scatter the sprouted seeds across it. Saves transplanting.'

That will put Zhang Hongren's transplanting team out of work, I thought to myself. 'Isn't it better to transplant? Doesn't transplanting make the plants stronger and improve the final yield?'

Old Wu wiped a hand over his eyes, then reached for the cigarette pack and lighter in his jacket pocket. 'Smoking's my only pleasure,' he wheezed. 'Only began in the 1980s; none of us could afford smokes or liquor before that.'

Li Wei and I both hate cigarette smoke, but we could hardly say so.

'Cao's trying to cut costs,' Old Wu said, lighting up. He breathed the smoke out through his nostrils. 'You're right, the yield won't be as good, but he'll save money: he won't need to hire labourers for the transplanting.' He erupted in a hacking cough. 'And he'll get a subsidy for planting this new type of rice. Doesn't matter to him if the yield's no good; he only cares about money.' He shook his head in disgust.

I bent down to take my water bottle from my daypack. 'Who is this Mr Cao?'

Old Wu grunted. 'Former Party secretary.' He pushed himself up off his stool, shuffled over to the doorway and hoicked a gob of phlegm outside. Li Wei wrinkled her nose and I suppressed a laugh.

He came shuffling back and eased himself onto his stool again. 'He was Party secretary from just after the return to family farming till 2013. For 30 years, he cheated villagers and embezzled village funds.' He sighed. 'Everyone knew. But the village committee didn't keep accounts; we couldn't prove anything. It was Xi Jinping's anticorruption campaign that made the difference. The higher-ups finally had to heed our complaints. They forced Cao to retire.' He paused and tapped the ash off his cigarette onto the floor.

'After that,' he said, folding one thin leg over the other, 'Cao subcontracted almost all of Gao Fields' paddy land and merged it into one large field. It used to be our land. Every household in Gao Fields had a plot down there. But Cao took almost all of it. Most of us don't grow rice anymore. We just have a bit of dry land. Mine's back there.' He waved behind us. 'I just grow a few vegetables for myself.'

*

Li Wei tilted her head. 'Why did you give up your paddy land?'

Old Wu took another sharp puff of his cigarette and pushed the smoke out through pursed lips. ''Cos we're too old to farm it ourselves! Cao pays 300 yuan per mu.[11] It's not much, but better than nothing.'

'For how long do the contracts last?'

'Twenty years. But who knows what'll happen after that. No-one expects their land back.'

'So, you've given up your land?' I said, distressed. 'What happens if your sons lose their jobs? Without any land, they'll have nothing to fall back on!'

Old Wu frowned. 'That'll never happen,' he said shortly. 'They're never coming back. I'm here all on my own and I can't afford to hire labour. Might as well get a bit of rent for the land.'

'And others?' Li Wei said after an awkward pause. 'Has everyone been willing to contract to Mr Cao?'

'Not everyone. One old couple refused. They're penniless; they need the money from farming. It doesn't matter 'cos their plot is near the edge. But it's different with others. Take Zhang Hongren. She didn't want to let go of her land but Director Zhou[12] forced her.' He took a drag on the remains of his cigarette, pinching it between bony thumb and forefinger. 'Her plot was right in the middle. It would've mucked up all Cao's plans if she'd refused. He's merged all the land into one big field. That way it's easier to use tractors and harvesters. He saves on labour costs.'

---

11   The equivalent of US$690 per hectare.
12   Zhou is the director of the village committee.

Li Wei looked up from her notebook. 'Grandpa, you said it was Director Zhou who forced her to give up her land. Why was he involved?'

Old Wu finished his cigarette and dropped the smouldering butt on the floor.

I stared at it.

'He and Cao are mates. We've only ever negotiated with Director Zhou; he was the one who signed the contracts. Cao doesn't live in the village anymore. We never see him. He pays Director Zhou to manage his land. Director Zhou is the one who hires labourers and organises the farming.'

'Are the labourers all locals?' I asked.

Old Wu nodded. 'From around Red River.'

'So, how much land has Mr Cao contracted altogether?'

'About 100 mu.[13] Another guy, Huang Dajun, controls 200 mu: 50 mu in Ginkgo Hamlet and 150 mu running through Green Riverbend and into Deng Inn. He has more land on the other side of Deng Inn as well. He's an outsider: a big boss from Macheng.'

Old Wu got up and hoicked out the door again. Li Wei and I scarcely noticed. We were pondering the villagers' loss of land.[14]

***

The following morning, Li Wei and I went to watch Zhang Hongren and her team transplant rice in Bitter Hollow.

It's a 30-minute walk from Yang Yurong's house to Bitter Hollow. Up the main road past the village government office compound, we turned and climbed a steep hill. The deep green of the tea plantation was on our left. Houses cascaded down the hill on the right. Strips of vegetables lined the concrete path and we could see down into villagers' courtyards. One family had a jolly black piglet in a concrete pen. There was a warm smell of manure.

---

13   6.7 hectares.
14   For further discussion of land transfers, see Jingzhong Ye, 'Land Transfer and the Pursuit of Agricultural Modernization in China', *Journal of Agrarian Change* 15, no. 3 (2015): 314–37, doi. org/10.1111/joac.12117; Qiangqiang Luo and Joel Andreas, 'Mobilizing Compliance: How the State Compels Village Households to Transfer Land to Large Farm Operators in China', *Journal of Peasant Studies* 47, no. 6 (2020): 1189–210, doi.org/10.1080/03066150.2020.1822340.

Further along, the road straightens out and runs alongside a playful stream. To the right, some of the flat fields needed a haircut: they were covered in unkempt canola, yet to be harvested. Others lay freshly flooded and harrowed, ready for their transplanted rice seedlings. To the left was a slope of luxuriant grass, bushes, saplings, bamboo and vines. The road verge was thick with tall weeds. The velvety air was thrumming with insects and frogs creak-creaking on the edges of the paddy fields. Oriental magpies along the muddy embankments chittered and wagged their tails.

It was 8.30 in the morning when Li Wei and I found the rice-transplanting team just outside Bitter Hollow. The sun was already high and we were tired and hot. My forehead was sweaty under the rim of my sunhat.

The transplanters had been working since 5 am and had already dug the rice seedlings from the nursery field. As we arrived, a woman came staggering up behind us with two trays heaped with sodden seedlings suspended from a shoulder pole.

Plate 4.2 Transplanting rice
Photo: Tamara Jacka, 2015.

The new leader of the team, she had short hair and tanned, muscled arms. Like the others, she wore long grey-green rubber boots that reached above her thighs and were held up with straps clipped to the waist of her trousers.

The seedlings were tied together in small bundles, which she flung out across the water, where they landed with a splosh. Zhang Hongren and the others bent and untied each one. Breaking apart the seedlings, they plunged each fine strand through the water and fixed it in the mud.

They worked side-by-side, replanting the seedlings in straight rows across the paddy field. They would toil until lunchtime. In the afternoon, they would move to another field and keep working until the sun went down.

***

We left Ginkgo Village a few days after that and didn't see Zhang Hongren again until December 2016. The village had a very different look and feel about it then. As we walked to Gao Fields one afternoon, the fields were wintry and grey.

Cao Fuguo's super rice was being harvested that afternoon. Most rice is reaped in late August when the plants are still green. You don't want to delay the harvest until the leaves and stalks have dried out because the grains drop off before then. This super rice is different: not only is it planted late, but also the grains still cling on long after the rest of the plant has died. So, you can wait until the beginning of December to harvest. By then, it's the farming slack season, so there are more labourers available and they're cheaper to hire.

From the road, Li Wei and I could see six middle-aged people—one man and five women—standing in a sea of dry grey rice-grass. They were wearing trousers tucked into boots and long-sleeved jackets and gloves. One woman cut the rice with a sickle. The others bundled the rice and loaded it into a carrier on the back of a tractor, half-sunk in the mud in the middle of the field. A middle-aged man slouched in the tractor's driver's seat.

I nudged Li Wei with an elbow. 'What was it Wang Xinran said—men do the heavy work? Look at all the heavy work those blokes are doing!'

She grimaced. 'They'll get paid more, too. Men get 100 yuan[15] a day. Women only get eighty.'

We watched as the tractor ploughed a trough through the mud and crawled onto the road, its fat wheels dripping. Three other men waited with a combine harvester. Compared with the combine harvesters used in Australia, this one was tiny: a chunky little dragon with a front feeder only about 1.5 metres wide. It hadn't been used in the field; it would've stuck in the mud if they'd tried driving it down there. So, instead, the women reaped the rice by hand and a man pulled sheaves of it off the back of the tractor and into the feeder.

A second man stood at the back of the harvester with a long wooden two-pronged fork, collecting the chaff that was being spat out. The third man, sitting in the harvester's driver's seat, wore a facemask. The air was full of chaff, dust and noise.

*

We arrived at Zhang Hongren's house to find her in a fuggy heating-room, warming herself by a woodstove. She wore a dark-red jacket with her grey slacks and felt slippers on her feet. There was a small sagging old couch on one side of the room, underneath a window. Li Wei and I shunted over to it. Zhang Hongren shut the door and sat on a stool facing the woodstove.

That day Li Wei and I finally learned about shifts in farm work during the post-Mao period.

'Once people started going out to work,' Zhang Hongren said, 'we didn't have enough labour. We had to pay someone to do the ploughing for us.' She shuffled her feet.

'But not everyone could afford that,' she added, straightening her back. 'One widow learnt how to plough for herself. She taught a few others as well.'

I leant forward, excited. 'Did you learn to plough?'

Zhang Hongren smiled. 'I tried it. It takes a while to learn to steer. But it's not hard. The water buffalo does all the work.'

I wrote that down.

---

15   US$14.

'But I didn't do it for long,' she continued. 'We had my husband's salary as a doctor and the money I brought in from rice transplanting. So, we could afford to hire someone to do the ploughing for us.'

'You set up the rice-transplanting team in 1995, right?' Li Wei asked.

'That's right. Before that, we helped each other. I'd help my neighbours one day and they'd help me the next. But later, too many people were going out to work. A lot of the older folk didn't have anyone to help them. Right across the village it was like that. That's why I set up a team.'

She held her hands to the woodstove. 'I got together with a couple of my old friends from Horse Ridge and went around looking for others to join us. I picked only the strongest, most skilled transplanters—the ones with the best reputations.'

Li Wei also sat forward to warm her hands. 'Aunty,' she said, 'does your team make a lot of money?'

'We used to. Three other, smaller teams started up after us, but they've never been as good. We always get the most work. In one day, we can each complete 1.6 mu[16] and earn 160 yuan[17] for ourselves. That's much more than you usually get as a farm labourer.'

'Do you all earn the same amount?' I asked.

'Yes.' She grinned. 'We divide the earnings up equally; each person gets exactly the same amount.'

'But there's been less work recently. One of the other teams folded last year and this year the other two have only four people each.'

She sat back and wiped a hand over her eyes. 'Not so many villagers grow rice these days. Here in Gao Fields, most of us gave up rice farming and contracted our land to Cao Fuguo. That was in 2013. And now he's introduced a new planting method. He doesn't transplant. Others are starting to copy him.' She sighed heavily. 'We used to get 20 days of transplanting work each year. But next year we'll be lucky to get ten.'

*

---

16   1,100 square metres.
17   US$25.

'Elder sister,' I said after a pause, 'did you contract your land to Cao Fuguo?' I didn't want to reveal that we'd talked with Old Wu about this already.

'It's not that I wanted to,' she murmured.

'Were you forced into it?' Li Wei asked quietly.

Zhang Hongren winced. 'If I hadn't agreed, it would've made things difficult for Director Zhou and the other villagers. And my son put pressure on me. He kept saying I was too old to farm.'

'If my husband helped, I could manage,' she said firmly. 'We used to do it together. He'd come home and do the ploughing. I did the rest. But his health has deteriorated. He has very high blood pressure. He can work in the clinic still, but he's not strong enough for physical work.'

She sat twisting her hands. 'Director Zhou came so many times to persuade me, I had to give in.'

I turned to the small window behind the couch and then back to Li Wei. 'It's getting dark,' I said in English.

Li Wei nodded. 'Aunty,' she said, 'it's getting late. We have to go.'

Zhang Hongren grunted and eased herself off her stool. She opened the door and the cold air gusted in.

Halfway out, Li Wei suddenly turned back. 'Aunty,' she said with a puzzled frown, 'who signed your contract with Cao Fuguo?'

'My old man was meant to—he's the head of the household. But he wasn't here, so Director Zhou wrote his name for him.'

Li Wei and I felt sad and angry walking home.

***

It's August 2019.[18] *Zhang Hongren is napping in her son's apartment on the edge of Wuhan. This is where she lives now. She's lying flat on her back in a flaccid T-shirt and pyjama pants. If she turns her head to the right, she'll be able*

---

18   The next several paragraphs are italicised to highlight the fact that they describe an individual's thoughts and emotions and, as such, are necessarily speculative and fictional. While I can imagine based on direct observations, interactions and other kinds of research, I cannot truly know what goes on in another person's mind.

to see out the door of her small room to a narrow hallway. If she turns to the left, she'll see the heavy sky through the window. But she doesn't turn her head. She just stares up at the blank expanse of ceiling. This mattress is much too soft. She's like a log sinking in a paddy field.

Through the window comes the chaotic sound of the city far below: incessant, muffled drilling, the beeps of motorbikes, the rush of cars, a siren pulsing in the distance. She often stands by that window, staring down. Opposite is a long-distance bus terminal, with crowds of people queuing, bundles slung over their shoulders, trailing kids and bulging bags and suitcases. So many people on the move.

What an adventure it was, that time she and her friends went to Beijing! So long ago. Perhaps she could go to the capital again and see her daughter, Aihua. But Aihua's too busy. Anyway, how would she get there? Her son brought her to Wuhan in his car, but she'd have to get to Beijing on her own. It's too far and too difficult. She can't read and she's too old for adventures now.

From the other end of the hallway comes the laughter of her daughter-in-law and her friends in the living room. They're like exotic birds, with their perfume and gaudy dresses; their sing-song chatter. They visit each other every day and gossip. They have nothing else to do. Her daughter-in-law has no job, her six-year-old daughter is in school and the four-year-old boy is in kindergarten.

Zhang Hongren lies with her hands flat on her stomach, recalling her own time in kindergarten: the starving inmates too weak to lift themselves off the floor, the dirt yard with the thick wall around it, the poplar looming outside. For so many years, she'd kept that memory buried. Then the foreign professor and her student came along and asked all those questions. So many simple questions. But scattered in among them, those ones about her childhood. They cracked her open. Why did they ask about the past? Why did they dig it all up again?

She remembers the poplar and the strange look on Laoshi's face when she mentioned it. She remembers sitting against the wall under the tree with her cousin from Horse Ridge. She didn't tell Laoshi and Li Wei about that. It must've been early autumn, just before they closed the kindergarten and sent everyone home. She felt happy that day, watching the yellow leaves twirling down. The wall was warm at her back. But when she turned to her cousin, he looked so pale and still. He slid sideways and she realised he had died. Just like that.

*

She smooths the floral bedsheet beneath her. Times have changed. Now she has two children, including a son. And a grandson, too. She's so fortunate. Her son is a businessman, importing and exporting something or other. For so long, she and her husband struggled to feed and clothe the kids and put them through school. But now their son provides for them. They can buy whatever they want.

The air in here is stale. She's trapped in this apartment—trapped and pampered. Useless. Her son pushed her into giving up her land and told her to stop transplanting rice. 'Why do you keep toiling in the mud?' he said. 'People will think I don't support you. They'll say I'm a bad son. Why don't you come live with us in the city? You can help with the kids.'

She had to go with whatever he thought best. But her daughter-in-law doesn't want her here—she can feel it. She doesn't blame her. Zhang Hongren is not used to the electric stove, so she's not much help in the kitchen. And she's so clumsy. She's afraid she'll break an expensive vase or something. Or she'll slip on the shiny tiled floor.

The one thing she can do is take her grandson to kindergarten and pick him up again at the end of the day. She enjoys the little boy's company and it's a relief to get out. But her legs are not what they were; climbing up and down seven flights of stairs is such an ordeal. And it's tiring being in the city, surrounded by strangers and noise, the confusion of stores and signs she can't read. All that traffic on the road; the petrol fumes in her nose.

This morning, her daughter-in-law said she would pick up her son from kindergarten herself from now on. 'You stay home and rest,' she said. Zhang Hongren knows her daughter-in-law just wants something to do. She, too, gets bored.

Her eyes are drawn to a damp patch spreading across the ceiling. She's no better off than those poor sods in the new elderly care home in Red River, she thinks. At least they have a vegetable garden to keep them occupied. Their living quarters are quite spacious, too, and they're served good food. Or so she's heard. It would be lonely though. And so shameful having no family to care for you.

*

She thinks again about Laoshi and Li Wei. She enjoyed telling them about collective labour and about her rice-transplanting team. Her family show no interest. She sighs loudly.

It's time she went back to the village. Her old man plans to retire and join her here next year, but she'll tell him that's not what she wants. For as long as they can look after themselves, she'd rather be in Gao Fields than here. She'd rather be surrounded by trees, mountains, water. The smell of black soil. The good earth. She can grow vegetables again. She can care for her old man and grow their food. They won't need to depend on their son so much then.

She curls onto her side, eyes squeezed shut. She'll be home soon. She'll be sweeping up the sunflower seed husks from around her friends' feet. Little Wang will be holding forth. Maybe Laoshi and Li Wei will be there, plying them with questions. She'll stand in her doorway, looking out to the great green sweep of paddy fields beyond.

5

Two funerals

How I imagine Hu Xiaoming's suicide[1]

Hu Xiaoming has not planned to kill herself on this ordinary heat-soaked day. That's not how it happens. The thought has not coagulated in her brain. She has not finally seen that there's no other way to end the constant drip of humiliation, the yellowing bruises, the wearying weight of it all. She has not been pondering her pregnancy or the factory job she gave up. Or the move to her husband's village to prepare for the birth. Or the miscarriage. Or her husband, also out of work and home from the city, thumping her and blocking out the light. Bashing her so hard, her brain is a haze, pierced by the never-ending insect-whining in one ear, the metallic taste of blood.

Nor has she been thinking of her mother-in-law nagging and abusing, on and on and on. She hasn't been reliving the monstrous walls caving in on her at night. Or thinking through the fact that she has no money; she can't escape. Her father on the phone, shouting about marital duty, refusing to let her come home.

Her mother-in-law comes in from pulling up the peanuts and finds her slumped on the kitchen floor. The older woman yells at her to raise her useless carcass and prepare their midday meal. She groans and gets to her feet. Her mother-in-law keeps snarling and spitting and Hu Xiaoming can't stand it anymore. Something

---

1   The following story imaginatively re-creates the inner world of a woman about to commit suicide. Again, I have used italics to indicate that the story is purely speculative and fictional. To reiterate: while I can imagine based on research, I cannot truly know what goes on in another person's mind. This limitation is compounded in the case of someone who has died by suicide, because I cannot talk with that person herself, but must rely on others whose accounts may be skewed by personal interest. This issue is explored further later in this tale.

inside short-circuits. The fury burns off the haze. She's fighting and screaming, the rage building and building. The older woman slaps her, and she slaps her back. She whips to the bench, retrieves the knife. Her mother-in-law lurches away, screeching through the house and out the front door, down the winding path to the peanut field, where her son still toils in the mud.

Then Hu Xiaoming is running, too. Her battered body drives her across the backyard, past the dog, who's sprung up, growling and baring his teeth. Hu Xiaoming doesn't hear. Fast and unseeing, she stumbles through the damp, stale heat to the ruined hut over there. Sparrows rush up as her broken body pushes through. Into the dark she blunders, around the peanuts laid out to dry, a mouldering pile of straw, the dust-covered wreck of a bicycle, a flat wicker basket knocked over. She's making straight for the spattered shelf at the back, shards of fury driving her. Quickly, she reaches for the pesticide and clasps the cool, clean bottle to her ribcage. Quickly, she unscrews the lid and lifts the bottle to her mouth.

***

Wang Shifu (Master Wang) is a *zhuchi ren*: a master of ceremonies (MC). He directs funerals and occasionally weddings[2] for people in his lineage. When Li Wei and I first met him in March 2016, we warmed to him immediately. 'He has a lovely open face,' I wrote afterwards. 'We felt sorry for him.' I cringe to read those fieldnotes now.

Wang Shifu was born in 1956 in Bitter Hollow. He said his family didn't suffer as much as the former landlords. By the end of the collective era, those Wang families were so poor and miserable, none of their men could find a wife. His family were poor peasants. He didn't have enough to eat, but he went to school for a few years, married just after the return to family farming and ventured out as a migrant labourer. Life was full of promise.

But fortune has a fickle heart. His father died, so he came home to care for his mother. He started a shoe store in Red River Township but couldn't turn a profit. Then he fell off his motorbike and had to have surgery. 'See my scar?' he said, twisting around and pointing to his neck. 'It runs all the way down my spine.' His stay in hospital cost 50,000 yuan (US$7,200). Medical insurance meant he received 30,000 yuan (US$4,300) back, but he

---

2   With increasing prosperity since the 1990s, more and more villagers have preferred to hire a company to direct their son's wedding.

had to pay the rest. Now he has coronary disease. His wife is two years older than him. She has stomach problems. Illness has reduced them to paupers: 'too poor to live; too poor to die'. He gave a sad smile.

Worst of all, he was given no sons. He only has two daughters. One is 33, the other twenty-eight. 'Daughters bring nothing but trouble,' he said. The older one rents a place in Red River. His wife has been staying with her and helping with the grandson. 'The husband wants a divorce.' He wiped a hand over his eyes.

'And the younger one?' I asked.

He shook his head. 'Still hasn't found a husband. She's hundreds of miles away, working in Guangzhou. She never phones home.' He sagged on his stool.

He and his wife are stuck in poverty and there's no-one to help them out. No-one cares. 'See what a rundown old ruin we live in?' he said, sweeping his arm round the room. Li Wei and I took in the dingy furniture, the greying walls. 'Our oldest sends a bit of money, but it's not enough.'

'What about the younger one?' I asked.

'Nothing.' He heaved a sigh. 'We can hardly pay for our pills.'

'Poverty alleviation funds?'

'Not a cent,' he moaned. 'It's because we have no sons. No sons, no future. The cadres think that if they give the money to us, it'll go to waste. We have no sons to start a business and make something of it. No-one will help us 'cos we've got nothing to give in return.' He sighed again and bowed his head.

Li Wei and I didn't like the way he talked about his daughters, but that scarcely dented our sympathy for him. We didn't question the reason he received no poverty alleviation funds. So many villagers talked about cadres embezzling those funds or favouring their relatives when distributing them. So many complained that 'the deserving don't get those funds; the ones with connections do'. We had no reason to doubt Wang Shifu.

*

Our second visit in December gave us an awful shock. Fire had ripped through Wang Shifu's house, reducing it to a ragged shell. He said something about ancient, faulty electrical wiring. The wooden beams supporting the roof were consumed and the roof crashed down. The kitchen stove—its chimney standing miraculously intact in the chill air—survived amid an ocean of broken bricks, shattered glass and plaster.

Wang Shifu had no time for talk. He was clambering through the chaos, retrieving a blackened pot, a singed coat, a broken chair from underneath the rubble. He refused to leave in case something was stolen. A neighbour had dragged over a mattress and some bedding for him. We saw it in a corner that still had a bit of roof. The neighbour came back every day with cooked food and water for him. He was cold and exhausted and stank of charcoal. But he insisted he would be okay.

Afterwards, Li Wei and I were shaken, which Yang Yurong could see as we sat down to lunch. 'What's happened?' she asked.

'Did you know that Wang Shifu's house burnt down?' I asked.

'Over in Bitter Hollow?' She frowned as she turned to the kitchen. 'Did he tell you how it happened?' she asked, coming back with the rice.

'Faulty electrical wiring.'

She frowned again. 'People say he did it himself.'

Li Wei and I looked at each other, eyes wide. 'Surely not!' I cried.

Li Wei tucked her hair behind her ear. 'Aunty,' she said, taking a deep breath, 'are you sure?'

Yang Yurong grimaced and dumped a spoonful of rice in my bowl.

'Enough, enough!' I protested.

'He's been complaining for months about not being accepted for the housebuilding subsidy. Going on about how others were given funds to rebuild their old house and he wasn't. He must think they'll give him the money now.'

'Will they?' I asked, adjusting my chopsticks.

She shrugged. 'Who knows?'

Li Wei and I fell silent. Would such a nice man do such a thing? Maybe desperation had driven him to it? We just couldn't believe it.

But perhaps that was when my doubts began to form.

***

We visited Wang Shifu again on a sunny afternoon the following September. By then, he had a newly built two-storey house standing behind the ruins of the old one. Inside, the walls were unpainted and there wasn't much furniture. But it was still impressive, I thought, taking in the vastness of the front room, the fat new black-and-yellow striped couch, the proud grin splitting Wang Shifu's broad face.

Perhaps it was the grin that did it. Or the couch. He'd said that he and his wife were mired in poverty with no-one to help them. So, how could they now afford this new house and expensive new couch? It didn't make sense. Others had said that the housebuilding subsidy only partially covered the cost of a new house. So, even if Wang Shifu and his wife received the subsidy, they would have had to draw on savings or have a friend or relative help them with a loan.

'Come in, come in,' he said. 'Sit down.' He motioned to the couch. Such an ugly thing and uncomfortable, too. Hard and unyielding. The fabric had an unpleasant synthetic smell.

He pulled up a wooden chair. 'I can't talk long,' he said with a quick smile. 'I've a funeral to organise.'

I sat up with interest. I'd never been to a Chinese funeral.

In fact, Wang Shifu had two funerals to organise recently—the first was in Horse Ridge three weeks earlier. The main banquet for this one would be the next night and the burial the day after. 'You're lucky you caught me,' he said. 'I've been over there all day; only just got home. One of the sons will drive me back again this evening.'

I took my notebook from my daypack. 'Whose funeral banquet is on tomorrow?'

'Widow Zhou's, over in Bamboo Glen.'

I turned to Li Wei: 'That's Wang Xinran's natal village, isn't it?'

5

She nodded.

Wang Shifu smoothed a hand over his balding head. I noticed his new black nylon jacket and brown fake-leather shoes.

'Widow Zhou's husband was a Wang. Her funeral's been a huge job. Six sons and two daughters, all with families of their own. That's more than 50 descendants!'

'Could we go, too?' I asked, leaning forward.

He shook his head. 'No, only relatives and friends go to funerals.'

Li Wei tilted her head. 'Don't you want as many guests as possible? Doesn't that bring face to the family?'

Wang Shifu shook his head again. 'If you came with someone close to the family it'd be okay, but it wouldn't be right otherwise.'

I doodled a sad face in my notebook.

'*Shifu*,'[3] Li Wei said after a pause, 'are funeral rituals complicated?'

He leant forward. 'More so than for a wedding. There are four days of rituals. Shall I tell you about them?'

Li Wei and I nodded eagerly.

On the first day,[4] Wang Shifu explained, the corpse is washed, changed into new clothes and laid in the coffin. The coffin is then placed before the family altar in the main room of the house. A man's coffin goes to the left of the altar, a woman's to the right (when looking towards the front door from the altar).

'Is the corpse in a white shroud?' I asked.

---

3   *Shifu*, meaning 'master', is a term of respect, used when addressing craftspeople or others with valued skills, including masters of ceremonies.

4   The *core* elements of the funeral rituals described in the following section match a funeral that Li Wei and I attended and a second that Li Wei attended without me. Most also match the description of customary funeral rituals given in the *Xin County Folk Customs Gazetteer*. Chang Zhaoqi and Zhu Jiefan, 新县民俗志 [*Xin County Folk Customs Gazetteer*] (Zhengzhou, China: Xin County Bureau of Civil Affairs, 1991), 178–90. However, as I'll indicate in later notes, some of the *details* are different to those provided in the gazetteer and the second funeral Li Wei attended. For discussion of historical and regional variations in funeral rituals, see James L. Watson and Evelyn S. Rawski (eds), *Death Ritual in Late Imperial and Modern China* (Berkeley, CA: University of California Press, 1988); and Kipnis, *The Funeral of Mr Wang*.

'No, no. Just ordinary clothes. Three layers on top: an undershirt, a dress shirt and a jacket. Then trousers and cloth shoes and socks on the bottom. Most old people buy their own coffin and burial clothes before their death. It's a source of shame if you can't afford to do that.'

'What colour are the burial clothes?'

'In the collective era, they were blue. Nowadays they're blue or brown—whatever colour the old person preferred. Not black though. In the otherworld, black means iron. That's too heavy for the soul—it'd drag it down.'

I smiled to myself. 'What about the mourners: do they wear white?'

'Close relatives do. The men put a white scarf round their neck and the women wear a white cap. The sons and daughters and their spouses wear white gowns, tied at the waist with a white hemp rope and white shoes. They must wear those until after the burial. The women wear white leggings, too. They used to wear them for the whole mourning period—49 days—but not anymore.[5] Nowadays, they take them off after the burial.'

Li Wei and I jotted this down.

Once the coffin is in position, Wang Shifu continued, the deceased's sons and daughters keep vigil over her soul (*shou ling*). They set up a makeshift altar in front of the coffin: a small table with a paper spirit-tablet standing on a plate. Every morning they put three cups of sacrificial liquor next to the spirit-tablet. In the morning and evening, they also put out a bowl of sacrificial rice and one of other food.[6] Each morning and evening, they burn incense and spirit-money and kowtow to the spirit-tablet.

After the burial, the deceased's sons and daughters take away the makeshift altar. They move the spirit-tablet to the left of the main family altar (facing away from the altar) and set out the sacrificial food and liquor next to it. Every day for seven days,[7] they replace the food and liquor, burn incense

---

5   The *Xin County Folk Customs Gazetteer* sets out different and more detailed customary rules for the funerary clothing of the deceased. It also gives more detailed specifications for the white clothing worn by different relatives of the deceased. However, it notes that these clothing customs have been simplified since the 1960s. Chang and Zhu, *Xin County Folk Customs Gazetteer*, 179–83.

6   According to Wang Shifu, any food except green vegetables is acceptable. He couldn't explain why green vegetables are not allowed. Perhaps it's because the green symbolises fertility, growth and other aspects of life.

7   The day of death counts as the first day.

7

and spirit-money, and kowtow to the spirit-tablet. After that, they keep burning incense and kowtowing every morning. Every seventh day they also put out the rice and other things. Through the mourning period, they kowtow and burn spirit-money and incense in the morning and evening of each seventh day.

Wang Shifu sat up and folded his arms. 'In the past,' he said, 'people also burnt small paper figures—servants to help the soul in the otherworld. Some people still do that.'

I wanted to ask more about this, but he kept talking.

'You're supposed to keep vigil for 49 days. But not everyone does that. They work far away in the city. They don't want to stay home so long, just to observe the mourning rituals. Some old folks get upset at that.'

'And you?' I asked. 'What do you think?'

He shrugged. 'What can you do?'

'*Shifu*,' Li Wei said, looking up from her notebook, 'how long is the paper spirit-tablet kept on the family altar?'

He grunted. 'It's meant to be kept till the first anniversary of the death. But nowadays, it's often burnt after the forty-ninth day. So few people are around to pay their respects to the dead. Families can't be bothered keeping it longer than that.'

He bent his head and shuffled his feet on the concrete floor, arms still folded.

'What else happens on the first day?' Li Wei asked.

Wang Shifu looked out the front door and Li Wei and I followed his gaze. We could see the remnants of the old house from where we sat. In among the rubble, weeds were sprouting. A couple of saplings, too.

'As the MC, I must find a lay Daoist priest to fix the date for the funeral.[8] We try to have it either three or five days after the death. Widow Zhou's is on the fifth day.'

---

8   There are three teams of lay Daoists in the Red River district, each with five or six priests.

He saw the puzzled look on my face: 'It has to be an odd-numbered day; an even number would bring bad luck. Sometimes, there's a delay. Maybe the priest can't find an auspicious date. Or maybe they can't find a good gravesite. It's not a problem for Widow Zhou; she'll be buried in the Bamboo Glen cemetery, next to her husband. Each hamlet has its own cemetery.'

I stared out the door, recalling clusters of tombs behind the houses, watching over each hamlet.

Wang Shifu cleared his throat. 'But those cemeteries are getting crowded. Sometimes they can't find an auspicious place in the local cemetery, so they look elsewhere. But other hamlets don't want them to use their land. Or villagers object to a grave close behind their house; they don't want the bad luck. So, there's conflict. It can take months to find a spot.'

'Do you always have a burial?' Li Wei asked. 'Is anyone cremated?'

Wang Shifu nodded. 'If a migrant worker dies away from home, he has to be cremated. It's illegal to transport a corpse, so you must cremate. Then you bring home the ashes in a casket. You still bury the casket.'[9]

'Once the funeral date is decided,' he continued, 'I help the family contact their relatives and friends and hire caterers for the banquet. Performers as well.'

I turned to him with a start: 'What sort of performers?'

'In the 1970s and 1980s, we just had relatives; every lineage had a few men who could blow a suona[10] and beat a drum. Nowadays, we mostly hire professionals. There'll be three military bands for Widow Zhou's funeral: one from Poplar Hamlet, hired by her sons; one from Deng Inn, hired by her daughters; and one from Gao River, which is Widow Zhou's natal village. Her siblings' families will pay for that one. Before and after the banquet, the bands will sing songs and keep the guests entertained with local Chinese opera: *didengxi*.[11] They'll do the weeping and keening, too.'

I raised my eyebrows. '*Performers* do the weeping and keening?'

---

9   Land shortages have led some local rural governments to ban burials and make cremation mandatory. At the time of writing, this is not the case in Xin County.

10   A double-reed Chinese horn.

11   *Didengxi* is a type of Chinese opera specific to Xin County.

Wang Shifu nodded and smiled sadly. 'When I was young, the women in the family did it. The keening was much fiercer then.'

'Did the men weep and keen, too?'

'Not so much. It's a women's thing. The deceased's daughters and sisters wept the most. They'd keen for three or four hours. They knew all the words—all the women learnt them.'

He let out a long sigh. 'But hardly anyone knows them anymore. That's why they get a performer to do it. The daughters pay for that. For Widow Zhou's funeral, they'll pay 400 yuan, plus another 100 yuan for a carton of high-grade cigarettes.[12] That's just for an hour of keening.' He shook his head and looked at his shoes.

Fascinating, I thought to myself.

Wang Shifu waited patiently as Li Wei and I wrote notes.

'Would you like tea?' he asked with a smile when we lifted our heads.

Li Wei declined and took her water bottle from the daypack at her feet. I accepted; I'd forgotten my bottle.

*

Wang Shifu went out a door at the back of the room, his shoes tapping on the concrete floor as he walked. He made a couple of trips to fetch a thermos flask and a mug with tea-leaves and then a stool to put them on. I felt guilty for creating so much fuss.

'*Shifu*, what happens on the second day?' I asked as he poured. I noticed the sides of the thermos flask were dented, its cork stopper soggy and dark.

Wang Shifu rubbed his nose as he sat down. 'The closest relatives arrive. Most of Widow Zhou's arrived this morning. We had 50 people at lunch. Some of them sat with the deceased. Others went shopping and cooked. A bunch of men went up the hill to dig the grave. They'll add her name to her husband's tombstone afterwards.'

He turned aside to cough. 'When I left, they were setting up the two marquees for the main funeral day tomorrow.'

12　In 2017, 100 yuan was equivalent to US$15.40.

I reached for my tea and Li Wei took a sip from her water bottle.

'Yesterday and today,' Wang Shifu continued, 'Daoist priests have joined Widow Zhou's sons and daughters keeping vigil. They sit next to the coffin and chant all through the day. That helps her soul travel to the otherworld. The soul needs to be accompanied by relatives, so the priests chant the names of all the gift-giving relatives. They read from a list.'

He paused and scratched his knee. 'We used to have priests chant for three days before the main funeral day. But nowadays it's only the wealthiest who hire them for that long. Most just do it for a day or two.'

*

I was struggling to follow all this talk of souls and the otherworld and chanting. I decided to stop taking notes and concentrate on what Wang Shifu was saying. I could check Li Wei's notes later.

'Chanting wasn't allowed in the collective period,' Wang Shifu said. 'But it started again in the 1980s. They had more priests then—seven or eight. Nowadays, it's only if the deceased is a cadre or the family are in business that they have so many. Usually, there are just five or six. The priests all get paid 100 yuan a day.'

'And the MC—do you get paid?' Li Wei asked.

'No, not a cent.' Wang Shifu gave a sad smile. 'To tell the truth, I didn't want to do Widow Zhou's funeral; it's so much work. But there was no-one else. There aren't many who know the customary rules nowadays. Not like I do.'

'The third day is the most work for me,' he said. 'When the guests arrive, they pay their respects to the deceased. The younger generations must kowtow three times. Anyone older than the deceased just bows. I must guide everyone. There'll be so many guests tomorrow, I'll have to divide them into groups. I'll let only one group into the room at a time.'

'And there's the gift register,' he added. 'I'll need to draw up separate gift lists for each of Widow Zhou's sons.'

'Do you record just the cash or other things, too?' I asked.

He smiled. 'Big things, like quilts, are recorded, too. You must record everything; gifts need to be repaid. You give a gift at my family funeral and, later, I'll give one at yours.[13] Normally, the MC does the gift register. But I'll be too busy. Bamboo Glen's hamlet head will do it instead. He's a Wang, too.'

*

Wang Shifu paused while Li Wei wrote notes. Then he explained the two rituals performed by the deceased's descendants on the morning of the third day. His account was convoluted, so I'll draw on Li Wei's notes to summarise here.

In the *song qiao* ('seeing off at the bridge') ritual, you farewell the soul before it crosses the bridge to the otherworld. The oldest son stands outside in one of the marquees set up for the banquet. He brings out the makeshift altar and stands behind it. On the small altar is the plate with the paper spirit-tablet along with a corner of the deceased's bamboo sleeping mat.

These things represent her soul. The bit of sleeping mat is cut off after the death and wrapped in a piece of paper, tied with white thread. Then the package is hung from a tree to let the insects gather. Just before the *song qiao* ritual, it's unwrapped. If insects are found inside, it means the soul has successfully reincarnated.

I had to ask Li Wei to interpret this. Once I understood, I became agitated. 'What if there are no insects?' I blurted.

Wang Shifu grinned. 'You leave it out for a day, there are bound to be insects.'

He explained that the oldest son stands facing the family altar inside the house. He lifts the plate with the spirit-tablet and bit of mat and the daughters, sons-in-law and daughters-in-law bow before him. Behind them stand the grandchildren and great-grandchildren. To the side stand four Daoist priests. One waves a flag and reads out the names of all the guests giving gifts. The other three play music.

---

13   The significance of gift exchange and reciprocity in Chinese culture is discussed in Mayfair Yang, *Gifts, Banquets, and the Art of Social Relationships in China* (Ithaca, NY: Cornell University Press, 1994).

This ritual lasts three minutes. It's just a prelude to the main *guo qiao* ('crossing the bridge') ritual, in which the deceased's descendants help her soul cross the bridge to the otherworld. In this ritual, those who were kneeling get to their feet. Together with the others who had been standing behind them, they line up on each side of a piece of white cotton cloth, stretching 6 to 8 metres from the makeshift altar towards the family altar room. The cloth is the bridge to the otherworld. The daughters help the soul cross the bridge by taking the plate with the spirit-tablet and bit of mat from the makeshift altar and sliding it down the cloth. The passage of the plate from one end of the cloth to the other marks the successful entry of the soul into the otherworld.

Then everyone turns and faces the family altar room. The Daoist priests stand to the side as before and continue to play music. The daughters stand on the other side, the oldest holding the plate. The sons and daughters-in-law kneel up front and the others stand behind them. This lasts another three minutes, and then the rituals are over and it's time for lunch.[14] The other guests start arriving after that, ahead of the main events in the evening.

Now, as I write this, I recall myself and Li Wei sitting there on Wang Shifu's new couch, straining to follow him. We both struggled to understand how the relatives are positioned in each ritual, how the white cloth is oriented and in which direction the soul moves along that cloth.[15] For all our difficulties, or perhaps because of them, we were completely absorbed in his account. So absorbed, we didn't think to ask whether villagers really believe there's a soul journeying to the otherworld.

---

14   The *song qiao* and *guo qiao* rituals are not described in the *Xin County Folk Customs Gazetteer*. This may be because they are not universally practised across the county.
15   Several villagers confirmed that the plate travels towards the family altar, but none could tell us why. My guess is that the soul is being guided towards her permanent home on the family altar, enabling her to join the ancestors, rather than become a wandering ghost. Villagers also couldn't explain how a soul can be reincarnated before travelling to the otherworld. A possible explanation is that there's more than one soul. See Myron L. Cohen, 'Souls and Salvation: Conflicting Themes in Chinese Popular Religion', in *Death Ritual in Late Imperial and Modern China*, eds James L. Watson and Evelyn S. Rawski (Berkeley, CA: University of California Press, 1988), 180–202. Alternatively, this may be an example of two different sets of religious practices and beliefs stitched together.

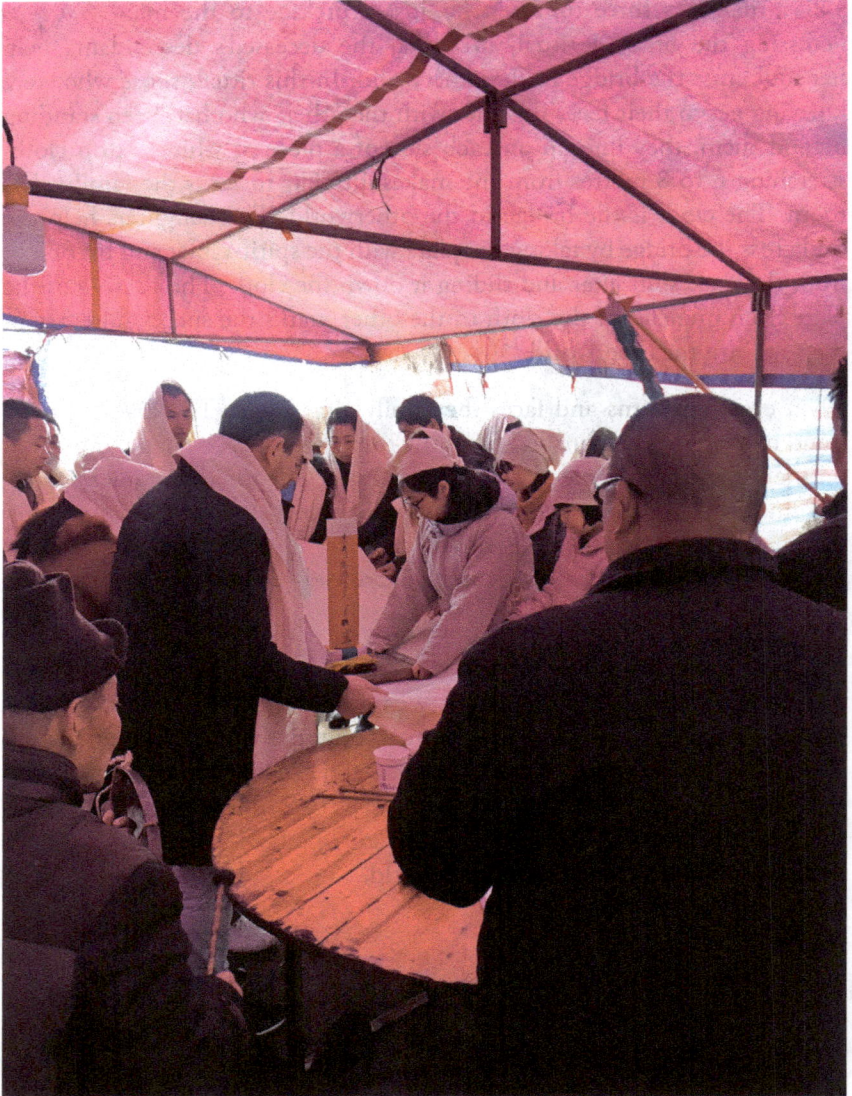

Plate 5.1 The *guo qiao* ritual
Photo: Li Wei, 2019.

Could they see her; could they feel her faltering steps? I could, though I'm not sure who it was. Perhaps Gao Xiuhua. Or my grandma. Or perhaps it was me inching along, my son at my elbow. My rational mind doesn't believe in souls or the otherworld. It knows they're not real. But I went on that journey all the same.

Perhaps rituals are like poetry and music: their symbolic, visceral truths make questions about what is real quite meaningless. I wonder what my dad would have thought. He was a fiercely atheist physicist. And he played the cello. Like my mum, he was passionate about books and music. If I told him the story of Widow Zhou's family helping her soul across that long, lonely bridge, would he hear it? If we could once again listen to Jacqueline du Pré playing Elgar's cello concerto, perhaps I could share the story with him then.

Or perhaps I couldn't. I miss my dad, but I don't remember him too well. To be honest, I'm not sure I ever really knew him. I'm also not sure whether I'm still the same person I was when he was alive. The young woman who inherited her parents' love of books and music left home and devoted herself to another culture. That has transformed her in ways she can't entirely account for. Would my father recognise me now, tracing the journey of Widow Zhou's soul? Would I recognise him?

***

Once he had finished telling us about the *song qiao* and *guo qiao* rituals, Wang Shifu got up to refill my mug. Li Wei and I adjusted our positions on the couch. It really was very uncomfortable.

'Tell us what happens on the evening of the third day,' I said as Wang Shifu poured the tea.

'There's the bonfire and then the banquet,' he said, sitting down again.

'The bonfire?'

'Uh-huh. To burn the things for the soul to use in the afterlife: spirit-money, cardboard houses, cars ...'

'You burn cardboard cars?!' I exclaimed in delight. 'What about other things: Cardboard clothes? Washing machines?'

He shifted on his chair and frowned. Maybe he thought I was laughing at him and other villagers. I stopped grinning.

'Some people burn cardboard washing machines,' he said shortly. 'But there's no need for cardboard clothes; you burn the deceased's real clothes.'

As I sat back, he continued: 'We used to have the banquet first and then the fire. The funeral would go on past midnight. But nowadays, it's the other way round. That way, the guests who've come over from Xin County City can drive home straight after the banquet.'

'So, tell us about the banquet.'

Wang Shifu wiped a hand over his eyes. 'We're expecting at least 180 people for Widow Zhou's. Getting the seating arrangements right will be a nightmare. Closest kin on the head tables. But men and women must be separated and relatives from adjacent generations mustn't be seated together.'

'Adjacent generations?'

He nodded. 'For example, I can't seat an uncle and a nephew at the same table.' He scuffed at the floor. 'If I don't get things right, there'll be hell to pay. The MC gets no recognition if a funeral goes well. But it's always me who gets blamed when anything goes wrong.'

'It must be very expensive to hold such a large banquet,' I mused.

'The whole funeral's expensive!'[16]

'How much?'

'The sons forked out 30,000 yuan[17] altogether. That's for the priests and performers, the food and catering staff, and other things like incense and spirit-money.'

'But they'll get more than that back in gifts,' he added.

'And the daughters—did they pay for anything?'

'They each spent 3,000 yuan[18] on hiring a band and buying incense, spirit-money and other things.'

'But they'll get that back in gifts, right?'

---

16   For a theoretical discussion of post-Mao China's 'ritual economy' and the 'waste of wealth' involved in funerals and other rituals, see Mayfair Yang, *Re-Enchanting Modernity: Ritual Economy and Society in Wenzhou, China* (Durham, NC: Duke University Press, 2020), 279–314, doi.org/10.1515/9781478009245.

17   US$4,600.

18   US$460.

Wang Shifu shook his head. 'If the deceased's husband was still alive, the gifts would all go to him. As it is, they go to Widow Zhou's sons. That includes the daughters' gifts; they gave 2,000 yuan[19] each.'

'On top of the 3,000 yuan they paid for the band and other things?'

'Uh-huh.'

'The sons will repay those gifts sometime, won't they?' Li Wei said.

He nodded. 'In the future, when there's a funeral in a daughter's marital family, each of the sons must pay back the same amount of gift money to her family. Six sons, so that's 12,000 yuan[20] just for one daughter.'

'So, you're right,' he said, grinning at me. 'Eventually, the daughters will get back far more than what they've spent on their mother's funeral.'

*

I scribbled a note and looked up again with another question: '*Shifu*, you have no sons. So, when you and your wife die, who will pay the funeral costs? And who will receive the gifts?'

Even as I spoke, I felt bad about being so insensitive. Both Li Wei and Wang Shifu looked away.

'Our daughters will cover the costs,' Wang Shifu mumbled. 'They won't accept any gifts. If my wife dies first, I won't accept gifts either. Some people might, but I won't 'cos I couldn't afford to pay them back. Same for my wife if I die first.' He let out a long sigh.

'But that's a long way off in the future.' He straightened his back and smiled at me. 'What's the time?'

Li Wei pulled out her phone. 'Three-thirty. Do you need to go?'

'It's okay. Not for a while.'

'Can you tell us about the burial rituals?' I asked quickly. 'Are they complicated?'

---

19 US$310.
20 US$1,800.

'Not really. It's done in the morning. The close relatives form a procession up to the gravesite. Eight strong men carry the coffin.' He scratched his knee. 'Sometimes there aren't enough male relatives, so they hire people. The others in the procession carry tall cloth banners—20 or 30 of them. They're made from gifts of cloth given to the deceased's family.'

'How tall are they?' I asked.

'And what colour?' Li Wei added.

'The cloth strips are 2 to 3 metres long. They used to be black. But nowadays any colour is okay, except red. They also use a piece of white cloth to tie a white paper crane on top of the coffin.'

Li Wei tilted her head in inquiry.

'Haven't you heard the expression "to fly on a crane to the Western Paradise [*jiahe xiqu*]?"'

'Oh yes!' Li Wei smiled and jotted a note.

'What does that mean?' I asked her in English.

'To go to Heaven,' she whispered hurriedly, before turning back to Wang Shifu. 'Is the crane buried with the coffin?'

'No, the white cloth is used to tie it to a small tree by the gravesite.'

I chewed the end of my pen and stared outside. In my mind, I was no longer sitting on Wang Shifu's couch. I was looking up at white cranes flying in a v-formation, high, high above me in the dawn light.

'Are there Daoist priests in the procession, too?' Li Wei was asking.

'Some people hire a band. Widow Zhou's family will just have three or four Daoist priests chant and play music on the way up there. And by the gravesite, too.'

*

'Any more questions?' Wang Shifu asked with a smile.

Li Wei looked at me and I thought for a moment.

I recalled the fireworks. Some mornings, before daybreak, I would hear firecrackers far away. I would ask Yang Yurong about them over breakfast and she would say, 'It's so-and-so's burial.' She almost always knew whose.

'When are the fireworks?' I asked Wang Shifu.

'Ah, yes,' he grinned. 'All through the funeral. But they must be finished by the time the coffin is buried. The soul can't take firecrackers into the otherworld.'

'You also set off firecrackers and burn spirit-money one year after the death,' he added. 'And then again three years after the death. Just at home—you don't set off firecrackers at the gravesite then.'

*

I reached for my mug of tea and took another gulp. 'Were funeral rituals the same during the collective era as they are now?' I asked, mug in hand.

Wang Shifu grunted. 'During the Cultural Revolution we couldn't perform the main funeral rituals. We didn't even dare burn spirit-money. But at other times we did. They were much the same, except the banquets weren't as big. They didn't hire performers or Daoist priests either.' He folded one leg over the other and rested his hands on his knee. I was distracted by his jiggling shoe and short blue nylon socks.

'Did the relatives wear white? And did you use a long piece of white cloth for the *guo qiao* ritual?' I was thinking about the desperate shortage of cotton during the collective era.

Wang Shifu nodded. As if reading my mind, he said, 'You had to borrow cloth and mourning clothes. And we were too poor to give money at funerals.'

'Did you give other kinds of gifts?'

'Close relatives gave a bit of cloth as well as spirit-money, firecrackers and wreaths. In the 1990s, we'd give a basket with some noodles, a piece of meat and a carton of cigarettes. And we might give a sheet or a quilt.'

'So, when did you start giving cash?'

'Some gave a bit in the 1980s and 1990s. But it's only in the last decade that large sums have been given.' He jiggled his shoe.

'Nowadays, close relatives give either quilts or cash. And they still give wreaths, spirit-money and firecrackers. They might give a basket as well. They pack it with a carton of cigarettes, a kilo of meat and one of noodles.'

'How much cash do they give?'

'Distant relatives give 200 yuan[21] or so. Close relatives give anything up to a few thousand.'

I put my mug down and took up my pen. But then I thought I better check who counted as a 'close relative' in this context. Wang Shifu's answer wasn't what I expected. He said the closest relatives, who give the biggest gifts, are the daughters and siblings of the deceased and, if the deceased is a man, his brothers' children. If the deceased is a woman, it's her husband's brothers' children who count as 'close'; her own are considered more distant. I wrote all these details, marvelling at how much of the traditional patrilineal system is built into funeral rituals, even today.

*

'*Shifu*,' Li Wei said after a pause, 'you said you organised another funeral three weeks ago. In Horse Ridge, wasn't it? Who was that for?'

Suddenly uneasy, Wang Shifu unfolded his legs and sat fiddling with his jacket zipper. He tugged it up and said: 'Hu Xiaoming. A young woman. She killed herself by drinking pesticide.'

My head jerked up. 'How old was she?'

'Twenty-seven. It was a huge shock to everyone.' He rubbed his nose. 'Her husband's a Wang. That's why I organised the funeral. Such a lot of trouble.'

'How common are suicides?'

Wang Shifu frowned at his feet. 'Quite common in the collective era, mostly 'cos of quarrelling. But nowadays they're very rare—none in Ginkgo Village in the past 10 years.'

'Why the change?'

'Life's so much better now! What's to quarrel about?!'

---

21   US$30.

I stared at my notebook. We have no reliable figures for suicide in China before the 1990s, but research shows extremely high rates in that decade, especially among younger rural women. In the 2000s, though, the rates fell dramatically, probably because outmigration and urbanisation led to decreased access to pesticides—the most common and most lethal method of suicide in rural China.[22]

Thinking about this, I suddenly recalled how few women under the age of 35 we had seen in Ginkgo Village. Most were either migrant labourers or lived in Xin County City. What was 27-year-old Hu Xiaoming doing here?

Li Wei interrupted my thoughts: '*Shifu*, is the funeral for a suicide the same as for a person who's died of old age?'

'Not quite. The funeral itself is simpler—no performers are hired.'

'Why is that?'

'If it's an elderly person's funeral, you can celebrate a life lived well, but a young person's death is always tragic. You don't want entertainment at the funeral.'

'What about the keening? Do you hire someone to do that for a young person?'

Wang Shifu shook his head.

'Why not?' I asked.

'It's just not done,' he said and shrugged.

I lowered my head, deeply troubled.

'Are there any other differences?' Li Wei asked.

'Hu Xiaoming's parents and parents-in-law are still alive, so her corpse had to be dressed in white and she couldn't be buried in her husband's family grave-plot. We couldn't put the coffin near the family altar either; it had to go outside in a marquee.'

---

22 Michael R. Phillips, Xianyun Li, and Yanping Zhang, 'Suicide Rates in China, 1995–99', *The Lancet* 359, no. 9309 (2002): 835–41, doi.org/10.1016/S0140-6736(02)07954-0; Yongsheng Tong, Michael R. Phillips, Yi Yin, and Zhichao Lan, 'Relationship of the High Proportion of Suicidal Acts Involving Ingestion of Pesticides to the Low Male-to-Female Ratio of Suicide Rates in China', *Epidemiology and Psychiatric Sciences* 29 (2020): E114, doi.org/10.1017/S2045796020000244.

I looked up again.

'A young person without descendants becomes a ghost. You can't put their coffin next to the family altar if the parents or parents-in-law are still alive. Do that and you'll lessen the lifespan of the older generation!'

'What about the bonfire? Do you have that for someone who's died without descendants?'

'Uh-huh. And you keep vigil over the soul. A son of the deceased's brother-in-law makes the sacrifices and kowtows. He does all the things a deceased's descendants would normally do.[23] Sometimes, he'll even pay for the funeral expenses if the parents or parents-in-law can't afford it.' Wang Shifu wiped a hand over his shiny pate.

'And the *song qiao* and *guo qiao* rituals?'

He shook his head. 'If there are no descendants, you can't perform those rituals.'[24]

Oh no! I thought of Hu Xiaoming's soul, left to cross the bridge to the otherworld on her own. I almost cried out. An awkward pause lengthened.

*

Li Wei spoke eventually: '*Shifu*, you said just now that organising Hu Xiaoming's funeral was a lot of trouble. Why was that?'

He shifted on his chair. 'Unnatural deaths are always trouble. As MC, I must figure out if the husband or in-laws were to blame, whether they mistreated her, drove her to suicide.'

He folded his arms. 'But nothing like that happened in this case.'

Li Wei and I cast anxious glances at each other.

'How do you know?' I asked.

'I went over there—spent ages talking with the husband and his mother. They were grief-stricken.' He squirmed and shifted and stared at the floor. 'They didn't do anything to her.'

---

23 If a deceased person without descendants was unmarried, her brother's son performs the vigil.
24 As Wang Shifu made clear, Hu Xiaoming's funeral was different from others' not because she committed suicide, but because her parents and parents-in-law were still alive and she had no descendants.

He got up and went to the front door, leant out, pushed one finger to the side of his nose and blasted out a long, thin stream of snot.

Li Wei and I sat rigid, waiting for him to return. 'So, why'd she kill herself?' I asked in a hard voice.

He plonked down on his chair and folded his arms again. His face was closed.

'Something wrong with her. She came back to the village to have a baby but had a miscarriage. Her husband said she was wrong in the head before that and then she got worse.'

He shifted his legs, arms still folded. 'It must have been the grief. He got her some pills from the doctor and tried to get her to take them. But she wouldn't, she refused.'

Oh, no, I thought, reading abuse as well as grief between the lines. No, no, no! I looked outside. It was sunny out there. How could it be sunny?

'Did you talk with anyone else?' Li Wei asked softly.

He was curt. 'I talked with her father on the phone. And with their representative. Many times.'

'They had a *representative*?' I broke in.

'Of course. I represented the husband's family, so there had to be someone for her side, too.'

'What did they say?'

He wiped a hand over his forehead. 'The father was furious at first. He said the husband must have mistreated her. But he finally relented, accepted she was mentally ill. This side agreed to pay for all the funeral expenses. And they paid for her family to come over; 30 people stayed in a hotel in Xin County City for a week. The husband's family paid for everything. Her side was satisfied with that.'

He squirmed again and pulled at his jacket zipper. 'These things are so hard to negotiate.' He sighed loudly.

I stared at my notebook. Li Wei and Wang Shifu started talking again, but I wasn't really listening. I was imagining Hu Xiaoming. That poor woman's marital family mistreated her; I was sure of it. And I was sure that Wang Shifu knew. Look at how he squirmed. My attempts at empathy with him finally broke down. I hated him for going along with the lie that Hu Xiaoming's marital family had told.

*

Now, as I sit at my desk, hands poised over the keyboard, I see how irrational that was. How could I possibly know what happened? But I recall the stories of domestic violence I've heard over the years in villages all over China. I've rarely asked about it directly, but so many women have told me. I think it's because I'm an outsider, I'm not likely to gossip to other villagers. Awful, awful stories. So hopeless.

I recall, too, that researchers have found lower rates of mental illness among those who have suicided in China than elsewhere. But they have found that family conflict can bring on depression and hopelessness, which then heighten the risk of suicide. Family conflict is the most common trigger for suicide, especially among women.[25]

Of course, I didn't consciously think all this as we sat with Wang Shifu. But it hung in my mind. Was I wrong to take that broad understanding and apply it to this individual case about which I knew nothing? And to be so angry at Wang Shifu? To give up empathising with him?

I stare past my computer, out to my garden full of trees and birdsong. I think about Hu Xiaoming and the horror of her suicide. I think, too, about the gaps in power and privilege between myself, Hu Xiaoming and Wang Shifu. I think about the good fortune I've enjoyed as a well-off white Australian going to Ginkgo Village, and now as a writer in the comfort of my study. I worry over the ethics of my research and writing. Who am I to speak for Hu Xiaoming and challenge Wang Shifu? Who am I to use my writing to build empathy for the former but block it for the latter? I wield such power as a writer. Am I abusing it?

---

25 Liu Yanzheng and Zhang Jie, 'The Impact of Negative Life Events on Attempted Suicide in Rural China', *Journal of Nervous and Mental Disease* 206, no. 3 (2018): 187–94, doi.org/10.1097/nmd.00000 00000000727. For more on rural Chinese women's suicide, see Lee Hyeon Jung, 'Fearless Love, Death for Dignity: Female Suicide and Gendered Subjectivity in Rural North China', *China Journal* 71 (2014): 25–42, doi.org/10.1086/674552.

***

We were having dinner with Yang Yurong. 'Have you heard about Widow Zhou's funeral tomorrow?' I asked.

'Of course,' she nodded. 'I heard she had cancer. One of her daughters-in-law cared for her for months.'

'Do you want another *mantou* [steamed bread bun]?' she asked, standing up. 'There are two left. I'll go get them.'

'Can I have half a one?' I asked. 'Li Wei, do you want the other half?'

Li Wei shook her head.

Yang Yurong returned from the kitchen, holding a warm, fragrant *mantou* with tongs.

'I wish we could go to the funeral,' I sighed.

Yang Yurong paused, *mantou* in mid-air. 'I'll see if you can go with one of the bands that's playing for them if you like. The bandmaster lives in Poplar Hamlet. I'm friends with his wife, Zhao Ling. She can probably take you there.'

Li Wei and I grinned at her and each other.

*

The next morning, there was a burst of fireworks at 4.30 and a sustained run between 5 and 6 am. Their cracking echoed through the hills.

After lunch, Li Wei and I walked with Yang Yurong to the bandmaster's house. She introduced us to Zhao Ling, before returning home.

The band had already piled into a minivan and left for Bamboo Glen. Zhao Ling offered to walk us there and we would get a lift with the band on the way back.

It's a long trek to Bamboo Glen, cross-country past Twin Maidens Shrine. We trudged for more than an hour, up one hill and down another, then cutting through fields. In the distance, a house hid among dense trees. Closer by, a scarecrow guarded a single patch of corn, fenced off with sticks of bamboo. Otherwise, it was all just one big quiet plain of scraggly grass and weeds, a single-file dirt path running through it. I paused to catch my breath. Open eggshell-blue sky, dark hills in the distance. It was almost like Australia. I felt homesick.

'Why isn't this land being farmed?' I asked, stumbling after Zhao Ling.

'It's too remote,' she said, turning back to me.

I was red in the face and sweating. She looked as cool as a cucumber. I thought I was fit, I moaned to myself.

She resumed walking. 'The houses are too far away. Villagers don't want to trek out here anymore. It's dangerous.'

'Wait a minute,' I panted. 'Let's wait for Li Wei.'

She stopped.

'How is it dangerous?' I asked, as Li Wei came up to us.

'Wild boars. With so few people around, they get bold. They'll eat your crops and attack you. They're vicious. Humans can't outrun a wild boar.'

Li Wei edged closer to me. 'Let's go,' we both said hurriedly.

We continued across the plain and up another hill. Then down and up again. On the edge of Bamboo Glen, we paused to rest on a shaded slope.

Below us, funeral guests threaded their way towards Widow Zhou's house. Some were in ordinary clothes. Others wore white shoes and rough white cotton cloth, wrapped around them as a coat with a hood. The women wore white leggings. Some people carried quilts in square clear plastic bags. Others lugged colourful paper wreaths on long, thin poles and blocks of yellow paper tied with twine. That must be spirit-money. Several wreaths were placed at the side of the path. Most were white, but my favourite was a glorious big flower with blue, yellow and purple petals.

A band came marching along the path. There were a handful of men in khaki uniforms blaring trumpets and trombones, a woman beating a side-drum and another clashing cymbals. Zhao Ling said they were from Deng Inn. The Poplar Hamlet band followed them. The whole valley would be able to hear the cacophony. Coming up behind, I feared for my eardrums.

Plate 5.2 Going to a funeral
Photo: Tamara Jacka, 2016.

We reached Widow Zhou's house by three o'clock. We had a long afternoon and evening ahead of us. We would not return to Ginkgo Village until 10 that night.

*

As we arrived, we were each given a strip of undyed white cotton. 'What do we do with this?' I asked Zhao Ling.

'Just hang onto it for now.'

Crowds of people milled about. Some lined up to pay their last respects to Widow Zhou, lying in the coffin in the front room. Strips of white paper with couplets in black ink had been pasted around the open doorway. Li Wei asked whether we could go inside, but Zhao Ling shook her head. 'It'd be disrespectful. Only close relatives and friends are allowed.'

I was secretly relieved.

Two enormous marquees had been set up outside the house. There was a blue one for the caterers; we went into the red-and-yellow one next to it, which contained two long tables. At the first, a queue of people waited to hand over their gifts of quilts and wads of cash. The hamlet head, a middle-aged man in faded black, recorded the details with a fat marker pen. Later, we learned that 50 households were recorded as giving something. Several quilts and just over 50,000 yuan (US$7,700) were received.

At the second table, a handful of Wang men received guests' gifts of yellow paper. They stamped each sheet with a red chop shaped like an ancient copper coin with a square hole in the middle. Zhao Ling explained that the stamp turned it from ordinary paper into spirit-money: 'You can buy spirit-money readymade, but it's expensive.'

Some of the spirit-money was put to one side in a loose pile, but most was stuffed into large hessian grain bags. Ahead of the evening's bonfire, 85 bags of spirit-money would be prepared. Most would be burnt for Widow Zhou's soul, but about 15 would be burnt for her deceased parents, parents-in-law and other ancestors. The recipient's name was written on the front of each bag. The souls of these ancestors would have no financial worries in the afterlife! Most of the loose pile would be given to the deceased parents of other close relatives—just one deceased parent per person. If both parents are dead, spirit-money is burned for the father.

The inside of the marquee was filling up with people, cigarette smoke and noise. We could just make out the wall of Widow Zhou's house on the left. In front of it, a wide strip of dirt had been set aside as a stage, with a jumble of instruments and sound equipment parked around it.

Each of the three bands performing that night included four to six men playing brass instruments and a couple of women singing and beating drums and cymbals. There was not enough room for all three bands, so the one from Gao River went home. They returned much later in the night, after Li Wei and I had left.

The two remaining bands performed a bizarre range of songs. One woman in tight blue jeans and a frilly blouse trotted across the stage in high heels, mike in hand, rolling her hips and belting out a raunchy pop song. A second woman, with dyed red hair and a long red skirt, sang a mournful aria, accompanied by a man reproducing the ear-splitting noise of a suona and cymbals on an electric keyboard. The volume was turned up so high, the sound was distorted. I mushed up some tissue to plug my ears. Li Wei copied me. It didn't help much. Our ears were ringing for two days afterwards.

*

For hours, we sat on little red plastic stools while the marquee choked with guests. Finally, the performers took a break and Li Wei and I breathed a sigh of relief. Everyone began shuffling and jostling out of the marquee.

A long line of people snaked downhill towards the bonfire in the middle of a bare field. At the head of the procession was an open-backed van loaded with wreaths, boxed firecrackers and hessian bags of spirit-money. Several men in the procession also carried bags of spirit-money on their shoulders. Others carried large flat cardboard cars and three-storey houses, painted with windows and doors. It was quite dark; we had to use the light on our phones to see where we were going. The bands clashed their cymbals and blared their horns and a Daoist priest played a suona. The musicians lined up along the ridge above the bonfire and continued playing while it burned.

A crowd of guests stood alongside the musicians. Zhao Ling, Li Wei and I stood with them. Zhao Ling showed Li Wei and me how to drape our white cloths around our necks, like scarves.

Widow Zhou's sons and daughters and their spouses in their white gowns and hoods went down to the fire and threw in the spirit-money and other offerings. They threw from two piles. The larger pile, we learned later, was for Widow Zhou and her ancestors to use in the otherworld. It included the 85 bags of spirit-money, the cardboard cars and houses, and the deceased's clothes and bed quilt. The smaller pile was the spirit-money for the close relatives' ancestors, plus a handful of sheets to keep the wandering ghosts content.

Once the piles had been thrown in and the flames were leaping, Zhao Ling motioned for us to take off our white scarves. Others were taking theirs off, too.

The music stopped and a great volley of fireworks was set off into the night. The white-hooded figures circled slowly round the bonfire, over and over. I lost count of the number of times they circled. Zhao Ling said they were guarding the money and possessions on the journey to the other side, protecting them from wandering ghosts.[26] They looked like druids or the Klu Klux Klan. It was all very strange and disorienting.

Part of me felt a sense of achievement witnessing this. I must be a real anthropologist! But another part of me was truly spooked by those circling, hooded figures; the towering flames rearing and spitting into the blackness. I felt out of my depth.

*

It was a long time before we returned to the red-and-yellow marquee. Eighteen round wooden folding tables were assembled inside. We sat with Zhao Ling at one of two tables assigned to the band members.

Each of us was given a disposable plastic bowl, disposable wooden chopsticks and a plastic cup of green tea leaves. I groaned at the mountain of garbage being created. The food was plentiful but cold and very salty. Li Wei and I ate very little. We drank cupful after cupful of green tea instead.

After the meal, several people left, but the marquee remained crowded. Zhao Ling shunted us deeper inside and found a spot for us to park our plastic stools, not far from the stage. There was more loud singing. Li Wei and I plugged our ears with more tissue. Zhao Ling laughed and shook her head when I offered her some.

I took several photos of two performers—one stout, one skinny—to one side of the stage, painting their faces with Chinese opera masks. The skinny one, a man, applied pink blush under fine black eyebrow-wings. The stout one painted a pert little butterfly mouth onto a stark white face. Li Wei and I couldn't tell whether it was a man or a woman. Both performers wore drab army uniforms, but their masks made them look like drag queens— gorgeous Chinese drag queens! I kept my delight to myself.

*

Hour after hour we sat, watching the singers and opera performers. My back and legs ached. I wanted to get up and walk about, but I was trapped, surrounded by hunched dark-jacketed villagers, their faces blank. A few children were dotted here and there. One little boy had a peculiar bowl haircut.

---

26 At the second funeral Li Wei attended, relatives stood around the bonfire but didn't circle it.

Then the stout performer with the butterfly mouth knelt before Widow Zhou's makeshift altar in a tall headdress and white cape. On the altar were a candle, incense and a red-and-white paper spirit-tablet. I made to lift my camera, but Zhao Ling staid my hand and shook her head.

The performer chanted and wept. I could make out the words 'Mama', 'pitiable' and 'suffering', but nothing else. They drew in great harsh juddering breaths and let them out in jagged sobs. They keened and wailed, kowtowing and draping their body over the altar. A man and woman dressed in white knelt in silence on either side, heads bowed. Zhao Ling told us afterwards that they were Widow Zhou's oldest son and daughter-in-law.

The keening continued for what felt like forever. I don't have the words to describe how disturbing I found it. The sound was like my mother's endless screaming; like the whole world wailing on and on and on.

But the other guests showed no signs of distress or grief. They just sat there. I was unable to read their expressions. Three girls in colourful skirts stood at the edge of the stage area, to the left of Zhao Ling, Li Wei and me. They must have had a good view of the performer's made-up face from there. One held up her phone to take a picture. She showed it to the other two and they giggled and nudged one another. They took turns to grab the phone and snap more pictures. Perhaps they were photographing me, not the performer.

I stared at them, unnerved. My brain was unable to process the clash between the performer wailing at the altar, the giggly girls taking snapshots and the old grey guys sitting passive beside me. I thought of the funerals I'd been to before. My brother's, my dad's, my grandma's. Funerals are sad— heartbreakingly sad. So, why were these guests seemingly unmoved? I didn't understand.[27]

---

27   One explanation for the lack of overt grief may be that death and funerals are commonplace in the lives of villagers. On average, there's at least one funeral in Ginkgo Village each month. A second explanation lies in Widow Zhou's advanced age. According to our host's husband, Wu Jianfu, the funerals of those who have lived long lives involve more cheerful performances and fewer expressions of grief than those of younger people and those who die unexpectedly. The second funeral that Li Wei attended bore this out. The deceased was a man in his sixties, who died unexpectedly. No performances were provided and there was more crying among the deceased's wife and children. A third, less likely, explanation is suggested by Andrew Kipnis. A Buddhist priest told Kipnis that 'it's important for family members not to cry' because 'crying makes the soul of the deceased less willing to leave this world and transition to the Western Paradise' (Kipnis, *The Funeral of Mr Wang*, 120). Wu Jianfu denied that Ginkgo Villagers are customarily restrained from crying at funerals. But, he said, family members and close relatives should not touch the corpse or let their tears drip on it, as this would cause the deceased's soul to linger. Usually, a more distant elderly relative cleans, dresses and moves the corpse.

I was exhausted and confused—perched on a too-small red plastic stool, my ears still plugged with tissue, floating in outer space. I looked down at myself sitting there in a daze of hunger and incense and cigarette smoke. Utterly lost. Half my life I've been learning about China, yet a huge blank plain of incomprehension stretches before me. Tears leak through my closed eyelids.

I see myself sitting on the beach with my mum. 'I cannot be your mother anymore,' she says, and I stare down, eyes blurred. Too stunned to move.

Finally, she lets out a rough sigh. 'It's late,' she says and gets to her feet. Shakes the sand from her towel and rolls it up. Walks away.

I stumble to the water's edge, wash off sand and suntan lotion. She's out of sight by the time I turn back.

Then I'm swimming slowly outwards. There are no waves or wind. The ocean is vast and calm and silent. I'm a tiny speck dipping down, bobbing up, watching for the magic green flash on the horizon just before the sun disappears. The water is like mercury. I swim on and on and on.

*

As the performer's keening wound down, an older woman to our right started crying. It was Widow Zhou's sister-in-law. She moaned and wailed, her eyes closed, rocking back and forth on her stool. A few other women crowded around her.

The daughter-in-law, still kneeling at the altar, started crying, too. Her son strode over and helped her up, wrapping his arms around her as she wept. The girl with the phone—the daughter-in-law's granddaughter—joined them. The three of them stood in a quiet huddle.

I wiped my eyes in relief.

6

The road-concreting conflict

Roads mean progress. As the saying goes, 'If you want to get rich, you must first build roads' (*Yao xiang fu, xian xiu lu*).[1] Sealed concrete roads rolling effortlessly up and down the hillsides will take you out of poverty. You can cart your produce to market on a smooth, flat road. You can spread your canola seeds out to dry on it as well.

With a network of sealed concrete roads, the government can fund development projects. It can bring in trucks with cement to build new ponds, grand office buildings for the village government and hamlet squares with exercise equipment.

With good roads, you can send your kids to school. You can take a bus to Xin County City and go shopping, too. You can become a migrant labourer and go all the way to Beijing or Shanghai or Guangzhou. You can even get yourself to an airport and fly to Japan or America. You can leave Ginkgo Village and make your fortune.

You can also come back. With decent roads, a filial son can come home at New Year. He can drive his shiny car with his ageing parents cocooned in the back and glide all the way up to the Buddhist temple on Mount Phoenix. And if there's a smooth road out to the ancestors' tombs, even future generations with no-one left in the village can return at Qingming to sweep their ancestors' graves.[2]

---

1   Building roads was a key part of the state's poverty alleviation strategy in the late twentieth and early twenty-first centuries (Boullenois, 'Poverty Alleviation in China').

2   The Qingming festival, also known as Tomb-Sweeping Day, is held on the fifteenth day after the spring equinox (in early April). On that day, villagers customarily clear away the weeds from their ancestors' graves and tombstones, pray to the ancestors and burn incense and spirit-money for them.

Plate 6.1 Drying canola seeds on a hamlet road
Photo: Tamara Jacka, 2015.

With good roads, villagers can go out into the world and the world can come to the village. Even foreign guests, like Laoshi, can visit. Perhaps, one day, there'll be tourists and the village will thrive again.

Admittedly, sealed roads aren't necessary. If they're wide enough for a vehicle, packed-dirt roads will do. But only when it's dry. When the summer rains come, those dirt roads blossom with patches of impassable bog.

Before the mid twentieth century, there were no vehicular roads in Ginkgo Village. Or anywhere else in the surrounding mountains for that matter. Not even dirt ones. The bandits, rebels, revolutionaries and government soldiers who rampaged through the area journeyed on foot. So, too, did the villagers fleeing violence and the peddlers carrying fish fry, grain and salt. Maybe one or two generals had a horse or donkey, but everyone else went on foot.[3]

---

3   In the early 1930s, the Communists built a few dirt roads through the Eyuwan Soviet, but they were destroyed during the war.

The main dirt road from Red River Township to Ginkgo Village was opened to vehicles in the early 1950s. Villagers couldn't remember the date, but they remembered the jeep coming down the road the day it was opened. They had never seen a motorcar and didn't know what it was. Looking down from the hills, they thought it was a giant water buffalo and worried about their crops. They felt reassured when the beast kept moving steadily past their fields. Is that a true story? I don't know.

For more than three decades, the main road was the only one in the village. When Ginkgo Brigade bought its first tractor in 1976, it could only be used in the fields bordering that road. You couldn't get it to the hamlets in the hills because the paths leading up there were too narrow and rough.

Even the main road wasn't concreted until 2010.

It took even longer to widen and concrete the paths fanning out to the hamlets. You might expect the short paths to the closest hamlets would be done first. In fact, they first concreted the long road stretching to Bitter Hollow. Why? Because the village's main tea plantation lies along that road. Yang Jiefang, the plantation's owner, wanted smoother passage from the tea bushes to the tea processing factory in Ginkgo Hamlet. He demanded that road be given priority. The tea factory brings in revenue for the village government in the form of land rent. And the Yang lineage is very powerful in Xin County: three men surnamed Yang have positions of influence in the county government. So, Party Secretary Guo made sure that Yang Jiefang's demands were met. The concrete was poured in early March 2011, just in time for the tea-picking season.[4]

Most of the other hamlet roads were concreted in 2013. The first to be completed that year was the one that wends its way out past Five Hills Hamlet. It was finished quickly because hamlet residents made it a condition for their approval of the construction of a phone tower on one of the five hills behind the hamlet. They blocked construction workers' access to the site until the concrete had been poured and set.

---

4   The influence of lineages on the governmental provision of roads and other public goods in rural China is discussed in Lily Tsai, *Accountability Without Democracy* (Cambridge, UK: Cambridge University Press, 2007), 148–86, doi.org/10.1017/CBO9780511800115. See also He and Wang, 'Social Resources Transfer Program'.

The second road to be concreted in 2013 was the one running to Twin Maidens Hamlet. That's where the former Party secretary Cao Fuguo has a house. He doesn't live there anymore, but his ageing parents do. The third went to Poplar Hamlet, where Director Zhou lives.

By 2015, just two roads remained unsealed. The first was the one to White Cloud Hamlet, which is understandable: White Cloud is a long way from the centre of the village and all but one household had left the hamlet long before 2015.

The other road not concreted—or at least, not *fully* concreted—was the one leading to Old Pine Hamlet. It climbs the hill to the south-east from the main road and into a right-angle bend. That's as far as the concrete reaches. On the uphill side of the bend squats Old Pine Hamlet's roadside shrine, surrounded by hollyhocks. On the other side stands a Huangshan pine tree, right on the edge of a cliff.

The hamlet isn't really named Old Pine. I just call it that because of this Huangshan pine. It's like a pine tree in a Chinese painting, all angular and gnarled, extending southwards in a crooked curve over the paddy fields.

This is one of my favourite spots in all of Ginkgo Village. Li Wei's, too. On our first visit it was May. The hollyhocks were flowering lilac and pink. We stood in the pine's limpid cool, looking out over the fields and back at the shrine with its gentle flowers. It felt like a dream.

A resident of Old Pine Hamlet once told us the story of this shrine. It was first built in the eighteenth century. Until then, the land on which it sits belonged to a landlord in Stone Gully Hamlet. One day, a wandering beggar died by the side of the road. An Old Pine Hamlet man tried to force the Stone Gully landlord to pay for the beggar's burial rites by dumping his corpse on the landlord's land. But the landlord refused to take responsibility by disowning that piece of land. So, the land was claimed by the residents of Old Pine. They built the shrine on it. Originally, it was no bigger than a wardrobe and housed only a wooden tablet for the Earth God (*Tudi Gong*), standing on a narrow altar-shelf.

At the beginning of the Cultural Revolution, the head of Old Pine Hamlet's people's militia had the shrine destroyed. Afterwards, he felt terribly guilty. In 1996, on his death bed, he asked his wife to rebuild the shrine. She built a plain mudbrick one. But shrines still weren't allowed in those days, so the Red River Government had it demolished.

Plate 6.2 Inside a roadside shrine. From left to right: Grandmother Earth God, Grandfather Earth God, the Goddess of Mercy, the Maiden Who Brings Children and the God of Wealth

Photo: Li Wei, 2016.

The shrine that stands today was built in 2013. All the hamlet's residents chipped in to pay for it. The names of each of the family heads who donated funds, along with how much they gave, are engraved on the black marble plaque next to the shrine. They also bought five new porcelain statuettes: Grandmother Earth God (*Tudi Nainai*), Grandfather Earth God (*Tudi Yeye*), the Goddess of Mercy (*Guanyin*), the Maiden Who Brings Children (*Songzi Niangniang*) and the God of Wealth (*Caishen*).[5]

Just past the shrine and the pine tree, the road to Old Pine forks like the tongue of a snake. One road continues to the north-east, the other turns abruptly east. In 2015, these two roads were still just dirt.

---

5   For discussion of the roles of the Earth God and the Goddess of Mercy (*Guanyin*), see Feuchtwang, *Popular Religion in China*; and Yang, *Re-Enchanting Modernity*. In Chinese popular religion, the Maiden Who Brings Children is known as *Songzi Niangniang*. In Buddhism, she is known as *Songzi Guanyin* and is viewed as either a manifestation of *Guanyin* or *Guanyin*'s attendant. The name of the God of Wealth speaks for itself.

Here's why. Old Pine's households fall into three groups: one-third are headed by men with the surname Li and the rest by men surnamed either Yang or Chen. The Li families live mostly along the road that turns east at the pine tree. They wanted concrete for that road. Most, though not all, of the Yang and Chen families live in the northern part of the triangle formed by the two roads. These families have houses close to the road that runs to the north-east. Naturally, they were pushing for that road to be concreted. The problem was, the county government's funds were enough for only one more road, so the hamlet had to choose. Which was it to be: the road the Li families wanted (which I'll call the Li road) or the one the Yangs and Chens preferred (the Yang–Chen road)?

You might think that being more numerous, the Yang and Chen families should have had the greatest say in this decision. Certainly, that's what *they* thought. I mentioned that the Yang lineage has three men in the Xin County Government. You would think that would strengthen their case for the Yang–Chen road to be concreted, wouldn't you? But you see, the Li lineage also has two men in the Xin County Government—both with positions more senior than the Yang men.

When first approached by their Li brethren, these two gentlemen were reluctant to get involved. Why get tangled in a hamlet dispute and run the risk of being labelled corrupt? After all, neither had any *close* relatives in the hamlet. They didn't even bother to learn the details of the dispute.

Then someone told them that a few ancestral tombs of one branch of the Li lineage are at the end of the Li road. Neither had ever visited those tombs as they belonged to a different branch. But that didn't matter. It was now imperative that the concreting be done on the Li road, so their brothers could go to burn incense and spirit-money at the Li tombs. It was a matter of lineage pride.

The road-concreting conflict continued for three years. It seethed beneath the surface of everyday life in Old Pine, adding venom to other, apparently unrelated tensions between Li families and their Yang and Chen neighbours.

***

Chen Dajin is the man who first told Li Wei and me about the road-concreting conflict. His house is a short distance up the hill from the fork between the Yang–Chen and Li roads. The latter forms the boundary of his property.

He's a genial fellow, a jack-of-all-trades turned entrepreneur. Perhaps he inherited his entrepreneurial bent from his grandparents: his mother's father was a peddler, who walked from Guangshan to Wuhan and back, selling salt. His father's father was an inn keeper. Until 1947, he ran a small inn on the main road at the base of the track running up to Old Pine Hamlet. But the main road was a dangerous place in the 1940s. Soldiers were tramping back and forth along it, getting drunk in the inn and brawling each night. So, Chen Dajin's grandfather gave up the inn and retreated into the hills.

From then on, he and his family got by farming a bit of rented land, which was just as well. If he had still been running the inn after the CCP came to power in 1949, he and his family might have been persecuted as petty capitalists. As it was, they were deemed poor peasants, so they escaped criticism. They just suffered poverty, like everyone else.[6]

Chen Dajin was born in 1972, the youngest in a family of six children. When he was 10, his mother died of a stroke. She was just 40 years old. His father died in 1996, aged fifty-five.[7] Chen Dajin's three older sisters had married out by then. His two older brothers had also married, split from the family and gone out to work as migrant labourers. Since 1990, Chen Dajin, too, had been away from home, working on the outskirts of Beijing.

In his first year, he worked on the assembly line of a car factory. He earnt 7,000 yuan (US$1,300). 'It seems so little now,' he said. 'But it was a lot more than anything you could earn in the village back then.' In those days, the highest-paying village work was in the tea factory, but even the skilled tea processors earned only 5,000 yuan (US$950) a year. Anyway, Chen Dajin didn't have the contacts one needed to get a job in the tea factory.

He didn't get married until he was twenty-eight. His wife, Liang Anqin, is from Hong'an. She's two years younger than Chen Dajin. When she turned 21, she, too, became a migrant worker; the pair met in Beijing. She worked in the small noodle house where Chen Dajin had his lunch.

---

6   For more about the rise of entrepreneurship in post-Mao Henan, see Camille Boullenois, 'The Self-Made Entrepreneur: Social Identities and the Perceived Legitimacy of Entrepreneurs in Inland Rural China' (PhD diss., The Australian National University, Canberra, 2020b).

7   Among those born before the 1950s, such short lifespans were not unusual. Talking with an elderly Ginkgo Villager about the Maoist period, I asked whether people worked in collective labour after the age of sixty. He said, 'No. Most were dead by then.'

'He always ate the same thing,' Liang Anqin laughed. 'Noodles in beef broth—the cheapest dish on the menu!'

Chen Dajin grinned. 'Freshly made noodles with chopped coriander leaves on top—delicious!'

'Oh, that's my son's favourite, too!' I cried. 'We lived in Beijing for six months when he was four. On weekends, we often went to a noodle house for lunch. He loved noodles in beef broth.'

Li Wei smiled to herself. She knows Misha.

I became quite nostalgic, thinking about the little noodle joints that he and I had visited. Poky little places, ripe with sweaty bodies. We would squeeze in and find a stool, between the migrant construction workers slurping noodle soup. We would sit there, mesmerised by the noise and bustle: the crowds of people inside and out; the honking, beeping traffic rushing by. When we went to a posh restaurant, the waitresses would come burbling and stroke Misha's fair hair. But in the noodle joints, they left us alone. It was a relief.

'What year were you in Beijing?' Chen Dajin asked.

'With my son? 2001. We lived at Peking University, Haidian.'

He and Liang Anqin exchanged glances and laughed. 'We lived in Haidian, too! Right on the edge of the suburb, in a migrant settlement.'

'I know the place!' I said. I'd been doing research in precisely that migrant settlement.[8]

'We might have crossed paths!' Liang Anqin laughed. 'You might have been in my noodle house!'

We swapped notes about the migrant settlement. 'You know it doesn't exist anymore, right?' Chen Dajin asked.

I nodded. I went back in late 2002 to find almost all the migrant shacks demolished. Officials had razed them ahead of the 2008 Olympic Games. They pushed out the rural migrants and put in green parks and golf courses.

---

8   See Tamara Jacka, *Rural Women in Urban China: Gender, Migration, and Social Change* (Armonk, NY: M.E. Sharpe, 2006).

Chen Dajin and Liang Anqin were among the last to leave. They moved to the edge of Chaoyang, even further from the city centre, and stayed there for several years.

*

Just after they moved to Chaoyang, Liang Anqin gave birth to a daughter, Huifen. She stopped working then, until after their son, Guotao, was born in 2004. But it was impossible for four people to survive in the capital on one migrant worker's wage. So, when Guotao turned one, the couple sent both children to live with Liang Anqin's parents. Liang Anqin returned to work as a waitress in another small restaurant. Gradually, she and Chen Dajin began to save a bit of money.

At the beginning of 2008, they celebrated New Year at Liang Anqin's parents' place. Afterwards, they took Huifen and Guotao to live in Xin County. They did it for the children's sake: it wasn't good for them to be estranged from their parents.

They didn't go to Old Pine Hamlet as they had nothing to return to there. Chen Dajin's family house was falling down and they had only a tiny amount of land—just 0.7 mu (470 square metres). That's because at the time of the final land readjustment in 1998, Chen Dajin's siblings had already left the household and his father had died. He had not yet brought in a wife, so he was assigned land for only one person.

For a while, the couple rented a two-room apartment in Red River and the kids went to primary school there. Then, in early 2009, Chen Dajin demolished the ruin in Old Pine Hamlet and had a new house built. It cost 160,000 yuan (US$23,400), most of which they had to borrow. It took two years to build.

Those two years were a real low point in Chen Dajin's life. 'I was destitute,' he said. 'I had no parents, no house, no land and no money.' To earn enough to repay his debts, Chen Dajin went to Luanda, Angola, and worked in a Chinese state-owned furniture factory. He got the job with a friend's help and by paying a private intermediary agency.

But working conditions in the factory were truly miserable and the pay was much less than he and his Chinese workmates had been led to believe. They'd been promised reimbursement of their return flights to Luanda and a salary of 100,000 yuan (US$15,900) to be paid at the end of each year.

They'd also been told they would receive free food and accommodation and a bit of spending money each month. They would work eight-hour days, with two rest days a month, plus an extra month of paid leave at the end of their two-year contract.

For the first six months, though, they had no contract and were required to work nine hours a day every day plus overtime. They didn't mind. The Angolan civil war was over by that time, but there was still a lot of violence and lawlessness.

'It was very dangerous out on the streets,' Chen Dajin said. 'Like in China before Liberation.' So, he and his workmates preferred to work than go out.

When they finally received a contract, it included an annual salary of only 70,000 yuan (US$11,000)—not much more than they could have earned in Beijing at that time.[9] Chen Dajin and his workmates fought back, refusing to do any overtime. But it was no use. They hadn't yet been paid anything and the manager told them that if they left, they would not receive their pay. They wouldn't be reimbursed for their plane tickets either. Chen Dajin lasted out the year, received his pay and went home.

*

Back at home, Chen Dajin and his family had no source of income. So, what were they to do? As he recounts the story, Chen Dajin was in Deng Inn one day when he saw a man selling noodles from the back of a three-wheeled cart. He watched and thought, 'We could do that!'

Using the money he'd earned in Luanda, he and Liang Anqin had a shack built next to their house and installed noodle-making equipment in it. They then paid a master 4,000 yuan (US$640) to teach Liang Anqin how to make *mantou* and *baozi* (stuffed steamed bread buns) as well as noodles.

The couple opened their noodle business in mid 2013 and were soon run off their feet. Liang Anqin's parents agreed to come live with them and help with the business. With them came Liang Anqin's sister, Meiling, with her nine-month-old baby. Meiling was three years younger than Liang Anqin.

---

9   The factory employed 50 local Angolan workers and 150 Chinese workers. The Angolans were paid even less than the Chinese, receiving no more than the equivalent of 12,000 yuan (US$1,900).

She had a congenital defect and couldn't walk without the aid of crutches, so she relied heavily on her mother to help care for her child. Her husband was a construction labourer, working in Cambodia.

It was an unusual household: Li Wei and I had not come across two sisters living together. What's more, while we knew of older women living in an urban apartment with a daughter, Liang Anqin's parents were the first elderly couple we had met who lived in their son-in-law's village.[10]

'It's not permanent,' Liang Anqin's mother told us. 'When we're too old to look after ourselves, we'll go live with our son.'

I asked why they wouldn't stay in Ginkgo Village and she laughed: 'It's not our home! Your home is with your son, not your daughter.'

All sorts of unconventional living arrangements were acceptable, it seemed, if you could think of them as temporary.

Chen Dajin might have been the one with entrepreneurial ambitions, but it was his wife and parents-in-law who did most of the work. Each morning, they slaved away, making noodles, *mantou* and *baozi*. During the day, Liang Anqin's parents sold their produce from the shack. Liang Anqin sold it from a three-wheeled cart, which she pedalled around Ginkgo Village. Her father also grew a few vegetables on the narrow strip of land between the house and the Li road. Chen Dajin supplemented their income with odd jobs around Ginkgo and neighbouring villages, laying bricks, installing plumbing and electricity in newly built houses and repairing electrical appliances. He only helped his wife and in-laws occasionally in the evenings. That's when they made dough and *baozi* stuffing in readiness for the next morning.

*

The noodle business went from strength to strength. Chen Dajin and Liang Anqin quickly paid off their debts. Then, at the end of 2013, Chen Dajin borrowed again and bought himself a truck. It cost 60,000 yuan (US$9,900). Through 2014, as well as continuing with his other work, he sometimes earnt money by trucking rock, sand, timber and other building materials across Xin County.

---

10   Occasionally, though, a newlywed with a baby whose husband was a migrant worker would return to her parents' place for a time, rather than live alone in her husband's village.

During the week, Huifen and Guotao went to school in Red River. They lived with Chen Dajin's sister there. Every Friday, Chen Dajin picked them up in his truck and took them home for the weekend, returning them first thing on Monday morning.

By the time Li Wei and I met him in 2015, Chen Dajin was struggling to find work. He couldn't even earn enough to pay back the money he'd borrowed to buy his truck. The state had tightened restrictions on the use of land for building, making it much harder for villagers to gain permission to build new houses. That meant there were fewer people wanting plumbing and electricity installed or building materials transported. Tightening restrictions on mining and logging also cut demand for the trucking of rocks and timber.

The other problem was the unsealed roads, which meant Chen Dajin couldn't take his truck out in wet weather. It was bogged once near their house. He, Liang Anqin and his father-in-law cursed and struggled for an hour trying to lever it out, the warm rain sploshing down on them. Another time, he nearly went over the cliff trying to avoid the worst potholes.

But the noodle business was going strong. Each day they were open, Liang Anqin and her mother turned a 25-kilogram bag of flour into noodles and other goods, which they sold for a net profit of 200 yuan (US$30). Working almost every day, from before dawn until late afternoon, they managed to cover the family's expenses. That included a few thousand yuan a year for Huifen and Guotao to live and attend school in Red River. And they paid another 10,000 yuan (US$1,500) each year for New Year expenses and gifts for weddings, funerals and other special occasions.

'Meeting obligations and maintaining good social relations are our single biggest expense,' Liang Anqin said. 'There's no escape from gift-giving. Everyone says, if you don't have money, sell your wok. Do everything you can to maintain good social relations. Otherwise, you'll have no-one to lend to you or help you out. We'd lose our customers.'

*

The noodle business was the family's lifeline, but it caused conflict with their neighbour Mr Li. Mr Li's mansion was built close to the edge of his property. When Chen Dajin and Liang Anqin built their noodle-making shack right up against the stone wall on the other side, Mr Li objected vociferously. He claimed its construction was illegal and took the couple to court.

It was true, Liang Anqin admitted, that they'd not received permission to build the shack. But that was the case for a lot of buildings in the village. She was sure that wasn't the real reason for Mr Li's objections. 'It's just because he's a Li and my husband's a Chen,' she said crossly.

Maybe it also had to do with image. Mr Li's mansion is very grand. It's three storeys and white like a wedding cake. A sweep of steps leads up to a portico with a triangular white roof, supported by white Roman columns on each side of the front door. Perhaps Mr Li didn't like living next-door to a ramshackle noodle shack, with a truck and a three-wheeled cart parked in the dirt yard and customers traipsing across it, hailing each other and coming together in gossipy clumps.

Not that he would have seen much of that. He and his family lived elsewhere most of the time. Once, Li Wei and I saw a man unlocking the gate, but he gave us such a filthy look as we walked past, we didn't dare approach.

That was in 2016, after the court case had been resolved. To my surprise, it was settled in favour of Chen Dajin and his wife. I've no idea how they pulled that off.

*

The year 2016 was big for them in other ways, too. Worn out by the noodle business, Liang Anqin decided to cut down on sales. She and her parents still sold their produce from the shack but, after New Year, she stopped peddling her wares around the village.

Meanwhile, she and Chen Dajin embarked on a new project: opening a restaurant on the second floor of their house. They had a single enormous room up there, into which they put one large round table that could seat 20 people and four smaller ones, each seating ten. They didn't get a permit and they were only open two or three evenings a week, when they were asked to hold a banquet.

Most of their customers were village cadres. Since the start of Xi Jinping's anticorruption campaign, there had been a ban on cadres using public funds to wine and dine. This meant the death of many small restaurants in villages and townships, especially those set up on busy thoroughfares. Cadres didn't dare risk being seen going into those restaurants. But Chen Dajin's place was much less visible; it was away from the main road and there were no signs to show it was a restaurant.

The men—they were nearly all men—would come in the late afternoon or evening. They'd walk through Chen Dajin's front room and up the stairs at the back. While their meal was being prepared downstairs, they'd sit smoking, drinking and playing cards. They'd continue drinking until long after the meal, getting louder and more obnoxious as the night wore on.

I know, because Li Wei and I were invited to a cadre banquet each time we visited Ginkgo Village. Mostly we went to a more formal restaurant in Deng Inn, but a few times we ate at Chen Dajin's place.

The food was good. I particularly loved the *mapo doufu*—a dish made with soybean curd with an eyewatering chilli sauce and tongue-tingling fragrant Sichuan pepper, which melted in your mouth. Li Wei was not so keen on that dish. Typical of northerners, she ate less spicy food than southerners, including Ginkgo Villagers. Her favourite was a simple dish of stir-fried egg with *xiangchun* (the tender new leaves of the Chinese toon tree).

Despite the delicious food, Li Wei and I disliked those meals with the cadres. The more they drank, the more they forgot us. You might think that would be a good thing; we'd learn more by eavesdropping than in an interview. Li Wei did pick up a few titbits, but I couldn't. Their loud rapid-fire dialect was almost incomprehensible to me. I would strain to follow, then give up and just watch them. You can learn a lot from merely observing, but I'd get too tired and bored and switch off.

*

Running a restaurant was Chen Dajin's idea. But again, it was mainly Liang Anqin and her mother who did the cooking. Like most village men, Chen Dajin knew how to cook, but he only helped when a particularly large banquet was being prepared.

There was no menu; the guests ate whatever dishes were made that evening. Liang Anqin and her mother used nearly all local produce: chickens bought from one villager, ducks from another, canola and peanut oil from a third. They cooked carp, loach, lobsters and shrimps that Chen Dajin and Liang

Anqin's father caught in the hamlet pond. They bought *doufu* from a peddler and vegetables from another, to supplement the bok choy, broad beans and chilli peppers that Liang Anqin's father grew.

They also cooked wild plants. Apart from *xiangchun*, Liang Anqin and her mother picked shepherd's purse on the embankments between the nearby paddy fields and foraged for leafy greens in the hills. Foraging is common among villagers of Liang Anqin's age, especially women. Yang Yurong also does it.[11] I have fond memories of the two times she took me and Li Wei foraging in the hills behind Ginkgo Hamlet. It gave me a special pleasure to be surrounded by the forest, continuing a centuries-old practice of sharing its bounty.

For middle-aged women like Yang Yurong and Liang Anqin, wild plants are good, cheap food. Yang Yurong and her friends swap WeChat videos explaining their health benefits. For others, they're a source of income. The physically disabled man in White Cloud Hamlet scraped a living for himself and his elderly mother from the sale of medicinal leaves, roots and flowers. And a few women in Poplar Hamlet supplement their husbands' migrant-labourer incomes by selling kudzu-root flour, which fetches a high price as a tonic for lowering blood pressure. But it's time-consuming to prepare: to make 1 kilogram of flour, you must dry and grind 10 kilograms of kudzu root.

These people learnt to forage from their mothers, but few in their mother's generation have any interest in the practice anymore. In this, Liang Anqin's mother is unusual. For most, foraging is too much trouble and wild plants are too strongly associated with extreme suffering. That's because when they were younger, eating kudzu root and other wild plants was sometimes the only way to fend off starvation.[12]

---

11 Yang Yurong could name 26 leafy plants, shoots, flowers, roots and fungi that she picked around the village and in the hills. The list included shepherd's purse, purslane, dandelions, purple shiso, golden needles (the flower buds of the citron daylily), *xiangchun*, wild celery, kudzu root and lalang grass rhizomes. She named another 14 types of edible fruits and berries found in the forest, including acorns, hawthorn fruit, yellow Himalayan raspberries, akebia fruit and the fruit of the Chinese raisin tree. For a more extensive Chinese-language list of edible and medicinal wild plants in Xin County, see Xin County Gazetteer Compilation Committee, *Xin County Gazetteer 1986–2005*, 75–78.

12 For another discussion of food and memory, see Ellen Oxfeld, *Bitter and Sweet: Food, Meaning, and Modernity in Rural China* (Oakland, CA: University of California Press, 2017), doi.org/10.1525/california/9780520293519.001.0001.

It might also be that they don't like the taste. Personally, I enjoy foraging, but I can only eat wild greens in tiny quantities. They're too bitter for my liking. As for kudzu-root flour, it's disgusting! At our request, Liang Anqin once used it to make dumpling balls in soup for Li Wei and me. Neither of us could finish even one small bowl. Eating those dumpling balls was how I imagine eating cement would be. Perhaps our palates have been spoilt by sugary processed foods and the bland but sweet fruit and vegetables we buy in supermarkets these days. It's easy for me to see why older villagers are no longer interested in foraging.

Younger people are not interested either. I suppose it's possible that, in the coming decades, a craze for foraging will develop among Liang Anqin's children's generation. But it's not likely. Most will leave home to go to boarding school, university and jobs outside the village. Their mothers will have little chance to teach them to forage. Nor will they see any use in doing so. They won't want a future in the village for their children.

Once they've settled in Beijing or some other sprawling, polluted metropolis, a few of the adult children might hanker for an idyllic country life, but they won't move back to the village until they retire. Most won't even do that. They'll stay in the city and buy herbal teas, tonics and medicines in a supermarket or pharmacy. Just like Li Wei and me.

***

By our third visit to Ginkgo Village in December 2016, Chen Dajin and his family seemed more relaxed than previously. In fact, Chen Dajin had always seemed laidback. He complained about corruption among the village cadres and about the conflicts with Li neighbours, but his complaining had no sting in it.

Despite his money and job worries, he was also remarkably optimistic. Once, when he was talking about his difficulties finding trucking work, I told him about the high rates of unemployment in Australia, especially among migrants and Indigenous folk. 'Many people feel hopeless,' I said.

He couldn't understand that. 'You can always earn money if you're willing to work hard,' he said, shaking his head.

His tone reminded me of the Australians who rail against those living off welfare payments. I thought about intergenerational trauma among Indigenous people; the erosion of dignity among the unemployed and working poor, struggling to make ends meet year after year, generation after generation; widening social inequalities; and the increasing precarity of employment in my son's generation.

But I didn't know how to talk about all that. I said nothing.[13]

Liang Anqin, too, seemed less stressed in 2016 than before. But even so, she was still more anxious about the future than her husband, and her complaining was more bitter. The road-concreting conflict made her furious. If they concreted the Li road, she said, they would first want to widen it and that would destroy her father's vegetable patch. But I'm not sure that was the main reason for her anger; I suspect it was more about loyalty to her husband's lineage. And the clash with Mr Li next-door.

I found Meiling and her parents easier to get on with than Liang Anqin. They always seemed cheery. Sometimes, if Li Wei and I arrived when Meiling and her baby were napping, we'd find her parents watching a small TV in the side heating-room of the house. Their dumpling-like bodies would be slumped there, exhausted. But they'd perk up when they saw us and invite us to join them.

*

The whole family is well liked. Aside from the village cadres who come to dinner, women often drop round during the day. They come to buy noodles and then stand around chatting. Or they sit in the front room gossiping with Meiling, while Liang Anqin and her mother come and go. When Li Wei and I visited, we would often find them hunched on wooden stools, leaning towards each other, guffawing and chewing sunflower seeds and spitting the husks on the floor.

One cold grey afternoon, we thought we'd try a formal focus group discussion, but it was no good. We would ask a question and three or four women would all yell their answers at once. Others would be having their own separate conversations at the same time. We gave up after a while and just listened.

---

13   For more on perceptions of social mobility and the future among rural Henanese entrepreneurs and others, see Boullenois, 'The Self-Made Entrepreneur'.

At one point, two middle-aged women sitting close by started talking about washing machines. One had an old machine that had broken down. She wasn't sure whether she should buy a new one.

'Are washing machines expensive?' I asked.

'Yeah, maybe it's not worth buying a new one,' she said. 'Machines don't clean as well as if you do it by hand.' She sighed loudly.

The others in the room had gone quiet at that point, so I tried some questions about decision-making among husbands and wives.

'When you're considering something big, like buying a washing machine, who makes the decision: you or your husband?' I looked around the group.

Liang Anqin spoke up: 'In some older couples, it's still the man who decides. But most people make decisions together. Men and women are equal, right?'

'But the man has the final say,' Meiling said, baby at her breast.

'Depends on what it is,' another woman said. 'I make all the decisions about the kids, including their schooling. My old man leaves that to me.'

I tried another question: 'If your husband wants to buy something big— a car, say—but you don't want him to, can you stop him?'

Laughter broke out. 'We don't have the money for anything like that,' a grey-haired woman said. She was standing by the doorway, a toddler twined around her legs. 'We just live from one day to the next. There aren't any big decisions to make.'

'It's his money, he's in charge,' someone else said.

The washing-machine woman spoke again: 'When my father-in-law was alive, he was in charge. But now my old man is. If we buy anything, it's he who decides.'

Everyone laughed again. I don't think they believed her; she was the one in charge, not her husband.

Liang Anqin's mother wandered out. She had seen a customer outside the noodle shack and went to serve her. I turned to Liang Anqin, who was sitting next to me. 'Who's in charge in your family?' I asked.

She looked down and smoothed one hand over her flour-dusted apron. A woman sitting on the other side of her leant forward and said: '*She* is. She does everything. That husband of …'

Liang Anqin turned and glared at her. Meiling's baby started whimpering.

The other women were talking among themselves. I waited for a lull, before trying again. 'What about the rest of you: who's the boss in your family— you or your husband?'

There was a flurry of laughter. Some women reached over to a plate of sunflower seeds on the tea table. Others straightened their jackets or looked down. They were shuffling their feet and nudging with a toe at the husks on the floor, giggling and murmuring with the women next to them. Others were standing up and wandering over to the open doorway, then coming back and sitting in another spot. They were like a flock of birds milling and flapping about.

'Why are you laughing?' I asked. They laughed some more.

Li Wei said afterwards, it must have been because of the way I asked the question. They were probably nervous or embarrassed. They probably all managed their household affairs, including those whose husbands were at home, as well as the widows and those whose husbands worked away from home. But they didn't want to come out and say so. Not in public like that. They didn't want to claim themselves to be 'the boss'. Saying such a thing would show up their husbands as unmanly. It also wouldn't reflect well on them to reveal such a departure from patriarchal norms.

Liang Anqin turned to me: 'Laoshi, what about you? Are you in charge or is your husband?'

I hesitated about how much of the truth to tell her. 'I don't have a husband,' I said. 'We separated years ago when my son was 18 months old.'

'How old's your son now?' Liang Anqin asked.

'He just turned twenty.' I smiled proudly. I didn't tell her that Misha's dad and I had never married. Nor did I mention my many aborted relationships before and since, with women as well as men.

Some of the women were frowning. 'Why haven't you remarried?' Meiling asked.

I didn't know how to answer, so I laughed and shrugged my shoulders: 'Men are no use; they're too much trouble. I'm better off by myself.'

There was a gaping silence. I wondered what they were thinking. Did they disapprove or did they pity me? Or did they envy me, perhaps? Did they think me foolish or strange or did they secretly agree with me and marvel at my frankness?

Most of the women looked away, but Liang Anqin's eyes bored into me. I couldn't hold her gaze.

'You're right,' the washing-machine woman said eventually. 'They're not much use. My old man spends all his time playing cards and gambling.'

A wave of muttering, shifting and rustling rippled through the room.

'But don't you get lonely?' Liang Anqin said. 'You need a husband!'

'No, I don't!' I laughed. 'I'm fine without one.'

She frowned and looked away, leaving me feeling uncomfortably exposed.

The grey-haired woman bent to pick up her toddler and left. A couple of others pushed themselves up off their stools and followed her.

'Li Wei, do you have a boyfriend?' Liang Anqin said suddenly.

Li Wei looked up with a start and reddened. 'Yes,' she said softly, 'but we have no plans to marry.'

'That's okay,' Liang Anqin said. 'There's still time—you're 23, right?'

'Twenty-five,' Li Wei mumbled, head down. She pretended to be writing notes.

*

Afterwards, I felt bad about what I'd said. I worried it would make things even more awkward between Liang Anqin and me. But it didn't seem to have that effect. If anything, our exchange seemed to loosen things up. It somehow made it easier for both of us to relax. But I may have been imagining that.

***

Through the last two months of 2016, the road-concreting conflict heated up because of the state's poverty alleviation campaign. One afternoon, Village Director Zhou planted himself in Chen Dajin's yard, legs akimbo, arms firmly folded. 'The road-concreting has to be finished,' he said to Chen Dajin and his wife. They folded their arms, too.

'Everyone knows Xin County is aiming to end poverty by 2017,' Director Zhou said. 'And you know what *that* means. Every hamlet will be swarming with inspection teams. They'll be driving out to check the progress of poor households receiving money, including here in Old Pine.'

Liang Anqin and Chen Dajin shuffled their feet in the cold.

'You must agree,' Director Zhou said, 'it wouldn't do for a county official to get his car stuck on the unsealed road.'

*

On our last day in Ginkgo Village that year, the women in Liang Anqin's front room were once more flapping and shifting about. But this time, their agitation had nothing to do with me. They were angry because they had heard the day before that concreting of the Li road was about to begin. A bunch of furious Yangs and Chens had taken the bus to Xin County City that morning. They barged into the Letters and Petitions Office to complain, yet again. But it was too late. 'Go home,' they were told. 'The decision has been made. Be thankful you're getting concrete at all.'

But the Yangs and Chens were not thankful. That night, after Li Wei and I had gone back to Yang Yurong's house, Chen Dajin drove his truck down to just before the fork in the road and parked it across the middle, blocking it.

Li Wei and I didn't see what happened the next day; we were on our way back to Australia by then. But we heard all about it from Liang Anqin the following year. I'll reconstruct the story for you.

Early in the morning, Liang Anqin and her mother were hard at work in the noodle shack, preparing to load up the three-wheeled cart with just-made *mantou* and *baozi*. The warm, rich scent of freshly cooked *baozi* followed Liang Anqin outside. Her breath made little cloud puffs in the crisp air. Apart from her niece crying inside the house and her mother turning on a tap to wash the dough off her hands, all was quiet.

Then suddenly, Liang Anqin heard, and a moment later saw, a bulldozer grinding its way along the main road. As soon as she saw it turn into the road up to Old Pine Hamlet, she let out a yell, dropped a steamer of *baozi* onto the three-wheeler and ran. First, she ran into the house and shook her husband and father awake. Then she rushed along the Yang–Chen road, yelling to her friends.

By the time the bulldozer had reached the fork in the road, all the Yangs and Chens were massed together there in front of Chen Dajin's truck. Liang Anqin had pedalled her three-wheeler into place alongside the truck as an extra barrier. For four hours, the villagers—mostly middle-aged women and older folk—stood hurling abuse at the two men on the bulldozer, waving their hoes and carrying poles at them. Liang Anqin's three-wheeler was still half-loaded with *mantou* and *baozi*. She and her mother handed them out to their friends for free that morning.

Soon, Director Zhou came up the hill to talk with the crowd of angry Yangs and Chens. He handed out cigarettes to the men and tried to reason with them. To no avail. Then, one of Red River's deputy heads, accompanied by a few of his men, drove up and parked his big white car by the shrine. The villagers refused to listen to them. Eventually, the two men on the bulldozer were forced to abandon the machine and stomp down the hill, arms raised in surrender.

The men returned the next day. They told the assembled crowd: 'The plans have changed. We've been told to do the other road.'

The crowd cheered and let the men through. Over the next few days, several labourers worked with the bulldozer and other equipment to widen and smooth the Yang–Chen road. Then they brought in the sand and cement and made and poured the concrete.

When Li Wei and I next visited, a lovely smooth pale concrete road stretched all the way to the northern tip of Old Pine Hamlet. But then it did something unexpected: it angled sharply to the south-east, continued to the base of the hill at the top of which the Li tombs lay and joined up with the Li road. The village government had paid Chen Dajin's family compensation for the strip of land taken to widen, as well as concrete, that road. So now, new concrete roads extended on all three sides of Old Pine Hamlet, and everyone was satisfied.

*

So, this story has a happy ending, doesn't it?

Not quite. When Li Wei and I paid a visit to Old Pine Hamlet at New Year 2018, we saw that the needles on the pine tree were brown and dropping off. The tree was dying, if not dead already.

Li Wei and I were heartbroken. We sat in Chen Dajin's front room with Chen Dajin, his father-in-law and a few of Chen Dajin's male relatives, who had come to pay their respects for the New Year. They had brought red gift bags with liquor and cigarettes and were sitting, smoking. They, too, were upset about the pine tree.

I thought perhaps the tree had died of old age, but Chen Dajin scotched that idea. He said it wasn't as old as it looked. Those pine trees can live for up to 800 years in the right conditions. But this one was less than 100 years old. He thought it might have been infected with the same disease as the other pines in the mountains. But the scrawny old man perched on a stool next to him shook his head. This is different, he said. There's no sign of disease. A second, younger and more solidly built man, smoking and pacing, said the tree's roots must have been disturbed by the bulldozer widening the roads.

Another, older guy hunched opposite muttered that the dying pine was simply a symbol of the times. 'The whole village is dying,' he said.

I cried out in protest at that. But no-one else did.

7

Yang Yurong's house

At the turn of the twenty-first century, Yang Yurong still lived with her in-laws on the outer edge of Ginkgo Hamlet. But she longed for her own, new house and eventually she got one: the house in which Li Wei and I stayed when we visited Ginkgo Village. It's a grand brick and concrete edifice fronting the main road.

Opposite are three young Chinese toon trees bordering a fat strip of riverbank soil where Yang Yurong grows green vegetables, corn and broad beans. The river is sluggish and grey. Fish swam in it once, but not anymore—too much chemical fertiliser has seeped into it from adjacent fields. On the other side, there's a long stone wall painted with a blue-and-white advertisement for China Mobile.

Yang Yurong is a feisty, swarthy-faced woman from Deng Inn. Born in 1974, she married Wu Jianfu, a migrant labourer of the same age, in 1997. The couple has a solid social status and a strong network of relatives and friends. Their house is a symbol of their prosperity. It's a multistorey 'Western-style' house or *yanglou*, with a large courtyard and a carport.

The main front room is just over 50 square metres in area—roughly the same size as the front room in an old-style village house. But it looks completely different. Yang Yurong has arranged it like a Western living room. Next to the front door, under a window looking out to the courtyard, she's placed a large couch with royal-blue fabric upholstery. There are matching armchairs on each side, forming a U shape.

1

Sitting in the middle is a low, rectangular tea table with a glass top and a floral cloth wrapped around the sides, hiding its legs. Above the tea table is a chandelier: an elaborate affair with one central light, surrounded by four smaller lights on curved arms, strung with glittery beads. 'It's all glass,' Yang Yurong stressed to Li Wei and me, 'not plastic.'

Most village houses, including *yanglou*, have a family altar in either the front ground-floor room or a second, central ground-floor room. But this house has no family altar.[1] Instead, on the back wall of the front room opposite the lounge suite, there's a large flat-screen television on a stand. Above it hangs a cross-stitch tapestry of galloping horses made by Yang Yurong.

In the corner, next to the TV, stands a tall, narrow set of shelves. On the top are bottles of vitamin pills and a tea cannister. The middle shelf holds a tray of glass mugs. On the bottom stand two thermoses.

Yang Yurong and the youngest of her two sons, Baoli, spend most of the year rattling about on their own in this house. Yang Yurong takes Baoli to the village primary school each morning on the back of her pink electric scooter. When Li Wei and I first visited, Baoli's older brother, Renkai, was in boarding school in Xin County City. Later, he started university in Wuhan. Wu Jianfu spent most of each year living in Beijing. He did the interior work—plastering, painting, plumbing and electrical wiring—in newly built city apartments.

Normally, Li Wei and I only met migrant labourers when they returned to the village for the Lunar New Year. But on our first visit, Wu Jianfu was home, his left leg in plaster—broken when he fell off a ladder. He would stretch out on the couch in the front room and Li Wei and I would take the adjacent armchairs. He seemed pleased to have us as a distraction.

*

The couple has struggled to get where they are today. Wu Jianfu told us their story one afternoon. All through his childhood, he said, he lived in a three-room mudbrick house built in the 1940s. His grandparents had

---

1   The lack of a family altar is due to a local customary rule: while there's a member of the older generation alive and living in their old house, the family altar must not be moved or installed in another house. Wu Jianfu's mother still lives in their old house, so he goes there to perform the ancestral rituals.

begged their landlord for a piece of land on which to build it. By the time they returned to family farming, the walls were worn and the tiled roof leaked. He remembered it as dark and smelling of damp.

There were 10 people in his family: his grandparents and parents, his three older sisters, two younger sisters and himself. His grandfather was unwell and Wu Jianfu and his younger siblings were too young to help with the farm work. 'We had too many mouths to feed and not enough workers,' he said with a sigh. 'Even after the return to family farming, we couldn't climb out of poverty.'

To increase the family's income, his father did odd jobs around the village and his mother raised five pigs. In this way, the family earned just enough to cover the school fees for Wu Jianfu and his younger sisters. But there was little money for anything else.

'How much schooling did you get?' I asked.

'My oldest sister only did three years. The rest of us finished junior secondary school.'

He shifted slightly and one of the pillows on which he was leaning slipped sideways onto the floor. Li Wei jumped up and retrieved it for him, easing it back into place. He smiled at her in gratitude.

By 1987, he continued, their house was collapsing. So, his parents had most of it demolished and rebuilt. 'That's the house my mother has now,' he said.

They extended one bedroom and added another on the other side. They also dismantled two separate mudbrick shacks behind the old house and rebuilt them, tacking them onto each side of the house. The main part of the rebuilt house had a concrete floor, rather than an earthen one, and a new roof of baked-clay tiles. The wooden lattices and shutters over the windows were replaced with glass. All the added rooms had mudbrick walls at the back and sides. Only the front walls were built with factory-made baked bricks. 'We couldn't afford more than that,' Wu Jianfu said ruefully.

'Did you have electric lighting in the rebuilt house?' I asked, looking up from my notebook.

'Yes, but we didn't use it much—it was too expensive. Even now, my mother hardly ever turns on the lights. She still thinks electricity is expensive!' He laughed.

'She's right!' Yang Yurong called out. She wandered in from the kitchen, wiping her hands on her red chequered apron. 'He wouldn't know,' she said, jutting an elbow at her husband. 'He's hardly ever home.'

Wu Jianfu shrugged. I couldn't read his expression.

'Uncle,' Li Wei said, 'how much did it cost to rebuild your old house?'

'Just over 1,000 yuan.[2] We had to borrow from relatives. In 1991, after I'd finished school, I went out to work to help pay off our debts and cover my younger siblings' school fees. I've been a migrant labourer ever since.'

Yang Yurong went to make tea for us.

'By the time we got married,' Wu Jianfu said, watching his wife put four glass mugs on the tea table, 'only my parents and younger sisters were left at home. My grandparents had passed away and my older sisters had married out. My father's health was poor. So, he and my mother were glad I was bringing in a wife; they really needed help with the farming and housework.'

Yang Yurong rolled her eyes but said nothing. She dropped a pinch of tea-leaves into each mug.

Wu Jianfu continued: 'We spent all our money on the wedding and had to borrow again, too. It took me years to pay back the debts.'

'Yurong,' I said, 'tell us about *your* childhood. Was your family poor, too?'

'Not as poor as his!' She pushed at her husband's plaster cast and he eased his legs sideways so she could sit on the edge of the couch.

'Why was that?' I asked, watching the two of them.

Wu Jianfu snorted. 'The Yangs are a powerful lineage. Her father was a brigade cadre, so they were well-off even before the return to family farming. Afterwards, he made use of his connections—quite a few Yangs have jobs in the county government. He pulled strings.'

Yang Yurong frowned: 'It wasn't like that. Our family made money by working hard. And my dad was smart.'

'He had contacts!' Wu Jianfu said with a laugh.

---

2   US$270.

'Well, of course,' Yang Yurong snapped. 'Everyone relies on contacts. But it wasn't just that; you need abilities to be successful.' She scowled at her husband and adjusted the rubber band around her ponytail.

I darted a look at Li Wei. She was blowing on her tea. Just that morning, we'd been puzzling over the relationship between our hosts. Sometimes, they seemed affectionate. At other times, Yang Yurong looked ready to scratch out her husband's eyes.

'It's true. Her father *was* smart,' Wu Jianfu conceded. 'He contracted a large piece of forest land, chopped down all the trees and sold the timber for a tidy sum. Then he started a business making *doufu*.'

'When was that?' I turned to Yang Yurong.

'I was about twelve.' She reached for her tea. 'He built a shack on the side of our house and we made the *doufu* there.'

'There were very few stores then,' Wu Jianfu said, 'so the Yang family *doufu* business did well. Villagers were just starting to get a bit of money in their pockets. They could afford some *doufu* now and again.'

'We worked so hard,' Yang Yurong murmured, staring into her tea. 'My grandfather, father and older brother worked in the fields. My grandmother, mother and older sister made and sold *doufu*. When my sister married and left home, I took over from her. I helped with the farm work, too.' She smoothed a couple of loose strands of hair from her face. 'My younger brothers were no help. They were in school. They both finished senior secondary school.'

'How much schooling did *you* get?'

'Three years. Same as my older brother. My older sister didn't go to school at all; my father didn't believe in educating girls. I didn't like school anyway. I got bored.' She went to the kitchen for a plate of sunflower seeds.

'Aunty,' Li Wei said, as Yang Yurong put the plate on the tea table, 'tell us about your marriage. Was it arranged?'

She nodded. 'Finding a spouse by yourself was still frowned on in those days.' She sat down again. 'We were engaged at the age of sixteen. I didn't even know about it. I came home one evening and saw a strange woman coming out of our house. I asked my mother who it was and she said, "Your mother-in-law." She'd given a gift of cloth to seal the engagement.'

5

She brushed at her apron. 'I was so upset. But there was nothing I could do. I had to marry the man they chose, even though I'd never met him.'

Wu Jianfu shifted uneasily on the couch.

'But then I ran away to Shenzhen,' Yang Yurong said with a laugh. 'I worked in a doll factory.'

'What do you mean, you *ran away*?' I asked.

'I went against my parents' wishes. They thought it wasn't safe. They feared I'd get taken advantage of or I'd shame the family.'[3]

'When was that?'

'I went to Shenzhen in 1992. I'd just turned 18 and I was sick of being at home. I wanted to get out and see the world before I got married.'

'How did you get the job in the doll factory?'

'I had an uncle working in Shenzhen. He found it for me. I earned only 400 yuan[4] a month and the workdays were long: 14, 15 hours sometimes. And the glue we used to stick the dolls together was toxic; the fumes made me sick. After a year I went home again. Most of my earnings went to pay for my older brother's wedding.' She stared for a moment at her slippers.

'After the New Year, I went to Guangzhou. I stayed there almost five years. I had a string of jobs, mainly as a kitchen hand and waitress. I didn't mind that work. It was exhausting, but more fun than in the factory. And I was lucky—the bosses were mostly okay.' She straightened her back and smiled.

'I was working in Guangzhou then, too,' Wu Jianfu chimed in. 'She and I went out a few times with a bunch of other friends, and then I asked her out by myself.' He laughed. 'She refused at first—said she had to have her friend with her. We were engaged, but she still thought she needed a chaperone!'

Yang Yurong's eyebrows creased: 'I was afraid of what people back home would hear about me.'

'But I was persistent!' Wu Jianfu cut in with a grin. 'We got married just before New Year in 1998. Renkai was born 12 months later.'

---

3   The implication is that she would engage in sexual behaviour.
4   US$70.

***

Wu Jianfu's plaster was removed and he went back to work. Over breakfast the next morning, Yang Yurong told Li Wei and me about the early years of their marriage. They moved to Ginkgo Village for their wedding, but shortly afterwards, Wu Jianfu returned to migrant labour. This time, he went to Beijing. She wanted to go with him, but he wouldn't let her.

'You go out in our first year of marriage,' he said, 'and you'll make my family look bad. Others will think you're unhappy living with them.'

Li Wei and I sat with a crispy *youtiao* (deep-fried pastry stick) in one hand, a bowl of hot soy milk in the other, watching Yang Yurong's darkening face. She stayed with her in-laws in Ginkgo Hamlet, but in truth, she *was* unhappy. She didn't say why.

Perhaps the reason was conflict with her mother-in-law. She told us their relationship was *yiban*, which means 'ordinary' or 'so-so'. A lot of women said that. It seemed to be code for 'bad, but others have it even worse'. Or sometimes, 'bad, but I'm ashamed to admit it'. Relations with her father-in-law were also *yiban*. He yelled at everyone in the family and, while he never hit Yang Yurong, he did hit his wife. But Yang Yurong's own father was the same. 'It was that generation,' she said with a shrug.

She was also upset by her in-laws' poverty. Three days after their wedding, she and Wu Jianfu returned to Deng Inn for the customary six days with her natal family. When her mother asked about her new home, she burst into tears. 'His family have nothing,' she complained. 'One broken stool, one broken chair and the house is all askew.'

She stood and her chair scraped loudly on the tiled floor.

'Laoshi, do you want another *youtiao*?' she asked, already halfway to the kitchen.

'No thanks,' I called out quickly.

Aside from poverty, there was something else that made Yang Yurong unhappy—something about her mother-in-law's house itself. She took us to see the house that afternoon.

It was about 20 minutes' walk up the hill behind Yang Yurong's house, along from Aunty Gao's, and just past where Old Liu and his ducks lived. Old Liu had 200 white ducks. He would shepherd them down to Red River every morning, and each evening they waddled and quacked their way back up the hill. Li Wei and I loved those ducks, but they annoyed Yang Yurong: they left faeces and muddy footprints all along the path and sometimes strayed into her vegetable patch and nibbled her seedlings.

The house was empty. In the past several years, Popo[5] had been living at home only for a few weeks either side of New Year. The rest of the time, she lived with her youngest daughter in Xin County City and helped care for her baby grandchild. It rankled with Yang Yurong that Popo cared for her daughter's child but offered little help in raising Baoli. But as the older woman pointed out once, when Li Wei and I spoke with her separately, she'd been the main carer for Renkai when he was little. Now, her daughter needed her because she had no-one else: her mother-in-law was too ill to be of any help.

The house is U-shaped. The main part is a row of four rooms facing south, in the middle of which is the front room with the family altar. There's no ceiling in this room. You can look right up to the roof, which is supported by a beautiful wooden dragon-gate frame. This central room is flanked by three side rooms: one on the eastern side and two on the west. These rooms are each about 25 square metres—half the size of the front room. Each has a ceiling of wooden planks running lengthwise across half the room. This creates an open storage space under the roof.

Jutting out from the main block, the rebuilt kitchen forms an eastern wing, while a heating-room forms a western wing. These rooms are smaller and rougher-looking than the others.

Apart from the family altar, covered in dust, the front room holds an old wardrobe against one wall. On the other side, there's a small wooden table and a refrigerator. When Yang Yurong first moved in after her wedding, neither the table nor the fridge existed, but a spinning wheel and a loom stood to one side. Nowadays, these are stored in pieces in the roof cavity of one of the western side rooms. Yang Yurong pointed out the wheel of the spinning wheel, poking out from a jumble of dusty rope and farm tools, a broken chair and other junk. Popo's coffin was parked there, too.

---

5   *Popo* means 'mother-in-law'. Here, I use Popo as the name of Yang Yurong's mother-in-law.

At the time of Yang Yurong's marriage, her parents-in-law slept in the eastern side room and her two sisters-in-law shared the room on the other side of the front room. The westernmost side room became the newlyweds' bedroom.

When Wu Jianfu was a kid, each side room contained nothing but a single wooden bed. Even when Yang Yurong moved in, the only additional furniture the newlyweds owned were the wardrobe and washstand she brought as a dowry. Today, Popo's bedroom on the eastern side is crowded with furniture, including a table with a small TV on top. But the other side rooms are empty.

In the kitchen is a wood-fuelled cooking stove—a hollow brick structure with a chimney and a wok set into the top. It has two holes in the back for feeding in the wood. Today, this stove looks old-fashioned and crude, but it's an improvement on what they had before they renovated the house. In the old kitchen, the wood fuel was piled on the floor and there was no chimney. Popo had to keep the door and window open to let out the smoke. In the current stove, the wood sits on a cast-iron grate, up off the floor.[6]

When Yang Yurong first moved in, the kitchen and heating-room had earthen floors. There was no woodstove in the heating-room. The family stayed warm in winter by huddling around a wood fire in a shallow pit dug into the floor in the middle of the heating-room. 'Our faces got scorched, but our backs stayed cold. Afterwards, our clothes would be coated in ash,' Yang Yurong laughed. 'To make full use of the firewood, we'd boil water and rice in a pot hung from an iron frame over the fire.'

'Did you fry things over the fire, too?' I asked.

'No, we didn't do much frying in those days.[7] But sometimes in winter, we'd give vegetables a light fry on the kitchen stove. Then we'd finish cooking them in a bit of water in the pot over the heating-room fire.'

---

6   The chimney and grate are innovations of the mid 1980s. Chimneys were built across the village on advice from village leaders, who also handed out cast-iron grates to each family. Both items, the leaders said, would make the stoves burn more efficiently and save wood. An added benefit of the chimneys was that they reduced the amount of smoke inhaled by village women, while the grates kept the wood separate from the ash, which could then be removed more easily and used to build up the soil in the vegetable plots. But these benefits were given little weight by either village leaders or women themselves.
7   Aside from the fact that villagers didn't eat much meat or vegetables before the 1990s, the high cost of cooking oil was the main reason frying wasn't common.

Plate 7.1 Popo's kitchen stove
Photo: Li Wei, 2017.

In 1999, Wu Jianfu laid concrete floors in the kitchen and heating-room and removed the fire pit. He replaced it with a metal woodstove, with a flue extending out through a hole in the top of the wall.[8] Popo now has a worn grey couch next to the woodstove. At New Year, she spends most of her time sitting there.

The house has neither a bathroom nor a toilet. Popo doesn't even have a water tap. Before the 1990s, she drew water by hand from the hamlet well. Instead of a toilet, she used a wooden pail, which she emptied onto her vegetable patch.

In the 1990s, villagers began to install electric pumps and waterpipes to take water into their house from a spring on the hill. Today, in most houses built since then, there's at least one water tap, either inside the house or outside in a courtyard. And there's a porcelain flush toilet. The recently built *yanglou* commonly have an indoor bathroom with either a squat toilet or a Western-style sit-down one. Most houses, though, have a squat toilet, along with a handbasin, in a separate outhouse.

But there are still some older villagers like Popo who don't have running water. There are no sources of water nearby that are high enough above Popo's house to enable a flow of water through pipes. So instead, she uses an electric pump to draw water from a well next to her house. She has no toilet of her own: she uses a public pit toilet nearby, which was built in the 1980s.

The only other structure linked with the house is a double-berth concrete pigsty, standing in front and to the right of the house.[9] 'When I lived there, it really stank,' Yang Yurong complained, wrinkling her nose. It stands empty now.

*

Li Wei and I stood in the main doorway of the old house, looking out at the rain and the lush foliage surrounding us. Something didn't feel right, but I couldn't put my finger on what it was.

---

8   This type of woodstove, used for heating, was not introduced to Ginkgo Village until the 1990s, after which it quickly became ubiquitous.
9   In the past, pigs were taken out to pasture during the day and were tied outside the house at night. The state provided funds for village families to build concrete pigsties in the 1980s.

Finally, I turned back to Yang Yurong and asked: 'Is there something wrong with the *feng shui*[10] of this house?' Li Wei raised a quizzical eyebrow; Yang Yurong eyed me warily.

On a previous occasion, she'd been hovering while we sat with Wu Jianfu stretched out on the couch, talking about popular religious practices. He had laughed at village women's 'superstitions' (*mixin*). 'They believe in all sorts of nonsense,' he said: 'Spirit mediums, mirrors above the doorway to ward off evil spirits[11] … Yurong even believes in ghosts—she thinks there's one in the river.' Yang Yurong had stood mute.

'Is ancestor worship superstition?' I had asked.

'No,' Wu Jianfu had said vehemently, 'that's completely different. The ancestor worship rituals, the rituals for weddings and funerals—they're all part of Chinese culture; part of what makes us Chinese. You must do them properly or you'll lose face.'

'What about *feng shui*: is that superstition?' Li Wei asked.

Wu Jianfu shook his head. 'I don't believe in it, but it's not superstition. It's part of Chinese culture, too, distilled from thousands of years of life customs and experience. It isn't just about the landscape. When the best position for your house or tomb is determined according to *feng shui* principles, your birthdate is considered, along with the lie of the land. But the way Yurong believes in it is incorrect. She thinks all sorts of bad luck can be explained by *feng shui*. That's just superstition.'

Yang Yurong fought back. 'I used not to believe in it,' she said loudly, 'but everyone tells of bad things happening because of poor *feng shui*.'[12]

Wu Jianfu had guffawed and I'm ashamed to say that Li Wei and I had laughed along with him.

On this occasion, though, Yang Yurong must have seen that my question was genuine. She said, 'Yes, you're right,' and proceeded to explain.

---

10   Chinese geomancy.

11   See Plate 9.1.

12   'Superstition' (*mixin*) is a pejorative word. It is considered separate from religion and ritual. See Feuchtwang, *Popular Religion in China*, 216–17. For more on *feng shui*, see Ole Bruun, *Fengshui in China: Geomantic Divination between State Orthodoxy and Popular Religion* (Copenhagen: NIAS Press, 2003).

When she was living there, the family kept getting sick and having accidents. Once, Popo fell down the front steps. Until then, they'd been quite solid, but on that morning, the big stone on the top came loose. It happened suddenly, for no reason. Popo sprained her ankle and had bruises all down her side. After that, they called in a *feng shui* master. He was a relative of Yang Yurong's, a 70-year-old gentleman from Deng Inn. He confirmed that the house's *feng shui* was poor.

'The hill in front is too close,' he said. 'It's not desirable to face into a hillside.'

There was nothing the family could do about that, of course. But the *feng shui* master told them to replace the stone steps with concrete ones.

'We did that,' Yang Yurong said, 'and it helped. We didn't get so sick and there were no more accidents after that.' She paused.

'It still feels bad in this house, though. Have you seen enough? Let's get out of here.'

***

By the time Renkai was a year old, Yang Yurong was fed up with living in Popo's house. She left the toddler in Popo's care and followed Wu Jianfu to Beijing. For six years, the couple rented a shack on the outskirts of the city. During the day, she sold *jianbing* (savoury egg pancakes) from a bicycle-drawn three-wheeled cart. Each morning, she would peddle the cart to a spot near a subway station to catch people rushing to work. But she had to keep an eagle-eye out for the cops and speed away if she saw any. She didn't have a business licence or even a temporary residence permit—they were too much trouble to organise. She was lucky: she was never caught. But the stress got to her after a while.[13]

In July 2005, her father-in-law had a stroke and died. Both Yang Yurong and Wu Jianfu returned to the village for the funeral. Afterwards, they decided that Yang Yurong should stay home, rather than go back to Beijing with Wu Jianfu. In fact, Yang Yurong said this was Wu Jianfu's decision, not hers. He didn't like it that she was earning almost as much as him in Beijing. He also thought Yang Yurong should help his mother with the farming now that his father was gone.

---

13 Rural migrant women's experiences in Beijing at this time are discussed in Jacka, *Rural Women in Urban China*.

She didn't mind staying behind. She was tired of Beijing and she worried that Renkai was too much of a handful for Popo. But she didn't want to live in the old house any longer than she had to. She said to Wu Jianfu, 'I'll stay in the village if you promise we'll build a new house. Everyone else has a new house; we'll be mocked if we don't build one, too.'

Wu Jianfu made the promise. But building work didn't begin until April 2007. They didn't move in until March 2008, a few months after Baoli was born.

One reason for the delay was the months it took to get building approval.[14] Wu Jianfu was away in Beijing, so it was Yang Yurong who did the necessary greasing of wheels. She went at it with gusto. She paid several visits to a relative in the Red River Land Office and invited both him and Ginkgo Village Party Secretary Guo to dinner with her parents. It only took a couple of meals, a few bottles of liquor and several packs of cigarettes and she had village and township approval.

But getting county government approval was more difficult. The problem was opposition from other hamlet residents. As Yang Yurong explained, the cause was 'red-eye disease' (that is, jealousy) connected with the redistribution of land in 1998 and the planned location of the new house on the main road.

In the 1998 land redistribution, Yang Yurong acted as the head of her marital household because Wu Jianfu was away and her father-in-law was ill. The final step in the process involved Yang Yurong drawing straws for plots of land, along with three other household heads: one man, chosen to be the group's leader, and two women, acting, like Yang Yurong, in place of their absent migrant-worker husbands. Each was to draw a straw for an equal number of plots of 'poor', 'medium' and 'high' quality paddy fields.

The flat land on either side of the main road was labelled poor quality. There were a few reasons for that: the strip between the road and the river had good, rich soil, but it was prone to flooding. Also, water buffaloes and pigs, as well as ducks, were taken each day to eat the grass on the riverbank. If you had land nearby, you had to be on guard all the time to make sure

---

14   Through the 1990s, officials became increasingly concerned about farmland being gobbled up by villagers' 'irrational' housebuilding craze and introduced a host of regulations to curb it. See Sally Sargeson, 'Subduing "The Rural House-Building Craze": Attitudes Towards Housing Construction and Land Use Controls in Four Zhejiang Villages', *China Quarterly* 172 (2002): 927–55, doi.org/10.1017/S0009443902000566.

the animals didn't stray and eat your crops. On the other side of the road, your crops were safer but harder to irrigate. You could terrace land on the hillslopes, so that water could be channelled and flow easily from top to bottom. On the flat land, you couldn't do that.

But Yang Yurong wanted the poor-quality land by the road because the plots were bigger than the others. She wasn't afraid of hard work and she knew she could buy an electric pump to take water from the river. Perhaps she'd also begun thinking of using some of the flat land to build a new house. She suggested to the other three that rather than draw straws, she would take only the poor-quality land by the road and no medium or high-quality plots. They could draw straws for the rest. The other two women eyed her sceptically, but the man leading the group agreed. He had the final say.

By the mid 2000s, the land close to the main road had become more desirable. Most villagers had little interest in farmland by then. It didn't matter how good your land was, prices were such that you couldn't make any money from farming. But with earnings from migrant labour coming in, more and more newlyweds wanted to build a large new *yanglou*. They wanted to build near the road, partly to avoid the cost of carting materials up the hill. But the main attraction was the convenience of living by the road: village stores were close by, as was the bus to Red River and Xin County City.

Some people paid the village leadership a large sum to obtain building land by the road. Yang Yurong said that since the land was already theirs, they didn't need to pay for it. Other hamlet residents countered furiously that it didn't matter if the land had been assigned to you. You still had to pay to convert it from farmland to building land. Yang Yurong tried to appease her neighbours, but to no avail. They remained implacably opposed and went all the way to the county government to vent their complaints.

Because of that, Yang Yurong never did get building approval from the county government. But she and Wu Jianfu went ahead with their building plans anyway. Once the house was built, they reasoned, there was nothing anyone could do.

Government approval wasn't all they needed to start building; they also needed a great deal of money for the grand house that Yang Yurong wanted. After saving for years, they still had to borrow 75,000 yuan (US$10,000) from her father. It would take them five years to pay it back.

Plate 7.2 Two *yanglou*[15]
Photo: Tamara Jacka, 2016.

Even then, Yang Yurong knew they couldn't afford a mansion like those the most successful entrepreneurs were putting up. But she was determined that her new house would be at least as big as the other *yanglou* already built along the main road. And both she and Wu Jianfu wanted a carport. Very few houses in Ginkgo Village had their own carport, but new apartment blocks in Xin County City did. Wu Jianfu dreamed they might get a car in the future.

To save money, Wu Jianfu designed the house himself. It was to take up 150 square metres—smaller than the area occupied by the old house. But it would have an additional second storey, plus an attic with a gabled roof on the back half.

15 Yang Yurong's house differs from these in being freestanding and having a carport. Otherwise, the size and design of her house are much the same as those depicted here. From floor to ceiling, the walls are 3.7 metres on the ground floor and 3.5 metres on the second. From the attic floor to the ridge of the roof is another 3.7 metres.

Altogether, the house would cost 200,000 yuan (US$27,000), which would cover the builders' wages (70,000 yuan; US$9,500) and the building materials. The steel and cement would be bought in Red River Township; the bricks would come from Guangshan. The 200,000 yuan wouldn't cover the labour for the interior work. They planned to complete only the inside of the ground floor and Wu Jianfu would do all the work himself. That would save 25,000 yuan (US$3,400). But, whereas the outside of the house would be finished in three months, it would take Wu Jianfu another eight months to do the inside. As he put it: 'Those with cash build quickly; those without are slow.'

Once they'd pulled together enough money, Yang Yurong called in a lay Daoist priest to determine an auspicious date on which to start construction. She further insisted on calling in her relative, the *feng shui* master, to check the design of the house. This time, he came with a *feng shui* compass (*luopan*) and spent a week on the job.

'The general orientation of the house is good,' he told Yang Yurong. 'The fact that it faces west, rather than south, is of no consequence.[16] Otherwise, the orientation is excellent: The hills are behind the house and the river is in front. You're fortunate there's a bend in the river immediately in front and the road curves, too; it would be inauspicious if they were straight.'

Inside the house, he approved of the siting of Yang Yurong and Wu Jianfu's master bedroom to the left of the main front room (when facing the front door from inside). But he disapproved of the placement of the kitchen on the northern, righthand side of the house. He advised them to move it to the south-eastern corner, on the left side of the house. Putting it there, he said, would bring them luck and they would do well if they went into business.

Reluctantly, Wu Jianfu accepted the *feng shui* master's advice.

For Yang Yurong, the height of the house was also a consideration. As she explained to Li Wei and me one morning over breakfast, the lefthand side is the green dragon, with more *qi* ('vital energy'). Houses to the left should

16 The notion that a house should face south dates back many centuries. It's an important principle in the 'orientations' or Fujian School of *feng shui*, which emphasises the directions indicated on the *feng shui* compass (*luopan*). However, it's given less weight in the 'forms' or Jiangxi School, which pays more attention to the configuration of forms, especially mountains and rivers, in the landscape (Bruun, *Fengshui in China*, 5, 131).

be the same height or taller than those on the right. 'Because our house is the furthest right, if we built a house much taller than the others, we'd all suffer bad luck.'[17]

Li Wei tilted her head. 'Your house *is* taller, isn't it?'

She frowned and bit her lip. 'Only a little. The front half has two storeys, the same as the neighbours. It's only the back half that has the extra attic on top. It's so useful having it like that!'

I recalled that the attic has a door leading onto the flat roof of the second storey. When Yang Yurong harvests peanuts and broad beans, she spreads them out to dry on that roof. Afterwards, she brings them back into the attic for storage.

'A house has to be a whole storey taller than the neighbours' for it to really count as taller,' Yang Yurong said. 'Our attic makes the house only half a storey taller, so it's okay. I checked with the *feng shui* master.'

'But our neighbours didn't understand,' she continued crossly. 'They thought we'd brought them bad luck by building our house taller than theirs. They're still mad about it, even now. They're always trying to get back at us.'

'How? What do they do?' I asked, sitting up.

Yang Yurong pointed out the back window. 'That's their land. See that row of Ginkgo saplings? The neighbours deliberately planted them right up close to our house, to block the flow of *qi*.' Her face twisted in disgust. 'And sometimes they dump manure from their water buffalo around the trees, so it'll stink out this dining room.'

I stifled a laugh and she frowned at me.

---

17   The green dragon (*qing long*) symbolises the left (the east, if the house faces south), while the white tiger (*bai hu*) symbolises the right. Vital energy or *qi* flows from left to right. Therefore, larger houses, which already contain more *qi* than smaller ones, should be located to the left of others. If the largest house is to the right, it will suffer from too much *qi*, while the others will have too little. The link between the left and a larger amount of *qi* also applies to the layout of a house interior. This explains the *feng shui* master's approval of the siting of the parents' master bedroom on the left side of Yang Yurong's new house. The parents' traditionally higher status entitles them to more *qi* than the children. The *feng shui* master's advice to place the kitchen on the left side of the new house is based on the same principle. The kitchen is accorded great importance because, being the place where food is produced, it's associated with wellbeing and prosperity.

'Have you complained to the village leaders?' Li Wei asked, with a commendably straight face.

'No, that'd only make the conflict worse. But it doesn't matter—the neighbours are just spiteful old fools; they can't hurt us. See how spindly those Ginkgos are? It doesn't matter how much manure is piled on; they still don't grow. As I said to the old lady once, "Heaven sees whatever humans do".'

***

Until the 1980s, the construction of a new village house was a community affair. A housebuilding couple would call on help from relatives, especially on the wife's side of the family. The men would cut wood from the forest for the frame and dry and prepare it months in advance. They'd make their own mudbricks, too. Only the master builders were paid. But the wife and her female relatives would cook three meals each day for everyone. It was understood that the couple would return the favour when a relative wanted to build.

By the time Wu Jianfu's parents rebuilt their house in 1987, this sort of reciprocal aid was dying out. They contracted builders to do the work. Still, kinship bonds remained important: most of the builders were Popo's relatives. They used wood and mudbricks they had prepared themselves and bought baked bricks and roof tiles from a factory in Deng Inn. That factory was set up in 1983, but it closed after six years when it ran out of good clay.

When Wu Jianfu and Yang Yurong built their new house, they also hired relatives. Yang Yurong hired six master builders—all her own relatives—and they, in turn, hired mainly relatives to lay the bricks. Yang Yurong didn't cook for the labourers every day, but she did provide them with meals at the beginning and end of the construction work and on days when a particularly large number of people was onsite.

For most of the housebuilding, Wu Jianfu was absent, working in Beijing. He returned only to do the interior work once the hired builders had left.

*

When the family finally moved in, the outside of the house was complete and much as Yang Yurong had dreamed. In front, the large concrete courtyard was surrounded by a tall brick wall, clad with red tiles. A double-wing red iron gate fronted the road. To the side was the carport, with a separate motor-driven metal roller door. Yang Yurong found it very satisfying to press the button and watch the roller door glide up and down, even if there was nothing inside. The front of the house was clad with white tiles; the back was plastered and painted white. Each room had a good-sized glass window with an aluminium frame.[18] Those on the ground floor had vertical steel bars across them to keep the house secure. There was also a heavy metal double-wing front door, the same colour as the gate.

The interior of the house was a different story. Even on the ground floor, the plastering and painting hadn't been finished and there were floor tiles only in the main front room. The rest was rough concrete. The flush toilet had been installed in the ground-floor bathroom, but the handbasin and shower fittings had not. The few pieces of furniture came from the old house. The front room was bare.

A week after they moved in, Wu Jianfu returned to Beijing. He had to start earning again, so they could finish the interior work on the ground floor, buy some furniture and begin to pay off their debts. Yang Yurong was left on her own with baby Baoli and Renkai.

One day, Village Director Zhou came round with the county birth planning officials to fine her 4,500 yuan (US$650) for having a second child. But she was able to say quite honestly: 'I can't—we have no money.'

They said, 'Okay, we'll take your new furniture.'

'What new furniture?' Yang Yurong shot back. 'Come look for yourselves, there isn't any!'

The second and third times they visited, Yang Yurong had the gate and front door locked. But the fourth time, both were open. They marched straight in. Emerging with the screaming baby in her arms, Yang Yurong yelled in exasperation, 'Look, we have nothing! All we have is the kid—here, take him.' They backed out in haste.

'You should have seen the look on Zhou's face!' she said to Li Wei and me with a laugh.

---

18   The kitchen window is 1.2 metres high and 2 metres wide; the others are all 2 metres by 2.4 metres.

The officials came a few more times, but then gave up. Other women were unable to register the birth of an 'out-of-plan' baby without paying a hefty fine. But Yang Yurong assured us she registered Baoli without any trouble. She had help from a relative working in the police station in Red River.

*

By 2011, the couple had still not paid off their debts. But they'd saved enough to buy some more furniture and whitegoods, as well as finish the interior work on the ground floor. Wu Jianfu decided that Yang Yurong needed a washing machine and she decided she needed a refrigerator. Each item cost 1,000 yuan (US$160). They bought the lounge suite that year, too. It cost 4,000 yuan (US$630).

They also completed a final step in the housebuilding process that had been left out in 2009: at Wu Jianfu's insistence, they conducted a ritual to 'raise the beam' (*shang liang*) and held a banquet to inaugurate the house.

Wu Jianfu told Li Wei and me about this on our first visit, as he lay on the couch with his leg in plaster. Ideally, he said, the inauguration should be conducted once the frame and walls of a new house are built but before the roof covering is finished. 'Before Liberation, everyone had a house inauguration. Even if your roof was just thatched, you had to raise the main roof pole, sacrifice to Lu Ban[19] and provide a banquet for the builders and other villagers.'

'And after Liberation?' I asked. I stood and fetched my notebook from the tea table.

'Few houses were built in the collective period. And when they were, they had only a simplified ritual and no banquet.'

'Were house inaugurations allowed during the Cultural Revolution?'

He hesitated. 'A lot of things were condemned then. The *feng shui* masters went underground and villagers burnt incense and spirit-money only in secret. But that's not why they didn't have house inaugurations. They just couldn't afford them. It's only since the 1990s that we've been able to hold big banquets for things like weddings and house inaugurations.'

---

19 The patron saint of builders.

He reached forward to scratch just above his plaster cast. 'Nowadays, these kinds of celebration are bigger than ever. We try to hold them at New Year—most people are home then.'

He and Yang Yurong held their house inauguration over two days in late January 2011. On the morning of the first day, he went with one of Yang Yurong's younger brothers, who was visiting from Wuhan, to 'steal wood for a beam' (*tou liangmu*): they went up the hill to his nephew's land and found a straight Chinese toon sapling to serve as a roof pole.

'You don't really steal it,' he said. 'It must come from someone close and you give them cigarettes in return for the wood. We chopped the tree down, brought it back here, planed it smooth and cut it in half.'

'Why'd you cut it in half?' I cried.

Wu Jianfu grinned. 'We raise more than one roof pole.'

In the past, he explained, when houses had a gable roof, there would be poles running just under the roof's ridge, between each dragon-gate frame. The focus was on raising the main roof pole above the family altar, but raising the auxiliary poles was also part of the ritual.[20]

Since their new house has no family altar and a gable roof only over the attic, they had to modify the ritual. They could have raised the roof poles under the gable roof, but chose, instead, to put two under the flat concrete roof on the second floor, with the main one above the spot where the family altar would be if they had one. When they built the house, they left holes in the concrete into which the roof poles were later slotted.

On the evening of the first day of the house inauguration, Wu Jianfu and Yang Yurong put on a banquet for their relatives and friends, including all the builders: six tables altogether—one each in the front room and dining room and the rest on the second floor. They hired a distant relative of Wu Jianfu's to act as master of ceremonies and direct proceedings over the two

---

20　The beam raised in this ritual varies regionally and according to architectural style. In Hubei, the ridgepole is raised. Hans Steinmüller, *Communities of Complicity: Everyday Ethics in Rural China* (New York: Berghahn Books, 2013), 78–86. In contrast, northern Chinese villagers ritually hoist the thick beam that sits at the base of the roof and runs across the middle of the room. For an example, see Zhang Yimou (dir.), 我的父亲母亲 [*The Road Home*] (Hong Kong: Beijing New Picture Distribution Company, 2000).

days of the house inauguration. Yang Yurong did most of the cooking, with help from her mother and Popo. They provided plenty of food, liquor and cigarettes.

Later that night, they 'sacrificed a beam' (*ji liang*).

'You're supposed to put the roof poles on the family altar,' Wu Jianfu said, running a hand through his thick hair. 'We just rested them on a trestle table in the front room.'

'Wait a second.' I scrambled to note down all the details.

He waited patiently.

In accordance with the customary rules, they tied red cloth around the main roof pole and red paper over the auxiliary one. Then the master builders lit incense sticks and burnt some spirit-money as a sacrifice to Lu Ban.

'You're meant to keep the incense sticks burning all night and until the end of the next day,' Wu Jianfu explained. 'But no-one bothers nowadays. We just went to bed and relit the incense the next morning.'

On the second day, relatives came again to help prepare for the actual raising of the roof poles. They took the trestle table and the poles upstairs and relit the incense there. Then the bricklayers climbed ladders to hoist the poles, while two master builders chanted a special song, full of auspicious symbols.

If they had done this ritual with the gable roof and before the roof tiles were laid, they would have had the four other master builders standing on the roof—one in each corner—while the roof poles were being pulled up. They would have thrown down sweets, cigarettes and *mantou* for the other guests to grab. As it was, Wu Jianfu said, the master builders stood near where the roof poles were being raised and threw the goodies from there. Then, they all went downstairs and set off firecrackers in the courtyard.

'We made sure there were plenty of guests, so it was warm and lively [*re'nao*],' he said with a grin. 'The kids were jumping up and down with excitement when we set off the firecrackers.'

***

Over the years that Li Wei and I lived in Yang Yurong's house, the interior work on the upper floors remained unfinished. But the ground floor had been completed and fully furnished. Each of the main rooms was full of light. The walls were painted white and the floor was laid with large, shiny white tiles. Whenever anyone came into the house, Yang Yurong ordered them to change into open-backed slippers or flip-flops lined up next to the front door. And when eating sunflower seeds in the front room, she would instruct us to spit the husks on the tea table and then would quickly whisk them away and wipe the glass top with a damp cloth. At least twice a day, she mopped the floor with a cloth mop kept in the bathroom.

Off the front room to the right (when facing the front door from inside), there's a bedroom with two single beds. It's meant to be Baoli's bedroom, but Baoli sleeps more often with his mother than in his own bed. 'We both get lonely by ourselves,' Yang Yurong said with a laugh. Further inside the house is a transitional space, merging into a dining area. To the left is the master bedroom: a large room with a king-sized bed, where Yang Yurong sleeps. To the right is a bathroom with shiny white tiles on the walls as well as the floor.

In 2011, Yang Yurong and Wu Jianfu teamed up with two neighbouring households and bought a pump and pipes to carry water into each house from a well on the hill. In early 2015, Wu Jianfu also installed a solar hot-water heater on the roof of their second storey. By the time Li Wei and I arrived, their main bathroom had all the modern conveniences we could wish for: a Western-style sit-down flush toilet, a basin and shower, both with hot and cold-water taps, and a washing machine behind the door.[21]

The dining room is at the rear of the house with a window facing east. Despite the ginkgo trees planted outside, this room is full of light. It's just big enough for six to eight people to squeeze around a large circular table. When guests come, Yang Yurong puts a glass lazy Susan on the table. Li Wei was surprised to see such a high-class item in an ordinary village home.

---

21 Like others installed in new houses along the main road, these amenities drained into an underground septic tank, built with a subsidy from the village government. Each septic tank in turn drained into nearby fields. For more about transformations in village bathrooms and toilets, see Santos, *Chinese Village Life Today*, 152–73.

To the left of the dining room is the staircase to the second floor. Tucked under the stairs is a large white refrigerator and an enormous box freezer containing several hunks of meat. Their meals today are so different from when she was a child, Yang Yurong reflected once. They never ate meat then.

Her kitchen sits in the auspicious south-east corner of the house. This kitchen puzzles me. The rest of the ground floor is sharp and modern, but the kitchen seems to hark back to the past. It's dominated by a traditional wood-fuelled stove. Yang Yurong also has a portable gas burner and an electric rice-cooker, but she uses them only sparingly. Gas and electricity are expensive. But in any case, she says, food tastes better cooked on a wood-fuelled stove.

The stove is a slightly larger, spruced-up version of the one in Popo's kitchen It has not one, but two woks set into the top. It's been plastered and the front and sides painted white; the stovetop is covered in white tiles. At the top is a metal flue, rather than a brick chimney, which pokes through a hole in the top of the wall.

Plate 7.3 Yang Yurong in her kitchen
Photo: Tamara Jacka, 2016.

For fuel, Yang Yurong uses chestnut husks and twigs she collects on the hill and larger branches that Wu Jianfu helps chop when he comes home at New Year. Most of the wood is stacked against the inner wall of the courtyard, with a smaller pile kept in the kitchen. Yurong feeds the wood through the two holes in the back of the stove.

When she deep-fries, she puts a bit of the cooked food into the holes for the stove god and his wife to taste: one morsel in one hole for Grandfather Stove God (*Zao Yeye*) and one in the other for Grandmother Stove God (*Zao Nainai*). Once over dinner, Yang Yurong explained that Grandfather Stove God is a cadre. 'Every year, he's sent down to check on each family and report back to Heaven. Villagers also say that the stove gods can heal a person by calling their wandering soul back to their body [*jiao hun*].'

'Do you really think that's true?' Li Wei asked cautiously.

Yang Yurong shrugged: 'I don't know. But when Baoli was sick one time, Popo said that if I stood him next to the openings in the stove, the stove gods would heal him. I did that and he did seem to get better.'[22]

Even without the old stove, the kitchen feels cruder than the rest of the house. The floor is just rough concrete, rather than tiles. The back of the stove is not painted or tiled. Yang Yurong keeps the benchtops wiped clean and in all but the space behind the stove, the floor is swept. But neither the floor nor the walls have the same glaring whiteness as the other ground-floor rooms. Around the stove, the walls are grimy and the back of the stove is black with grease and soot.

The kitchen smells different, too. Unlike the odourless front room, it's full of the aromas of frying food, woodsmoke and chilli oil. In 2014, Wu Jianfu installed a rangehood with an extractor fan, but it fails to remove the cooking fumes. He admitted that that's because he installed the rangehood too high. 'It'd work better if Yurong kept the window closed while the fan was on. I've told her that, but she keeps forgetting.'

---

22 The male Stove God is worshipped across rural China, but in many places, his wife is not. For discussion of the (male) Stove God's role, see Wolf, 'Gods, Ghosts, and Ancestors'; and Feuchtwang, *Popular Religion in China*.

Occasionally, Li Wei and I would go into the kitchen to watch Yang Yurong cooking. We would last no more than five minutes before the chilli fumes drove us out, coughing and spluttering. They didn't seem to bother Yang Yurong. She mostly kept the kitchen door shut though, so the fumes wouldn't spread into the dining room.

Apart from the kitchen, another thing that puzzles me about Yang Yurong's house is the lack of heating. With its high ceilings and thick walls, the house is cool in summer, but it's like a mausoleum in winter. When we visited in December 2016, Yang Yurong placed a small electric radiator under the tea table in the front room. Huddling around it afforded some warmth, but it still was colder inside than outside the house.

When we asked why she didn't have a wood heater, Yang Yurong said they were too dirty to have inside. She had asked Wu Jianfu to convert the carport into a heating-room, but he refused. He still wanted to buy a car one day.

*

While in Ginkgo Village, Li Wei stayed in Baoli's bedroom on the ground floor. I could have shared the room with her, but I wanted privacy. So, I slept in one of three cavernous second-floor rooms, where the walls were unpainted and the unpolished concrete floor was permanently dusty. In summer I stewed; in winter, I froze. But I had a small desk and a bedside table with a lamp, plenty of space and a wonderful view across the fields. On warm evenings, I'd lie with the window open, listening to the chorus of frogs and crickets.

Across from my room was a bathroom with a toilet and a handbasin with cold water. Every few days, I'd go downstairs to use the hot-water shower.

Neither Li Wei nor I spent much time in our bedrooms. We sat in the front room most evenings, writing up our fieldnotes with the life of the family going on around us. Sometimes, Baoli would ask Li Wei for help with his homework. At other times, he'd watch cartoons on TV or play games on his smartphone. If he was home, Wu Jianfu took control of the TV. It turns out, he and I both love Chinese melodramas, especially the ones set in the countryside during the collective era.

Yang Yurong would do the dishes after dinner, tidy up in the kitchen and sweep the floor. On warm evenings, she liked to go dancing in Five Hills or stroll through the village and meet up with friends. When it was too cold or wet for that, she'd be on her smartphone, exchanging videos with her friends on WeChat or playing games.

Through the middle of the day, the dining room became the centre of activity in the house. Of course, Li Wei and I spent most of each day visiting other people. But we usually ate meals at home with Yang Yurong.

My favourite meal was breakfast. It began once Yang Yurong returned from taking Baoli to school, which started at eight o'clock. Each morning, she prepared something different: congee with pickled vegetables on the side, homemade *jiaozi* (dumplings), piping-hot *youtiao* or noodles bought from Liang Anqin over in Old Pine Hamlet. Even now, my mouth waters recalling the warm tastes and smells.

But it was our conversation that meant the most to me. When Wu Jianfu was home, the talk over breakfast was constrained. But when he wasn't there, we had long leisurely chats. By that time of the morning, Yang Yurong had been up for two or three hours. She'd been cooking and cleaning and struggling to get sleepy, sullen Baoli dressed and fed. But having finally got him off to school, she would relax.

She was full of colourful stories. Often, she talked about the five years she spent working in Guangzhou before her marriage. 'Before that,' she said, 'I was extremely timid.' She laughed at our disbelief. 'It's true. I was very shy. But Guangzhou toughened me up.'

Around the dining table, she was an entertainer. In private, she confided in Li Wei and the two of them became close. I can't say the same about Yang Yurong and me. With other people around, it was easy. But on our own, we became awkward—more conscious of my language limitations and the differences between us in age, education and cultural background.

We had motherhood in common though. Misha is about a year older than Renkai. I showed Yang Yurong a photo of him that I kept in my wallet and, each time I visited, she asked after him. When he was a kid, I told her, he was like Baoli: impossible to rouse in the morning, but lively and demanding at other times. I didn't want to dwell on Misha's early childhood though.

I felt bad about the impact on him of my separation from his father. Yang Yurong, too, felt bad about having left toddler Renkai with his grandmother while she worked in Beijing.

We both preferred to share our pride in how well Renkai and Misha had turned out, despite their difficult beginnings. Yang Yurong seemed to see Misha as a model for her sons. He was doing well in his engineering degree at university and his job prospects were good. She hoped Renkai and Baoli could have the same bright future as him.

***

Over the time Li Wei and I spent with her, Yang Yurong grew increasingly restless. Once, she talked wistfully about getting Wu Jianfu to stay at home with Baoli so she could go back to work in Beijing or Guangzhou. 'But he'd never agree to such a thing; he'd feel disgraced.' She sighed. 'Anyway, I'd never earn as much as him.'

At that time, Wu Jianfu's annual income was about 70,000 yuan (US\$10,000), but his living costs in Beijing ate up more than half of that. Added to that, Renkai started university in 2016 and his father had to cover his tuition and living costs. He set up a bank account for his son and into it deposited 15,000 yuan (US\$2,200) to cover Renkai's costs for one year. When he came home for the New Year in 2018, Wu Jianfu brought only 1,000 yuan (US\$150) for his mother. The rest of his earnings went into his bank account.

Yang Yurong had access to that account, but she did her best not to withdraw from it. Instead, she used her own earnings to cover Baoli's expenses and her own. In 2013, she contracted their paddy fields to Huang Dajun, the businessman from Macheng. In return, she received an annual rent of 900 yuan (US\$130). She still had her vegetable patch by the river and another small plot next to the house, where she grew canola and peanuts. The family also had the rights to one mu (670 square metres) of chestnut trees up by the old house. In 2017, aside from producing all her own vegetables and cooking oil, she sold 1,000 yuan (US\$150) of canola oil. She also earned about 2,000 yuan (US\$300) picking tea and worked as a cook for the tea-factory workers for one month, earning another 3,000 yuan (US\$460). The chestnuts had been damaged by heavy rains, so the harvest was poor and she earned only 1,000 yuan—not worth the five days of work it took her and a friend to collect and peel them.

In November, she heard from a friend in the dance group about a job picking chrysanthemums for use in tea and Chinese medicine. She joined a group of 50 women flower-pickers from Deng Inn and Ginkgo Village. Together, they hired a few minibuses to take them into the mountains of Hubei, a few hours' drive from Ginkgo Village. Each day for 10 days, the bus drivers picked them up at five in the morning and returned them late in the evening. Once they deducted the 40-yuan bus fare, the women each earned 400 yuan (US$62) a day.

Yang Yurong earnt a total of about 20,000 yuan (US$3,000) in 2017, but much of that went on banquets, rituals and gift-giving. During the 2018 New Year festive period alone, she spent about 6,000 yuan (US$900) on gifts of cash and 2,000 yuan (US$300) on meat for visiting relatives. Wu Jianfu contributed another 9,000 yuan (US$1,400) for liquor, cigarettes, firecrackers, incense and spirit-money.

'New Year gets more and more expensive every year!' Yang Yurong complained.

*

It's my guess that Yang Yurong and Wu Jianfu accumulated about 15,000 yuan (US$2,300) each year between 2011 and 2017. So, what did they do with their savings?

For a while, they considered buying an apartment in Xin County City, but Yang Yurong was torn. She liked the idea of moving to the city, but even if they just rented, they would only be able to afford a small, shoddy place. And if she lived there, it would be harder to maintain their land in the village. She doubted she would find a job in the city; none of her friends had. Better to save money by staying at home, she finally decided.

Meanwhile, though, she tried to persuade Wu Jianfu to get a tourist visa and work overseas for a few years. It was the only way to earn the money they needed to buy an urban apartment. But Wu Jianfu resisted.

Once over dinner during our 2018 New Year visit, he told Li Wei and me that nowadays, migrant wages overseas weren't much better than those in China and working conditions were worse. 'I'm too old for that sort of thing,' he said. 'Besides, this house is good enough for us.'

Yang Yurong's eyes threw daggers at him. Li Wei and I pretended not to notice.

'What about Renkai?' Li Wei asked. 'We've heard it's difficult for a young man to marry if the family hasn't bought a city apartment for him.'

Wu Jianfu shook his head. 'That used to be true. The first thing a prospective mother-in-law would ask was, "Whereabouts in Xin County City is your apartment?" But nowadays, a lot of young men find their own wife. Quite often it's someone they've met at work.' He ladled chicken stew into his bowl.

'Once married,' he said, bending to eat, 'young couples want to keep living where their jobs are. There's no point going into debt over an apartment in Xin County City. After he graduates, Renkai will probably get a job in Wuhan and want to stay there.'

In short, Yang Yurong and Wu Jianfu decided against renting or buying new housing. Nor did they spend any money on improving their existing house. The rangehood in the kitchen wasn't modified and no heating was installed. The upstairs rooms remained unfinished. Aside from my bedroom, one other room stayed empty, while the third was piled with building tools and junk. The washstand from Yang Yurong's dowry lay on its side. It was made of wood, painted a delicate pale green, with a hole in the top for a washbowl. A dark green vine with tiny pink flowers twined around the edges of the two small doors of the cabinet underneath. I whispered to Li Wei how sad it was that it had been discarded.

Instead of renovating the house, Wu Jianfu took driving lessons and, in 2017, bought a large white car, costing 85,000 yuan (US$13,000). At first, Li Wei and I couldn't understand this purchase, for the car sat in the carport unused for most of the year. But on our 2018 New Year visit, the car's importance became clearer. Wu Jianfu drove the two hours to Wuhan to meet us at the airport and took us back to the village. In the following weeks, he also ferried several locals and their relatives between Wuhan, Xin County City and Ginkgo Village. Other than the cost of petrol, he received no payment for this driving. The car was a status symbol and acting as chauffeur was a favour, which helped cement his ties with friends and kin.

*

Another new development came after Li Wei and I left Ginkgo Village that year: the Xin County Government began a major project to widen the main road. In the process, they bulldozed several front yards and even some of the houses lining the road. For months, Wu Jianfu worried that their courtyard and carport would be demolished, too. Later, Yang Yurong confided to Li Wei that she hadn't been so concerned: if their property was damaged, they would receive compensation and she and Baoli could move to the city.

As it turned out, the courtyard and carport weren't touched. Much of the driveway was destroyed though, along with the bushes and flowers that Yang Yurong had planted around it. She was annoyed they weren't compensated, but they had got off lightly. Others had received only token compensation for much greater losses.

8

Motherhood

When Li Wei and I first met her, Tan Zimei was a wrung-out 30-year-old, dragged down by three young children: two daughters, aged eight and five, and a 14-month-old son. They lived in Stone Gully Hamlet.

Theirs is one of six two-storey houses strung along the main road, close to the bridge marking the boundary between Ginkgo and Carpenter villages. At the northern end of the row is a small general store, much like Widower Yang's. It's crammed with everything from dust-covered metal lunchboxes and bottle-openers to preserved fruit in glass jars to bottles of beer and packets of instant noodles. Old men buy the beer and schoolkids buy the instant noodles when they're home for the weekend. But the other stuff has sat unsold for years. That's because most of Stone Gully's men—including Tan Zimei's husband—are migrant labourers living far from home and most of the women are either migrant labourers or live in Xin County City. Except for Tan Zimei and a few others struggling with poverty, illness or other handicaps, all those aged under 35 have left. Only a dozen or so middle-aged and older folk remain. They like to gather outside the store, but they rarely buy anything. They prefer to spend their meagre savings in Red River.

Tan Zimei lives at the southern end of the row of houses. Opposite are three thin poplars and an electricity pole. Wrapped around the electricity pole is a torn handwritten advertisement for an STD clinic. Further along, the road to Old Pine Hamlet climbs steeply up the hillside.

Her house is the same as all the others in the row. At the front, the upstairs rooms jut over the footpath. Underneath, the double-wing doors open directly onto the footpath and road. Behind the row of houses is the river. Elsewhere in Ginkgo Village, a wide stretch of fertile soil graces the riverbank, which is not much lower than the road. But here, the water runs beneath a cliff. The houses' second-floor rear rooms extend over the cliff edge, supported by rough concrete pillars driven into the mud a few metres below. Every few years, there's a flooding downpour and the river swells up the pillars, perilously close to the top of the cliff. Most of the time, though, the pillars stand exposed.

Once, I slithered down to the water's edge from the side of the bridge. Li Wei stayed above; she said the slope was too steep and she didn't want to muddy her shoes. The river rippled mean and dark under the bridge. Spent firecrackers, instant noodle packets and plastic bags as well as leaves and twigs had caught around the base of the pillars. There was a smell of something rotting.

*

Li Wei and I first went to visit Tan Zimei one Saturday afternoon in late March 2016. It was tea-picking season. The old couple who run the Stone Gully store were sitting outside with measuring scales, receiving tea leaves picked by locals.

Tan Zimei's front door was ajar, so we could see into her front room. To one side, a wooden stool lay upended and kids' shoes and clothing were strewn over a faded couch and across the concrete floor. Towards the back was a low rectangular tea table with what looked like the remnants of a meal: bowls and chopsticks, a baby's bottle and an open jar of chilli paste. Next to the table, Tan Zimei and her two youngest were standing in a clump, with their backs to us.

They looked dressed up, as though they'd just come home from an outing. Perhaps they'd taken the bus to Xin County City to visit one of Tan Zimei's sisters-in-law. The five-year-old was wearing jeans and a grubby white jacket. 'Luv me' was written in fat sparkly pink letters across her back. Her little brother, who was screaming at the top of his lungs, was partly hidden from view by his mother bending over him, trying to peel off his tight red jacket. Tan Zimei herself wore a pale-blue and pink floral blouse with a short loud-yellow and black chequered skirt. Her matchstick legs were encased in shiny nylon stockings and she had red wedge shoes on her feet. Her hair hung in a stringy curtain.

It was a confronting scene, reeking of disadvantage and struggle. I should have empathised with the young mother. I shouldn't have passed judgement on her. Yet, in that moment, I did; I couldn't help it. In the blink of an eye, my bourgeois feminist brain shot from 'your clothes are cheap and nasty, your house is a mess' to pity and contempt.

The five-year-old saw us and patted her mother's side to get her attention. But Tan Zimei was busy, trying to pull the wailing toddler's chubby arms out of his jacket. He squirmed free and tottered away, surprisingly fast, towards the back of the house. The jacket was hanging off one arm and dragging on the ground. Tan Zimei uncurled and for a moment just stood there, slumped. Then she yelled 'get back here' and lurched after the toddler, hefting him onto her hip and turning back. She saw us then in the doorway. The little boy was still wailing, tears and snot streaming, little fists pummelling his mother's flat chest. Tan Zimei stood rigid and unsmiling, her body dwarfed by the bulk of her son.

'What's his name?' I asked, after Li Wei and I had introduced ourselves. I tried to take the boy's hand, but he wouldn't let me.

'His baby name is Little Dog,'[1] Tan Zimei said awkwardly.

*

We were able to talk only briefly with her on that occasion, snatching a few questions in between her getting up to attend to her two kids' demands. She didn't stay still long enough for us to have a real conversation.

Nor was there much chance to get to know her later that year. We visited a few times, but usually the curtains in the downstairs window were drawn and the two grey-steel wings of the front door were shut. We would knock and I'd call out, but without an answer. Sometimes, we'd pull at the metal handles, but the door would be locked.

If it was during the rest period after lunch, we'd go over to her neighbours and ask whether Tan Zimei had gone out. The old women would be sitting in the sun together, chatting and joking among themselves, washing garlic chives in a plastic bowl and watching the world go by. They would lift their heads and smile at us as we came over. Occasionally, they'd tell us that Tan

---

1   The practice of giving a child an unflattering baby name (*xiao ming*) was aimed originally at ensuring that the child did not attract the attention of evil spirits bringing death.

Zimei had gone to work in her vegetable patch on the hill. But usually, they thought she must still be inside; they would have seen her if she had gone out. It was all very strange. Villagers usually lock up when they go out, but unless they're resting or ill in bed, they keep their doors open when they're home. Neighbours wander in and out at will.

So, why did Tan Zimei keep her front door shut? Why did she not answer when we knocked and called out? When we asked the neighbours, they just shrugged, palms upturned, picking at the sleeve of their jacket or shifting about and shuffling their feet. They would laugh off the question and invite us to join them instead. One woman would stand up and motion for me to take her chair. Another would fetch a stool for Li Wei.

***

On our fourth attempt to visit her, Tan Zimei's door was closed and there was no answer when we knocked. I didn't bother calling out and turned away. But Li Wei knocked once more and waited quietly.

I stood, distracted by the poplar trees rustling in the breeze opposite. I will always love poplars. But since meeting Zhang Hongren, my childhood memories of a tall, twinkly tree protecting me had been overlaid with images from the Great Famine.

Eventually, Tan Zimei opened the door. She gave a start when she saw us, but let us in. She wore a filthy apron over her jeans. I could smell stale milk. Her daughters, she said, were in school and preschool and Little Dog was asleep in a back room.

She cleared a pile of clothes off the couch, dropped them on the floor and motioned for us to sit down. The springs in the couch must have had it; I sank much deeper than I'd been expecting. Tan Zimei brought over a stool from the back of the room and plonked down next to us.

She told us the reason she shut her front door was to keep Little Dog safe. He learnt to walk much earlier than her other two and was impossibly active and fast. She was afraid that if the door was left open, he would run out into the road when her back was turned.

The trouble was, she went on, she had no-one to help look after him. In the past, she sometimes asked a neighbour to mind him, but they were reluctant. Maybe he was too much of a handful for them or maybe there was another reason. They weren't very friendly. She paused and looked down at her hands. Li Wei and I saw chipped pink nail polish and fingernails bitten to the quick. We waited quietly.

Perhaps, Tan Zimei mumbled, it was because she was not a local, but from a poor village in Hunan Province, miles from here. She and her husband met when they were both migrant workers in Shenzhen. She had lived here almost 10 years, but Ginkgo Villagers still treated her as an outsider.

There was no-one else to whom she could turn. Her husband, a builder, now worked mostly in Beijing and other cities up north. At least he did most of the time. Recently, there had been a downturn in the construction industry and it was harder to find work. He earned up to 200 yuan (US$30) a day when on a job, but in the past few years, he had no more than 20 days of work each month. Some months, there was so little work, he gave up and came home. The previous year, his earnings were barely enough to meet their needs.

But even when he was home, Tan Zimei said, shifting on her stool, her husband wasn't much help. He refused to look after the kids or do any washing, saying those jobs were hers. He was not much help with the farming either. He'd been a migrant labourer since finishing junior secondary school and never learnt to farm. The first time he tried harvesting the peanuts, he went hard at it. He went out in the blazing sun and pulled so vigorously, he got heatstroke and had to lie down after a few hours. Tan Zimei looked up with a half-smile and a shrug.

I thought about my own pathetic attempt to help Yang Yurong pull up peanuts. I didn't last long either. It was more tiring than it looked.

*

Tan Zimei stood to make tea for Li Wei and me. 'It's okay, we don't need tea,' we cried. But Tan Zimei took no notice. She took mugs, tea leaves and a thermos from a shelf next to the couch.

While she was pouring, I continued with my questions: 'Are your older kids any help? Can they mind the toddler?'

Tan Zimei shook her head. 'The eight-year-old takes the bus to primary school in Red River every morning and comes home late in the afternoon.'

'Why does she go to Red River? Wouldn't it be easier to send her to the local Ginkgo Village school?'

Tan Zimei frowned. It turned out, she was in conflict with her husband over this question. He said the girl should go to the local school and they would save on the bus fare. And on school costs, too; they charged more for meals and things like pencils and notebooks in the school in Red River than here.

'But the local school is no good,' Tan Zimei said. She stared out the front door.

'Why, what's wrong with it?'

Her head jerked back to me. 'Have you been there?'

Li Wei and I shook our heads.

'It's completely run down. Go see for yourself. The yard's full of weeds and they have no equipment for science or sport. No English classes either. And everyone says the teachers are no good.'

There was the sound of crying from the back room and Tan Zimei darted off. She was still agitated when she came back, Little Dog on her hip. He was tousle-haired and his nose was running.

'My daughter has to go to Red River for grades three to six anyway,' Tan Zimei continued. 'Nowadays, the village school only goes up to grade two.'

'What grade is she in now?' Li Wei asked.

'Grade one. My husband says we should have kept her in the local school for as long as possible. But I want the best for her.'

Li Wei nodded and sipped her tea. I put my notebook on the couch and arched my back. It was already starting to ache.

'How many years of schooling did you yourself get?' I asked her.

'Only two. My family couldn't afford more. My older brother finished senior secondary school but then we ran out of money.'

That must have been in the 1990s, when Jiang Zemin was in power. Of all China's national leaders, Jiang Zemin was the only one about whom villagers complained. That's because, under his government, rural citizens were crippled by skyrocketing school tuition fees and a host of exorbitant taxes and charges. It was a tremendous relief when Hu Jintao finally abolished the taxes in 2006 and the following year removed tuition fees for nine years of compulsory schooling.

*

Tan Zimei stood with Little Dog on her hip. If she'd been a boy, she said bitterly, her parents might have found the money to keep her in school. But they couldn't afford it for a girl. Since girls marry out and the family loses their labour, spending money on them when they're young is like watering someone else's garden. That's what they thought.

Her brother had found a stable job and climbed out of poverty. But, with only two years of schooling, the best she could manage was poorly paid piecework in sweatshops down south. She worked 14-hour days and the bosses treated the workers like scum. She endured it for three years before she was married, but she was determined her daughters would do better. 'I'll give them the best schooling I can,' she said.

Little Dog was starting to squirm. Tan Zimei jogged him up and down.

'Hardly anyone sends their kids to the village school anymore,' she said to her husband, 'so why should we?'

'How many students still go there?' I asked.

Little Dog whined and clutched at his mother's limp hair. She yelled and pulled his arm away.

'Older sister,' Li Wei said, 'come sit down.' She patted the couch.

'No, I'm fine.'

Li Wei clambered up. 'Here,' she said, reaching her arms out. 'Let me take him; he can sit with us.'

But Little Dog was having none of it. He cowered away from Li Wei and started crying. Tan Zimei took him back out to the kitchen and I took the opportunity to stand up, straighten my back and look around.

Taped to the dirty grey wall behind the couch were three awards for 'best student' that Tan Zimei's oldest had won from the Red River primary school. They were pale-orange paper squares with black writing and a border of red flags and peonies. On the other side of the room was the squat cube of an

7

old television, with a picture above it in a hideous ornate frame. I went over to have a look. It was a studio photograph, showing Tan Zimei and her husband in Western-style wedding attire, posed against a nineteenth-century European landscape painting, bathed in warm, fuzzy light.

*

Soon, Tan Zimei returned with a bottle for Little Dog. He calmed down and she sat with him on the couch next to me. Li Wei moved to the stool.

We returned to the question of how many children attended the Ginkgo Village primary school.

Six years ago, Tan Zimei said, the school went all the way to grade five and they had 100 students. There were another 100 in preschool. This year, it had dropped to nine, including six preschoolers, two in grade one and one in grade two. All the other kids went to school in Red River.

Little Dog sat in his mother's lap, sucking his bottle. She tightened one arm around him as she spoke: 'I told my husband that our kids deserve no less than anyone else. When it comes time, the younger ones will also go to Red River, along with their sister. Anyway, they'll probably have closed the Ginkgo Village school by then.'[2]

'What about later?' Li Wei asked, tilting her head. 'Do you think they'll all go to senior as well as junior secondary school?'

'Definitely.' She gave Li Wei the empty baby's bottle and stood up with her son again. He lay his head on her chest and stared sideways at me and Li Wei, his thumb in his mouth.

'I want to rent an apartment in Xin County City, so I can be with them there and they can go to day school. That'd be much better for them than staying in boarding school. But we might not be able to afford it. It costs more than 4,000 yuan[3] a year to rent in Xin County City. They might have to go to Red River for secondary school as well as primary school.'

---

2   In the first decade of the twenty-first century, the Chinese state undertook a nationwide campaign to consolidate education resources in rural areas. The campaign resulted in the shrinkage or closure of most village primary schools. For more about consequent transformations in rural education and rural parenting decisions, see Rachel Murphy, 'Education and Repertoires of Care in Migrant Families in Rural China', *Comparative Education Review* 66, no. 1 (2022): 102–20, doi.org/10.1086/717449.

3   US$580.

Her voice trailed off. She put Little Dog on the floor and went over to fold the shirts and trousers she'd dumped next to the couch. Her son crawled over and plumped himself down on top of the clothes. Tan Zimei cried out in exasperation and pushed him aside. Li Wei and I winced.

Predictably, Little Dog started wailing again. Li Wei and I rummaged in our daypacks for something to give him, but we had nothing. Tan Zimei hauled him up and shoved him into a narrow, thin-framed pram parked at the back of the room. She wheeled the pram over and stood pushing it backwards and forwards. Gradually, Little Dog's wailing subsided.

I watched, distressed at the interaction between mother and child. Misha had been difficult as a baby. Was I as rough with him as Tan Zimei was with Little Dog? Maybe.

'Can the five-year-old mind Little Dog?' I asked, looking up at Tan Zimei. She looked so stressed.

Tan Zimei shook her head. 'He's too much for her. In any case, she's in preschool during the week.' She stopped pushing the pram. 'Perhaps it's a mistake to send her to preschool. It's expensive and it takes half an hour to walk there. I spend two hours every day taking her there in the morning and picking her up in the afternoon.'

'Oh, that's very hard,' Li Wei said. 'What do you do with Little Dog?'

'I leave him here. I lock the door and rush to the school and back as fast as I can. What else can I do? Other women take their kids on a motorised scooter, but I can't afford one of them. He's too heavy to carry all that way and the pram's too flimsy. The wheels would fall off.'

'What about your mother-in-law? Can you ask her to look after him?' I asked.

'I do sometimes,' she mumbled, going to the other side of the room for another stool. 'But she says she's too old and frail. My husband is five years older than me and he's the youngest; he has three older brothers and an older sister. My mother-in-law looked after all three brothers' kids when they were small, but now she says she's not up to caring for mine.' She let out a rough sigh.

'I do take Little Dog to her occasionally. She'll sometimes look after him while I do the farm work. We haven't divided the family—we still share the land. My mother-in-law looks after Little Dog while I do the heavy farm work. But that's about it.' She set the stool down next to the pram and slumped onto it.

'Does she ever come here?' Li Wei asked gently.

Tan Zimei gave the pram another push. 'Not often. She says her legs are too weak to walk down the hill to our house. I know that's not true. She's able to walk to the bus stop and go do her shopping in Red River!'

'I don't want her here anyway,' she added quickly.

'Why not?' I asked.

Tan Zimei chewed a fingernail. 'Once, she came to watch Little Dog while I went to pick up his sister from preschool. She left him and went next door to chat with the neighbours. The front door was open and Little Dog crawled straight into the road.'

Li Wei and I took a sharp breath.

'He was okay. One of the neighbours pulled him back just as a van sped by. She told me about it afterwards. She blamed me—said I was irresponsible. Everyone else has a mother-in-law who can look after their kids. But not me. So now I just keep the door shut.' She paused and looked away. 'Even when I'm home.'

***

Tan Zimei's explanation for the closed door made sense. Sometimes, though, we could hear both her and Little Dog inside, but when we knocked and called out, there was no response. Why didn't Tan Zimei open the door to us? Li Wei thought she must be too busy. I suspected there was more to it. Perhaps she was struggling with depression and avoiding people. Perhaps she was avoiding her neighbours.

During our next stay in Ginkgo Village in December 2016, my suspicions were partly confirmed. But Tan Zimei wasn't depressed and she hadn't just been avoiding her neighbours; she'd been avoiding me. Yang Yurong told us this. I don't think she's particularly friendly with Tan Zimei, but she likes company and talks with everyone. She makes it her business to know everything that goes on in the village.

'Laoshi,' she said one morning over breakfast, 'when you knocked on Tan Zimei's door and called out, she could tell it was you. She got scared.' She took a bite of the *youtiao* she was holding between thumb and forefinger and slurped a spoonful of congee.

'She thought your visit had to do with birth planning and you were going to report her for having three children. She's already suffered enough; she doesn't want any more trouble.'

I flinched, remembering that it was usually me, not Li Wei, who banged on Tan Zimei's door and called out. Li Wei was more patient and discreet. I also felt bad about the clumsy questions I'd asked Tan Zimei. The first time we'd met, I'd asked her why she'd given birth again when she already had two daughters. And when she said it was the wish for a son that made her try a third time, I pressed further. I went against my training and asked a leading question: 'Did your husband pressure you into it or was it your mother-in-law?' I suppose I wanted to assume that Tan Zimei was an innocent victim of her husband's or mother-in-law's patriarchal preference for a son.

But Tan Zimei had stared at me defiantly. 'No,' she said. '*I* wanted a son. Without a son, I'm nothing.'

I had dropped my eyes and concentrated on recording her words in my notebook. I pressed hard on that 'I'—so hard I left a groove on the next three pages.

I wanted to ask: 'Did you really think you'd be nothing? Or was that what others would think?' But I didn't dare. Later, I realised it was a foolish question anyway. If others put no weight on having a son, it's unlikely that Tan Zimei would feel such a need for one. Conversely, if other villagers looked down on families with no son, it would be hard for her to stand tall without one.

*

After talking with Yang Yurong, Li Wei and I decided it was best to not approach Tan Zimei again ourselves. We asked Yang Yurong to reassure her that we wouldn't say anything to the authorities and we didn't care how many children she had. We wouldn't visit her again unless she told Yang Yurong it was okay for us to do so.

To our surprise, a week later, Yang Yurong said that Tan Zimei had agreed to see us once more. That afternoon, we rugged up in hats, scarves and gloves and walked to Stone Gully. Yang Yurong had rung ahead to tell her we were coming. The air stung our eyes as we trudged along. I had a cold and was feeling weary. Opposite Tan Zimei's house, the poplars were pale broomsticks. Her door was shut, but she opened it when we knocked.

As before, Tan Zimei's daughters were in school and preschool. Little Dog was sitting on the couch, chewing a piece of cardboard. She picked him up and put him on the floor, so Li Wei and I could sit on the couch. There was a smell of urine and a damp patch where the toddler had been. I avoided that spot and sat at the other end. Li Wei and Tan Zimei sat on stools.

Both mother and son seemed calmer than they had been previously. But Tan Zimei was still wary. Li Wei wanted to ask about Tan Zimei's husband's experiences as a migrant labourer, so I let her do most of the talking.

Then, towards the end of our conversation, I tried a few questions about Tan Zimei's children. 'Was it hard to register your son's birth?' I asked.

Tan Zimei clammed up. She looked down at Little Dog, fingering a biscuit that Li Wei had given him. Suddenly, she got up and snatched the biscuit from him. She slapped him away when he started crying and reaching for it. Then, as the kid kept snivelling, she switched on the TV to distract him. It was impossible to continue talking after that.

***

Later, Li Wei tactfully said that perhaps Tan Zimei still found me too threatening. She suggested she try visiting by herself.

Despite my ego being bruised, I found it easy to agree. The truth was, I was enormously discomfited by Tan Zimei—by her dreadful, tasteless clothes and rough manner with Little Dog; by the chaos in her house; by her struggle with her three children. I could see she wasn't coping and I wanted to empathise. But I couldn't. I was torn between an urge to shake her in frustration and a need to flee. Each time we saw her, I would come away with a sore jaw from having clenched it so hard. It might seem strange, but I think the problem was that Tan Zimei reminded me too much of myself at that age.

Of course, the differences between us were enormous. Not only were we separated by age and cultural background; our life experiences also had been shaped by quite different circumstances. Compared with Tan Zimei's childhood and youth, constrained as it had been by poverty and sexism, my early years were couched in material privilege, even relative to others in Australia. From the age of five, I grew up in a comfortable middle-class house in a comfortable middle-class suburb. I enjoyed a solid secondary school education and undertook free undergraduate and postgraduate studies at the best university in the country. I had no firsthand experience of significant material deprivation. Nor had I suffered the kind of discrimination that had blighted Tan Zimei's youth.

In my mid-twenties, I moved to Western Australia for my first lecturing job. I lived in a share house in Fremantle—a fishing port gentrified into a trendy suburb. On weekends, I would stroll down to 'Cappuccino Strip'—a row of cafes along the main road outside which crowds of people sat sipping their coffees and appraising passers-by in much the way I had looked at Tan Zimei.

Then, shortly before Misha was born, his dad and I bought a house together. We couldn't afford Fremantle, so we moved further south, to Rockingham. We lived in a big old place with a rambling garden, one block from the beach. It was a few kilometres from an aluminium smelter, a power plant, an oil refinery and a fertiliser factory. Our neighbours were factory workers with thick northern England accents. On the weekends, we saw pot-bellied men in shorts and singlets washing their cars and obese women in tent-like frocks shouting at their kids. We didn't have much to do with them, but they seemed friendly.

It felt more real living there in that working-class suburb than in the privileged hothouse of Fremantle. My partner and I joked about how our Fremantle friends pitied us down in smelly, polluted Rockingham. They weren't aware that the wind blew most of the pollution away from us and towards them. In the evenings, we walked on the white beach and watched the blushing sunsets. It was glorious.

But everything changed after Misha was born. Suddenly, I was isolated with a difficult baby, far from my friends. In any case, they were busy at work. I was bent on breastfeeding but had insufficient milk, so Misha was forever hungry. He cried incessantly and refused to sleep. During his birth, I'd ripped my perineum and damaged my spine. I was in constant pain and utterly exhausted.

Misha's dad—also an academic—proved to have extremely conservative views on parenting. On leave from work, he spent all day sitting in his study. I would stand in the doorway and plead for him to take our squalling baby for a moment. But he'd hurl abuse, come raging across the room and slam the door in my face.

I thought of my mum then—how she was after Tommy's death, when Dad was in intensive care. And afterwards on the beach: my fearful mother, crazed and broken. At night, I snatched fragments of sleep, shot through with nightmares. In one, a gunman went berserk. Another night a landslide hit—a whole wall of rock came crashing down. I feared I'd be a bomb blast, brick and bone and flesh splattering. Nothing left but rubble. I feared I'd become my mother. I feared for my son.

It was midsummer and we had no airconditioning. During the day, the temperature climbed higher and higher. The baby screamed louder and louder. My T-shirt was blotched with stale milk. I stank and I couldn't breathe.

To escape, I'd put Misha in the car, turn the airconditioning on and drive around and around. Then one day, I took him to the local shopping mall. I hated the tacky consumerism of that place—the crowds and clashing colours, the claustrophobia, the syrupy music. But at least it would be cool.

It was a Wednesday morning and less crowded than on my previous weekend visits. But the babies still cried and the music still leaked through the glaring maze of halls. I scarcely heard. I discovered that with so many in school or at work, the mall was crawling with the worn-out and desperate: the strung-out drug addicts; the depressed, unemployed and homeless; the physically disabled and mentally disturbed; the dank and rickety old men; the obese middle-aged housewives; the hollow-eyed young mothers with jutting hipbones, wearing clothes like Tan Zimei's and pushing prams with screaming babies. And me.

So much reality, so unbearably close. I ran with Misha in his pram. I ran and ran. Two decades later, I was still running.

Reflecting on my discomfit with Tan Zimei, I saw all this. But there was something else: I had thought my mum's statement that 'I cannot be your mother anymore' was about me. I had felt it as a life-threatening rejection from the person to whom I was closest. But seeing myself in Tan Zimei, it suddenly came home to me that my mum was talking about herself.

My mother, Tan Zimei and me: three women with profoundly different life experiences—different troubles, different struggles. Yet, motherhood connected us. I should have done more to draw on that connection and deepen it, but I wasn't brave enough. Empathy was too painful.

***

Fortunately, Li Wei could empathise and connect with Tan Zimei in a way that I could not. How that happened I'm not sure. The two women are similar in age, but in other ways they are quite different.

Like other northerners, Li Wei is taller than the average southerner. She's about my height—several inches taller than Tan Zimei. She has grace and poise and the kind of self-assurance that comes with material security and a relatively privileged social status. Her clothes are always simple and discreet: a pale-coloured blouse or a fawn-coloured cashmere jumper with slim dark slacks or leggings—that sort of thing. Much classier than my loose jeans and T-shirts and far more expensive than Tan Zimei's synthetic trash.

As the only child of urban Han government employees, Li Wei belongs to China's up-and-coming middle class, whose material lives and life chances in the early twenty-first century resemble those of young middle-class Australians more closely than those of the poorest Chinese villagers like Tan Zimei. She's been nurtured in a stable, materially comfortable environment. Her life has not been narrowed by poverty, sexism or any other kind of social discrimination any more than mine has.

From the little that Li Wei has told me about her upbringing, I have the impression that she and I have also been inculcated with similar values. Like mine, her parents are atheists and emphasise the importance of education. Neither set of parents talked much of politics during our childhoods, but from them, both of us inherited concerns about growing inequalities and the excesses of the wealthy and powerful under capitalism.

In school, Li Wei did well. She was accepted into a prestigious university in Beijing and graduated with a sociology degree. Subsequently, her parents paid for her to do postgraduate studies in Australia. They wanted her to hurry, finish her studies, get married and have a child.

But in her mid twenties, Li Wei wasn't sure about either marriage or children. For village women like Tan Zimei, these things seemed essential. Young urbanites like Li Wei were getting other ideas. At her age, I'd yearned for a child, but Li Wei was in no rush. She even wondered whether she wouldn't be better off without one. A child, she knew, would be a heavy burden on her time and finances. In competition with childless women and men whose wives took care of domestic work and childrearing, she would likely be severely disadvantaged in her pursuit of a fulfilling career.

Given all this, she seemed no better placed than me to make a connection with Tan Zimei, but there's something about Li Wei. She's like a deep, still pool that draws people in.

Despite working side-by-side with her for months, I can't say I know her intimately. We regularly penetrated other people's personal lives—in my case, crashing through boots and all; in Li Wei's, more subtly, some might even say deviously. But we rarely talked about our own private troubles or joys. I have little understanding of Li Wei's inner emotional world.

I get the sense, though, that she's experienced some sort of significant loss or suffering. Perhaps the trauma of the Cultural Revolution has somehow passed down from her parents to her. Perhaps there's conflict between her parents. Or perhaps their ill health (apart from his injuries, her father has heart troubles and her mother is diabetic) has been a burden on her. She mentioned once that she had been her mother's main carer. It was a relief to be away from home, but she worried how her mum would cope.

I suppose we all suffer at some stage or other. But it hits us at different points on our life journeys and we respond in different ways. I'm still trapped inside my past hurts, while Li Wei's seem to have drawn her closer to others. At any rate, she's more able than me to reach beyond herself to those around her.

But perhaps I have it all wrong. Perhaps she's just good at interviewing. She knows which questions to ask—the ones you need her to ask, which will pull you deeper and deeper beneath the surface. She knows how to listen with all her attention and care. She makes you feel that she can see you the way no-one else can.

*

It didn't take long for Tan Zimei to relax with Li Wei. The two women met twice that December and a few more times in February 2017. Li Wei learned all about the conflict between Tan Zimei and the birth planning officials.

When she became pregnant for the second time, less than the mandated four years after the first, Tan Zimei knew the authorities would come after her. She fled to Beijing, where her husband was working, and hid until her daughter was three months old. But while she was hiding, township officials went to her parents-in-law. They harassed and fined them. They were like a criminal gang, Tan Zimei said. If you hid or you didn't pay up, they went after both your husband's parents and your own. It was lucky her parents were so far away.

When Tan Zimei finally returned to Stone Gully, the cadres caught her. They fined her an extortionate sum: 4,000 yuan (US$640). They came repeatedly, every few days, to bang on her door and force her to pay. And it wasn't just one or two of them. There were 20 people, including several township birth planning officials, as well as Village Director Zhou and Women's Director Liu. Sometimes, they brought along one or two beefy thugs as well to bully her into paying up. Each time they came, she'd pay them a few hundred yuan, but then she ran out of money. So, they took all her furniture and went to her parents-in-law and took their water buffalo. The whole family was reduced to penury. They were afraid and humiliated.

That wasn't the end of it. A few months later, when her husband returned for the New Year, they forced him to pay another fine, because Tan Zimei refused to have a tubal ligation. The couple also had to bribe a man at the police station in Red River to record their daughter's birth and have her included on their household's register.

'They won't register babies born out of plan,' she explained, 'unless you pay a bribe. We had no money left, so we had to borrow from my sister-in-law. We had to get our daughter registered; if we hadn't, she wouldn't be able to go to school or get a job.'

The birth of their son cost them dearly, too. They paid a doctor 1,000 yuan (US$150) to conduct an illegal sex test on the foetus and, after the baby's birth, they were forced to pay another hefty fine.

'We still need to get him registered,' she told Li Wei. 'We haven't managed to get that done yet; we ran out of money. We haven't even repaid our debts from our daughter's birth yet. We've got nothing.'

My heart went out to Tan Zimei when I heard all this. I covered my face with my hands.

*

I wish I could end this tale with a rapprochement between Tan Zimei and me. I wanted there to be one. The next time Li Wei and I visited Ginkgo Village, I wanted to see her. I wanted to apologise—to somehow make it up to her. But I chickened out. I didn't dare risk messing things up again.

Anyway, rapprochement was my desire, not Tan Zimei's. What good would it have done her?

9

New Year

At the beginning of each Lunar New Year, Ginkgo Villagers adorn their front doors and gates with fresh paper door gods and *duilian* (rhyming couplets) wishing peace and prosperity. The new *duilian* signal a grace period: once they're pasted up, no-one's allowed to demand the repayment of debts. Before they come knocking again, the debt collectors must wait until those who owe them have properly welcomed in the New Year.

That takes more than two weeks of vigorous festivities. Beneath the cold, white sky, the village balloons with home-comers and visitors, colour and noise. The usually hollow houses and quiet roads burst with rituals and reunions, fireworks, exchanges of gifts and boisterous celebratory banquets.[1]

Today is the sixteenth of the first lunar month, 2018.[2] We had the Dragon Parade three nights ago and the Lantern Festival last night. I'm exhilarated and exhausted.

---

1   In this chapter, I describe only the main customs observed in Ginkgo Village and elsewhere across Xin County between New Year's Eve and the sixteenth of the first lunar month. For a fuller account of the many rituals performed at the end of the preceding lunar year as well as during the New Year period, see Chang and Zhu, *Xin County Folk Customs Gazetteer*, 205–9. See also Charles Stafford, *Separation and Reunion in Modern China* (Cambridge, UK: Cambridge University Press, 2000), 30–52, 136–39.
2   All the dates in this tale refer to the lunar calendar.

Plate 9.1 Doorway with new *duilian* and door gods[3]
Photo: Tamara Jacka, 2018.

---

3   The mirror above the doorway is to ward off evil spirits.

***

Li Wei and I have been staying with Yang Yurong's family for just over three weeks. Wu Jianfu had already been home for a couple of weeks when we arrived and Renkai got back the day before us. He and Baoli have been camping on the floor in the upstairs room next to mine.

I've been waking before daybreak each morning. I can hear Aunty Gao's rooster on the other side of the fields and Yang Yurong downstairs. She's been getting up even earlier than usual. That's because she's not used to sharing the bed with Wu Jianfu and he wakes her with his snoring.

'I have to get up early anyway,' she says. 'I must cook and prepare for visitors. New Year is a holiday for the men, but not for us women.'

I imagine her tossing aside the bedclothes and plodding out to the kitchen, raking her hair into a ponytail as she goes. The air on her ears is icy. She closes the kitchen door, turns on the light and blinks for a moment in the sudden glare. Perhaps she feels better once she's started the stove. I imagine her on her stool, wedged behind the stove, planning what meals to prepare, what work needs to be done. She blows gently to get the fire going. The straw starts smoking; the twigs shift and glow. She watches the flames and feels the warmth on her face. Perhaps she whispers to the stove gods before getting up to prepare breakfast.

*

Each morning, I steel myself for the dash to the bathroom. There, I fill a plastic washbowl with hot water from a thermos, plunge in a cloth and use it to wipe my face and body. I wipe the bottom and top halves separately, peeling off layers of thermal underwear and long socks. While getting dressed again, I teeter on top of my flip-flops, trying not to touch my bare feet on the frigid concrete floor.

Once dressed—in down coat, woolly hat and all—I make my way downstairs with my laptop computer in my left hand and a thermos in my right. If Yang Yurong hasn't already put on the kettle to refill all the thermoses for the day, I do it myself.

Apart from Yang Yurong, I'm the only person in the household awake. I sit on the couch, huddled over my laptop, sipping hot tea. The steam fogs my glasses. I must look quite a sight.

Yang Yurong and I have learnt to leave each other alone before breakfast. She comes out of the kitchen and says a brief hello, but then she gets on with her tasks. I'm not so friendly first thing in the morning, but Yang Yurong doesn't seem to mind. Perhaps she appreciates that bit of time to herself as much as I do.

After I've drunk my tea, I go back upstairs for a while. Some mornings, I come down again with the wastepaper basket from my bathroom. I collect the one from the bathroom next to the kitchen, too. I take the bins outside and empty the smelly toilet paper into the garbage tank across the road.[4] I take my time walking back, feeling the cold nip my nose and cheeks and watching the world stir in the pale light. Sometimes, I wave to Mrs Cao next door.

I like taking the bins out. But it occurs to me now that perhaps it's a mistake to do so. What if Yang Yurong feels bad about not having emptied them? Or what if Mrs Cao tells others what a bad host Yang Yurong is, forcing the foreign guest to take out the garbage?

This reminds me of something else: the first time Li Wei and I stayed with Yang Yurong, I broke the plastic toilet seat. I must have sat on it too heavily and my weight was uneven. I broke one hinge and a great big crack appeared along one side. I was too embarrassed to say anything. Eventually, Yang Yurong saw for herself and asked me about it.

I blushed and stammered.

'It's not your fault,' she said quickly. 'The seat was poorly made. We weren't expecting to have guests up there when we bought it. We just got the cheapest one we could find. I'm so sorry.'

She spent ages fixing the seat, binding it with strips of rag, wound over and over, all the way around. She was proud of her work and I was very happy. It made the seat comfier. But Wu Jianfu said it looked shoddy and he'd have to buy a new seat. Then, for three years, he did nothing about it. It's only this year that he got around to it. The day after he got back for the New Year, he drove Yang Yurong into Red River and, while she was in the supermarket, he went to buy a new toilet seat. He bought the best available but complained that it was still no good.

---

4   To avoid blocking the plumbing, villagers put toilet paper in a bin rather than flushing it down the toilet.

Yang Yurong told Li Wei and me all this: 'He should've gone to Xin County City. I told him that, but he said it was too much trouble. Even though we have the car now.' She shook her head in disgust.

*

We ate homemade *jiaozi* (dumplings) for breakfast this morning. They were the last of a batch made on the sixth and stored in Yang Yurong's big freezer. *Jiaozi* are eaten throughout the New Year period. Some say that's because they're similar in shape to the gold and silver ingots used as currency in imperial times. They're symbols of wealth. Others say it's because the circles of dough with which *jiaozi* are made symbolise family reunion and togetherness.

This batch was filled with egg and shepherd's purse. Yang Yurong had taken Li Wei and me to pick the shepherd's purse the day before. This is the best time to pick it, she told us. After the fifteenth, it flowers and goes to seed.

We picked it from the roadside and the edges of the vegetable patches on the hill. It thrives there because Popo and her neighbours use plenty of fertiliser. 'Shepherd's purse likes lots of fertiliser,' Yang Yurong said. 'That's one thing the old folk have over us: they don't have flush toilets, so they have urine for fertiliser. Of course, Aunty Gao has chicken poo and Old Liu has duck poo, too.'

I had trouble identifying the shepherd's purse. So afterwards, Yang Yurong had to sort through the basket to make sure there weren't other weeds mixed in. Did that irritate her? Or did she smile to herself, recalling my clumsy delight in foraging?

She made a huge bowl of stuffing before breakfast on the sixth and that afternoon her sister-in-law and her daughter came round to help wrap the *jiaozi*. Yang Yurong rolled out the dough on the dining table and cut it into circles. The others spooned stuffing onto each circle, folded up the sides and squeezed the top between thumb and forefinger. They gently lined up the finished little crescents on a tray, ready for boiling.

Li Wei and I were sitting on the couch, typing up fieldnotes. Yang Yurong called for us to join them. Li Wei declined, but I jumped up. Yang Yurong grinned at me and I grinned back. I'm no better at wrapping *jiaozi* than

I am at picking shepherd's purse. But I love the camaraderie of *jiaozi*-making parties: the banter and laughter, even the other women's good-natured jokes about my misshapen *jiaozi*.

'Ignore them,' Yang Yurong says. 'Different places have different-shaped *jiaozi*.'

*

Wu Jianfu was the last one up this morning. That's normal; he usually emerges long after the rest of us have started breakfast. Once at the table, he sits in sullen silence, snapping occasionally at Baoli opposite and watching his wife, Li Wei and me from the corner of his eye. Renkai, by his side, is quiet. I'm conscious of being an interloper at family times like these. But perhaps Wu Jianfu feels the same. Perhaps he listens to us women chattering and feels like *he's* the interloper. In his own home.

This morning, Yang Yurong was telling Li Wei and me about all the meat she'd bought for the festive period: 30 kilograms of pork, 5 kilograms of mutton and 5 of beef, 10 ducks and 10 chickens. The only thing she didn't buy was fish; they received silver carp from the hamlet pond. A week before the start of every New Year, the fish are taken out and distributed among residents. Each person was given 1.5 kilograms this year. The pond has grass carp, too, but not enough to give to everyone. So, if you want them, you must pay at the market price. Yang Yurong doesn't bother.

Wu Jianfu joined the conversation. He said the money goes to buy more fish fry to stock the pond for the coming year. But Yang Yurong snorted. 'Most of it stays in the hamlet head's pocket,' she said.

Wu Jianfu frowned at his bowl of *jiaozi*.

Yang Yurong said her sister bought mutton and beef in Xin County City for her, but she bought the pork from Fang Wenli, her friend down the road, who keeps 20 pigs in a shed. The ducks came from Old Liu and the chickens from her uncle in Deng Inn. She bought roosters, because they're cheaper than hens. Her uncle killed them and brought them over and she plucked them.

'It's much better to buy meat from villagers, you know,' she said. 'You can't trust what's in the stores. It isn't always fresh and it's full of chemicals. You can taste the difference, can't you?'

Li Wei and I nodded dutifully.

But that got us talking about how few people raise animals nowadays. In fact, over in Twin Maidens Shrine it is forbidden. That rule came in after they cleaned up the hamlet for the Construction of a Beautiful Countryside campaign. Here in Ginkgo Hamlet, Old Liu has his ducks and Fang Wenli has her pigs. Some of the old folk, like Aunty Gao, keep a handful of chickens and a few have a pig. But that's about it. Only eight families in the whole village keep a water buffalo. It's much the same in Deng Inn; Yang Yurong's uncle has 30 chickens, but that's unusual. The state has introduced a two-year subsidy to encourage animal husbandry, but it's not working.

'No-one wants to raise animals anymore,' Yang Yurong said. 'We've stopped growing grain. We'd have to buy feed if we wanted to keep chickens and pigs. It's not worth it. And even if you're still growing rice, you're better off hiring someone to do the ploughing with a tractor. So, there's no point keeping a water buffalo.' She got up to clear away the breakfast dishes.

Wu Jianfu was fully awake by then. He took over. He said the animals' disappearance was a sign of modernisation and launched into a lecture about how fast the village was changing. I saw Yang Yurong's eyes lift skywards as she reached for my bowl. I struggled to keep a straight face. Li Wei was listening intently. Or pretending to. We both appreciate Wu Jianfu's engagement with our research and often his analysis is extremely helpful. This morning, though, he wasn't telling us anything we didn't already know.

Renkai and Baoli had long since left the table and Yang Yurong was coughing and clearing her throat. Li Wei and I were getting restless. But we felt compelled to stay put, listening politely to Wu Jianfu. We didn't want to hurt his feelings.

Then suddenly, I thought of Aunty Gao's rooster, strutting with his proud red comb and his black and green tail feathers. I waited for Wu Jianfu to finish his sentence and looked over to Yang Yurong. 'How come Aunty Gao's rooster is still alive? Why didn't she kill it for the New Year?'

Yang Yurong stood for a moment, bowls in hand. She shrugged. 'Maybe she didn't need to.'

Wu Jianfu's chair scraped loudly on the tiled floor. He left the table. Yang Yurong ignored him.

'Aunty Gao has probably had fewer visitors to feed than us,' she said.

***

Wu Jianfu doesn't always get up late. Take New Year's Eve, for example. He got up well before dawn, so he could take Li Wei and me, as well as his sons, to burn incense and sacrifice to the gods and ancestors at Popo's old house. We set out in the half-light, while Aunty Gao's rooster was still crowing. The bare paddy fields wore coats of sparkly white.

Popo was waiting for us in the front room, with the sacrificial fatty pork simmering on her portable gas burner. Wu Jianfu explained that his mother doesn't get involved in the rituals themselves.

Li Wei nodded. 'Women don't perform the ancestral rituals—only men do,' she said.

'Except if the men are away,' Wu Jianfu corrected her. 'It's okay for women to take men's place if they need to.'

Wu Jianfu began the rituals by arranging the bowls of sacrificial food and liquor on the altar. He explained each step as he went and Li Wei and I took notes. In between two large decorated red candles, he put out three sets of bowls: one set for the ancestors in the middle, another for the Stove God to the east and a third for the God of Wealth to the west. Each set included a slab of fatty pork with a pair of chopsticks stuck in it, a bowl with *doufu* and another with fish. At the back, he put cups of liquor and, in front, he lined up nine bowls of rice: three each for the ancestors and the two gods. In front of the rice, he put three sticks of incense, each stuck in a small bowl of sand. The Earth God in the cabinet underneath the altar also received incense, sacrificial food and liquor.

Next, Wu Jianfu told Renkai to go outside and set off one big firework cake[5] and a couple of firecracker sticks. Li Wei and I stood in the doorway with our fingers in our ears. There were others setting off firecrackers, too: the sky was lit up and the hills were echoing with whizzes and crackles and pops. Baoli was hopping around like a flea. Renkai had to hold him back. Li Wei and I were stamping our feet in the cold and cupping our gloves over our mouths. You could see our breath leaking out.

---

5   A firework cake is a box containing multiple tubes of explosive. When the cake is lit, it produces a barrage of shots, one after another.

Plate 9.2 Family altar with New Year sacrifices
Photo: Tamara Jacka, 2018.

After we'd all gone back inside, Wu Jianfu and his sons burnt spirit-money in a pile on the floor. Renkai used his dad's cigarette lighter to get the flames going. They had a stock of the coarse yellow spirit-money already prepared.

With the flames still bright before them, Wu Jianfu, followed by his sons, knelt and kowtowed, turning to each of the three positions on the altar in turn, and then to the Earth God underneath. Baoli looked like a little frog, grinning and bobbing up and down on the cold floor. Wu Jianfu then used his cigarette lighter to light the incense sticks on the altar and underneath, inside the cabinet. We stood for a moment, breathing in the woody fragrance.

'There are rules about lighting incense at New Year,' Wu Jianfu said, turning to Li Wei and me. 'According to custom, you must change the incense every hour. You do that every day for three days between New Year's Eve and the second day of the New Year. You light it again between the thirteenth and fifteenth days. You must always burn an odd number of rounds. In the past, most people burnt seven or nine rounds each day.'

He watched me screwing up my face, trying to follow.

'Are you really going to change it that often?' Li Wei asked. She did that thing of tucking her hair behind her ear and tilting her head.

He laughed. 'People aren't so particular nowadays. Most of us light no more than three rounds. Some light only one.'

Afterwards, Popo walked home with us and we all had breakfast together. Congee that morning, with mung beans. Wu Jianfu's favourite. While we were eating, I asked Popo whether villagers practised the ancestral rituals during the collective era. She smiled and said they did until the Cultural Revolution.

Wu Jianfu felt the need to elaborate: 'My father told me there'd always be three sets of sacrifice set out. Each set would include a piece of meat, a bowl of fruit and a bowl of *ciba* [glutinous rice cake]. Sometimes there'd be other things as well.'

His mother interrupted him: 'It wasn't fresh fruit. Usually, it was just a bit of dried melon. And the meat wasn't real—we used a piece of wood painted red. Villagers were too poor to have real meat. Some put a pig's head and tail on the altar to symbolise a pig. But no-one could afford a whole pig.'

'What about during the Cultural Revolution?' I asked her. 'Did your husband perform the ancestral rituals then?'

'You tell them.' She turned to Wu Jianfu.

He slurped his congee: 'My father didn't dare hang the ancestral scroll. He hid it and put a poster of Chairman Mao in its place. He didn't sacrifice to the gods and ancestors either. But he still burnt spirit-money and incense. He did it in secret at night. I was very little—I turned five in 1978—but I still remember him burning the spirit-money. He tried to shoo me away, but I hung in the doorway. I remember the flames.'

'*Ba* [Dad],' Renkai said to his father, 'did you have firecrackers when you were a kid?'

Baoli, sulking over his untouched congee, lifted his head.

Wu Jianfu told the boys there were string firecrackers and sticks, but not everyone could afford them. And the string firecrackers were different. Today's have hundreds of little red firecrackers strung together. When he was a kid, each firecracker was bigger, but there were only 20 or 50 on a string. He and his sisters were given a string to share between them at New Year. It was a special treat. They picked off all the firecrackers and lit them one at a time. It wasn't until the mid 1990s, just before Renkai was born, that they began to set off whole strings at once.

'What about firework cakes?' Baoli asked him.

Wu Jianfu shook his head. 'We didn't get them till the mid 2000s—just before *you* were born.'

*

New Year's Day was devoted to receiving guests and visiting relatives around the village. The day began with a bunch of youngsters coming over at eight in the morning to receive *hongbao* (small red paper packets containing gifts of cash) from Yang Yurong. Each kid was given 10 yuan (US$1.50). She said that was the standard amount for children, though close relatives sometimes paid more. Their grandfather gave Renkai and Baoli 100 yuan (US$15) each. Yang Yurong took the money from Baoli but let Renkai keep his.

'Do you give *hongbao* to adults, too?' Li Wei asked.

Yang Yurong nodded. 'Nowadays, we do. We give 200 yuan[6] or so to close relatives.'

We had a late breakfast of *jiaozi* that day. Afterwards, Wu Jianfu took me and Li Wei with him on his visits to his Wu relatives across the village. We set off on foot, but a short way up the hill, Wu Jianfu saw that other visitors had come by car. So, we had to hurry home to fetch his own vehicle. I confess, it was more comfortable being carried in a car than trekking up and down the hills. But it made Li Wei and me nervous, sitting in such a hulk, with a beginner driver navigating those narrow, winding roads.

Baoli and Renkai went separately, joining a big gang of kids and teenagers, roaming from house to house. They intersected with us from time to time. Baoli was grabbing sweets, mandarins and peanuts from the plates each woman had set out for guests. He shoved them into the big plastic bag he was carrying, grinning from ear to ear.

In most places, women and children were the only ones at home; all the men were out visiting. Wu Jianfu, Li Wei and I found Baoli in one house, sitting with a gaggle of other boys playing games on their smartphones. Wu Jianfu got angry and pulled him away. Walking out, he turned to Li Wei and me. He disapproved of Baoli having a phone and said he wished Yang Yurong wouldn't let him spend so much time playing games. 'It'll affect his grades at school, especially once he starts secondary school.'[7]

I sympathised. 'When my son was Baoli's age, I struggled with him over the same thing,' I said.

Outside, we joined the knots of men standing around, stamping their feet in the cold, exchanging cigarettes and sharing news: who had married, who had a baby, who had just come back from working overseas. A few times, Renkai had to come over to his dad to ask for a man's name and how to address him, but Wu Jianfu wasn't always able to answer. He wasn't even sure, in some cases, whether a particular house belonged to a relative or not. 'So many of us work away from home,' he said. 'We hardly know each other. It's good to come back each New Year and get reacquainted.'

*

---

6   US$30.
7   This is a common concern among parents and grandparents of school-age children. Smartphones are banned by local schools but used by children at home.

According to custom, men devote the second day of the New Year to visiting their maternal uncles. Maternal uncles play a central role in the extended family, Wu Jianfu explained. His maternal uncle died some years ago. But in the morning, he paid a visit to the deceased man's family. Meanwhile, Renkai and Baoli made the long walk to Deng Inn to visit Yang Yurong's older brother.

Back at home, Yang Yurong was busy preparing an afternoon banquet for the families of Wu Jianfu's three older sisters—put on so his nephews could wish Wu Jianfu a happy New Year. The sisters themselves didn't come, but their husbands, children and grandchildren did. Popo came, too, and Yang Yurong invited her older brother's son and his wife, who was nursing a baby boy. Altogether, 20 adults and four children came barrelling through the door, bearing red gift bags of liquor, cigarettes and sweets. Yang Yurong set up an extra table in the front room to accommodate everybody.

After a large, rambunctious meal, several guests left and the rest of us retired to the couch and armchairs. Some cooed over the baby boy. Others used their smartphones to send each other digital *hongbao*. It's a game, the rules of which are that each person can send between five and 10 *hongbao*, with 5 to 50 yuan (US$0.75–7.50) in each. The person who receives the most *hongbao* must send an additional one to someone else. There was no chatting between the players. They all had their heads down, their thumbs and fingers darting. Every now and again they'd call out, urging one another on. I watched wide-eyed, marvelling at this technological transformation of gift exchanges.

***

Over the next few days, Li Wei and I mostly went out by ourselves in the mornings and afternoons. But we came home for our meals and spent the afternoon rest periods and evenings with the family. After lunch, we sat in the front room and plied Wu Jianfu with questions about his life as a migrant labourer. We asked about his living and working conditions in Beijing, his wages and his costs in the city. He didn't seem to want to talk about these things and I couldn't help feeling we were asking the wrong questions. Something was eluding us.

One afternoon, I asked him about urbanites' discrimination against migrant labourers and the exploitation they face. 'I know it was terrible at the beginning of the 2000s,' I said. 'Has there been any improvement since?'

Wu Jianfu glanced up at me. 'It's not as bad as it was.' He ran a hand through his hair. 'But Beijingers are snobs. You get used to it.' He paused. 'Anyway, there's more to a labourer's life than that.' He lapsed into silence.

'What else is there?' Li Wei said gently. 'Can you tell us about it?'

He frowned and looked at his slippers. 'You wouldn't understand.'

Li Wei and I said nothing.

Wu Jianfu leant forward for the pack of cigarettes lying on the glass tea table. He stood, flicked his lighter at the cigarette in his mouth and plodded to the front door. 'Goin' for a smoke,' he mumbled. He went out to the courtyard, carefully shutting the door behind him. Li Wei and I didn't follow.

That evening, we sat in the front room with Wu Jianfu once more. I'd been thinking over what he said about us not understanding. I told him about my brother, Marcus. 'He's a carpenter. He builds tables and chairs. He says he gets great satisfaction from making things.'

Wu Jianfu and Li Wei looked up.

'Do you get that feeling, too, when you're doing the interior work on an apartment?' I asked Wu Jianfu. 'That feeling of satisfaction?'

He gave a brief smile. 'Sometimes. Like when there's a tricky bit of plastering and I get it just right.' He paused and looked down again. 'But it's not like working for yourself; there's no freedom. And it's hard work. You just push through each day.'

'It's not all about the work, though,' he said after another long pause. 'You relax with your mates at night. Have a smoke or a drink together. Play poker.' He let out a long sigh.

He looked forlorn, sitting there with his head down, kneading his hands— like a soldier home on leave, I said to Li Wei later. He's worked away from home his whole adult life, but he still doesn't belong in the city and he doesn't belong here.

She nodded thoughtfully.

Previously, Wu Jianfu had said that when he's too old for migrant labour he'll return to Ginkgo Village. Others retire to Xin County City, but he doesn't want to live there; it's not as pleasant. I wonder about that now. How will he readjust to village life?[8]

*

Wu Jianfu doesn't always seem such a fish out of water. Nor am I always conscious of such a gap between him and Li Wei and me. Sometimes, it's like we've been friends for decades. I'll give you an example.

After dinner one evening, Li Wei and I again went with Wu Jianfu and Renkai to light the incense at Popo's old house. We sat with Popo around the woodstove for a bit, chatting companionably. Then Wu Jianfu got up and started rummaging in a battered old wooden cabinet at the back of the room. He rifled through the contents of each drawer in turn.

'What are you after?' Popo said.

He didn't respond. 'Aha, got it!' he cried, pulling out a small tin box. The edges of the lid were rusting. Inside were three sheets of thin, worn paper, neatly folded. Two were charts indicating the property his family received during land reform, stamped by the county government and dated 1952. The other sheet was dated the twenty-ninth year of the Republic (1940). It set out the division of property among Wu Jianfu's grandfather and his three brothers. They had 2 mu (1,300 square metres) between them. Wu Jianfu gingerly handed each fragile sheet to Li Wei, and she, Renkai and I stood with our heads together, poring over them. Popo looked up from her old, worn couch. She gave us a little shake of her head and an indulgent smile.

'Have you got your camera?' Wu Jianfu said to me. 'Take a picture!'

'You should, too,' I said, reaching into my daypack. 'Use your phone. These are valuable historical documents.'

He nodded. 'Yeah, I should claim the land,' he joked. 'Or sell these papers!'

---

8   Wu Jianfu's 'retirement' came earlier than he anticipated. During the Covid-19 pandemic, rural migrant labourers were severely affected by travel restrictions and declines in industry. The construction industry, already slumping before the pandemic, was particularly badly hit. Wu Jianfu spent half of 2020 and most of 2021 and 2022 in Ginkgo Village. He was able to find only short-term casual jobs around Red River.

When we got back, Yang Yurong and Baoli were snuggled together on the couch, playing a noisy game on their phones. Every minute or two, there'd be clangs and explosions and cries of frustration.

Wu Jianfu poured tea for us before taking an armchair. He sat scowling at his wife. Renkai wandered away. Li Wei squeezed in next to Baoli and I sat in the other armchair and settled into typing up my fieldnotes. But I couldn't concentrate with the noise that Yang Yurong and Baoli were making. I perched on the arm of the couch next to Yang Yurong and asked her to show me how to play. It was a simple game, but I was too slow. I gave up after a while.

Then Wu Jianfu asked whether I wanted to watch TV and I said yes. The others moved so he and I could sit next to each other on the couch. Li Wei sat in an armchair with her laptop. Yang Yurong and Baoli left the room. Wu Jianfu put on a serial called *Ordinary World*, set in a village in China's north-west in the 1970s and 1980s. It's based on the novel of the same name. When he was in junior secondary school, Wu Jianfu said, his teacher gave him the first volume to read. Sadly, the teacher didn't have the second or third volumes.[9]

We both watched avidly, leaning forward with our elbows on our knees, mugs of tea and plates of melon seeds and mandarins in front of us, the radiator under the tea table warming our legs.

Wu Jianfu pointed out details of the characters' poverty-stricken lives. He was just like the protagonist, Sun Shaoping, he said. And his life was just like his. 'Only I didn't yearn to eat a white *mantou* like he did. I just dreamed of a great big bowl of steaming white rice.' He reached for some melon seeds. 'And see that metal washbowl? We didn't have one like that till the late 1980s. Before that, we just had wooden bowls, made by the local carpenter.'

I asked when plastic washbowls came in and he had to think about it.

'They would've had them in the city in the 1980s. But we didn't get them in the village till the 1990s. I brought one back from Beijing after my first year there. That would've been for the New Year, 1992. It was a gift for my mother.'

---

9   The novel *Ordinary World* (*Pingfan de Shijie*) by Lu Yao was published in 1986. The TV serial has 56 episodes and first screened in 2015.

We watched a few episodes and then sat drinking tea and munching melon seeds. Yang Yurong and the boys had gone to bed by then and Li Wei was still typing her fieldnotes. Wu Jianfu became nostalgic about his childhood. I asked what his earliest memory was. When he was four or five, he said, he and one of his older sisters were given the job of gathering up the just-harvested hemp stalks floating in the river. They'd been left in the water so their outer layer would rot away. His mother used the inner fibres to make rope. He and his sister waded barefoot into the mud to pull in the hemp and straight away were surrounded by swarms of little fish. They turned this way and that in glee, trying to catch the fish in their cupped hands. By the time they got home, their shirts and trousers—the only clothes they owned—were covered with mud and slime.

I asked how their mother reacted. 'She probably beat us,' he said. 'I've forgotten. I just remember the fish flashing in the water and my sister laughing and splashing me.' He sighed. 'Those were the days.'

We sat hunched close to the radiator, warming our hands around our mugs of tea. I said I was nostalgic about my childhood, too.

***

On the thirteenth, Li Wei and I joined the family to go see the evening Dragon Parade in Red River Township. The six of us squeezed into the car and Wu Jianfu drove us there. That was a mistake. We set out straight after lunch, but even so, there were so many people and cars on the road, we could only inch forward at a snail's pace. Eventually, Wu Jianfu parked the car on the outskirts of the township and led us on foot the rest of the way.

We walked through Red River and all the way up the tree-covered hill on the other side. From there, we had a fine view of the dragons going down the hill and along the main street. They moved slowly. By the time they'd reached the township centre, it was dark.

There were four long dragons. The two bigger ones had red and black spines and were covered with multicoloured stripes and swirls. They were held up by several young men. The other two, with smaller heads and blue bodies covered with yellow spots and spines, were held up by children. The biggest dragon at the front of the parade was accompanied by a band of older men beating drums and clashing cymbals. A stream of little kids marched on each side, carrying pink paper lanterns strung together with a red rope.

Li Wei and I thought the dragons were glorious, but Wu Jianfu was disappointed. In the past, he said, villagers made the dragons themselves and poured their hearts into the job. But for the past decade or so, they'd been bought in a store. 'They're nowhere near as good,' he said. 'They're too thin and the decorations are so crude.'

But even Wu Jianfu was infected by the parade's excitement. So many people were out. Even the lads in their twenties were there, hanging out in gangs, chewing gum and yelling and pointing. The whole of Red River was so choked with men, women and children, we could hardly move. We crawled for hours down the street behind the dragons, the air thick with the acrid smoke of the firecrackers exploding all around us.

Once in the centre of Red River, the two largest dragons stopped to dance in the quadrangle in front of the township's government offices. Music played on loudspeakers, the drummers beat their drums and the dragons whirled and twisted in time to the beat.

Over dinner afterwards, Wu Jianfu told Li Wei that the government sponsors the dragons each year as a way of supporting local culture. They provide 10,000 yuan (US$1,500) for each dragon, which is why they perform in front of the government offices. They also dance in front of a few private houses—those belonging to the wealthiest residents, who also sponsor the dragons. It brings high status to have the dragons perform for you, so the wealthy are willing to pay a large sum for the privilege. It costs 1,000 yuan (US$150) for one measly paper dragon that's going to be paraded for just one night on the thirteenth. You also get to have it dance again in front of your house on the night of the fifteenth, but then it's destroyed on a bonfire and 'sent back to Heaven' on the night of the sixteenth.[10] And you don't just pay for the dragons; you must provide the drummers with cigarettes and liquor and hand out juice-boxes, biscuits and sweets to the kids. What's more, you're not allowed to pay for only one New Year; you must cough up for three New Years in a row.

'It's such a waste of money,' Wu Jianfu said.

I didn't have dinner with the others after the Dragon Parade. By seven o'clock, the noise and fumes from the firecrackers had given me a nasty headache and I felt queasy. Yang Yurong made me sit on the kerb, next to

---

10   'Sending the dragons back to Heaven' (*song long shang tian*) is the last New Year ritual.

a spindly ginkgo tree. She and Li Wei sat, too, and Renkai hung around, looking worried. Fortunately, by then, we weren't too far from where we'd started. Wu Jianfu pushed through the crowd and back to the car. Then he managed to drive a bit closer, down a side street, so I didn't need to walk so far.

Once home, I just wanted to sit on the couch. I didn't want dinner and I didn't want to go back out to see the lion dance. Yang Yurong stayed behind with me and the rest went without us. We'd gone to bed by the time they returned.

*

Yesterday was another long day and it didn't start well. Firecrackers had been going off since midnight, so none of us had much sleep. Li Wei and I got up before dawn, ready to go with Wu Jianfu again to Popo's house for the sacrifice to the ancestors. But he and his sons slept in and Yang Yurong had to drag them out of bed. It put her in a bad mood and meant we were running late the whole day.

For breakfast afterwards, Yang Yurong had prepared the customary large meal. She'd made hotpot with meatballs and vegetables. But we didn't eat much; there wasn't time. Wu Jianfu drove us to the God of Wealth shrine, half an hour's drive west of Ginkgo Village. It's only a small shrine, but it was recently renovated, with a shiny 2-metre high statue of the God of Wealth installed inside. Yang Yurong and I went in to burn incense, while the others stayed outside and set off a firecracker cake. Yang Yurong wouldn't let Li Wei into the shrine because she had her period; she said that made Li Wei unclean.

When we came out, Yang Yurong and the boys went looking for firewood. Wu Jianfu explained that was because the word for firewood, *chai*, sounded like the word for wealth, *cai*. 'So, Yang Yurong thinks we'll get rich by collecting firewood around the shrine to the God of Wealth. She's so superstitious!' He laughed.

Yang Yurong came back to the car with a bundle of small twigs tucked under one arm, grasping one long, fat branch in the other hand. The branch was too big to fit in the car and Wu Jianfu looked tempted to throw it away. But he didn't dare. Instead, he made a joke about them becoming billionaires. He propped one end against a rock and jumped on the branch to snap it in half so he could squeeze the two pieces into the boot.

I couldn't help chuckling. I asked Yang Yurong, 'When you break the branch in half, does that halve your wealth or do you get twice as much?'

She laughed and said it made no difference. We all laughed with her.

After that, we visited the Purple Dragon shrine. It sits at the top of a long, steep hill just east of Deng Inn. Wu Jianfu drove us to the foot of the hill and we walked the rest of the way. It took us almost an hour to puff and pant to the top.

We were very late. Hundreds of villagers had been arriving at the shrine since before dawn, but we didn't even start climbing until midmorning. As we made our way up the narrow, rocky path, we had to give way to a steady stream of people coming down.

Many of the old women recognised Li Wei and me. They'd see us from up the hill and call out. Then, as they came alongside, they'd clasp my hands and say, 'It's so good to see you here. Keep going—not much further now.' But there were others—migrant workers—who had heard nothing about us. They were whispering and pointing at the *laowai*.[11]

Neither Wu Jianfu nor Yang Yurong had visited the Purple Dragon shrine before. It's just a rough, low-roofed stone building with a single narrow room with statuettes lined up on a shelf. Several people were jostling to get in, so Wu Jianfu stayed outside. Yang Yurong and I tried to squeeze in, but we couldn't get close enough to see which gods the statuettes were.

To one side of the shrine, there's a spring, with water welling up in a pool. Yang Yurong said the water has healing properties. As a child, she'd heard of people climbing the hill to drink the spring water. But she thinks the shrine itself was not built until the 1990s. Since then, crowds of villagers have visited each year. It's said that if you pray to the gods inside, all your problems will be solved.

'Don't drink the water,' warned Wu Jianfu. 'Think of all those dirty hands being plunged in. See all those people milling about? They're washing their hands and faces, but they're not actually drinking.'

11　An informal, sometimes derogatory term for 'foreigner'.

On the other side of the shrine, a shrunken old man sat on the ground, surrounded by villagers having their fortune told with divination sticks. I wanted to go over, but Yang Yurong said we didn't have time; we had to go home for lunch.

Squeezed into the backseat of the car on the way back, I asked Renkai next to me whether he'd ever had his fortune told. He described the time he went with his parents: he and his dad were told their future would be excellent, but his poor mum only got 'okay'.

Wu Jianfu let out a guffaw. 'The one person who really believes that stuff and she got the worst reading!' he called out. 'They never say your future will be bad; they'd lose customers if they did that. It's only ever excellent, good or okay.'

I couldn't see Yang Yurong's reaction. She was sitting in the front passenger seat with Baoli on her lap in his green puffer jacket. She had her head turned to the window.

We didn't get home till one o'clock. By then, Popo, along with Wu Jianfu's older sister, his nephew and his nephew's wife, were standing outside the gate waiting for us. Yang Yurong snapped at Popo when she asked why we were so late.

Lunch was hotpot with meatballs again, followed by bowls of delicate, mouth-watering *yuanxiao* (soft, sweet glutinous rice balls) filled with black sesame seed paste.[12]

Wu Jianfu's nephew said that New Year would be quite different in the future. The Xin County Government was planning to ban fireworks because of the danger and air pollution.

'What?! They can't do that!' Baoli cried out.

Yang Yurong was also dismayed, but Wu Jianfu approved.[13]

*

---

12 *Yuanxiao* are filled with a variety of pastes and served in a light syrup. The balls are eaten on the fifteenth day of the first lunar month because their round shape symbolises family reunion as well as the first full moon of the year. Meatballs are eaten for the same reason.

13 The ban didn't come into effect in 2019. Then, in 2020, all New Year festivities were cancelled because of the Covid-19 pandemic. In 2021, they resumed, but on a much smaller scale. Fireworks were banned that year.

After lunch, Popo went home and the rest of us walked to the Wu family cemetery for the Lantern Festival. It's just as well we walked rather than drove. Near the cemetery, the road narrows with mud and slush on either side. A few cars had tried to drive off the road and park there. One van was stuck in the mud and tilting over, alarmingly close to the cliff edge. As we approached, we saw a crowd of villagers surrounding the van. Some of the men were trying to use logs to lever it out of the mud and its spinning wheels were splattering them.

From inside the cemetery, fireworks were going off and the sky was a riot of noise, smoke and colour. Children were darting and jumping about and screaming hysterically. Baoli made a dash towards the van, yelling to a schoolmate he'd seen, but Renkai grabbed him by his jacket and jerked him to a halt, cuffing him over the head as he did so.

Wu Jianfu hastily moved us on, past the giant bronze incense holder at the front of the cemetery. It held several burning sticks and was surrounded by the blasted rubbish of spent firecrackers and the plastic bags in which they'd been carried. Other Wu men had already placed little battery-driven fake candles on top of the tombstones of their deceased fathers, grandfathers and other predecessors. They were burning incense and spirit-money in front of the tombstones and setting off firecrackers. Women and children were wandering around, on the lookout for their friends. Wu Jianfu asked me to stop taking photos of the tombstones. 'It's disrespectful,' he said with a frown.

He'd brought along a large knife, which he used to hack the grass and weeds away from his father's and grandfather's tombstones. It took a while. The rest of us stood watching, as he and Renkai put their fake candles on the tombstones, burnt some spirit-money and kowtowed before them. Then they set off a firecracker cake nearby. It had grown dark by then and a cold wind had blown up. Most of the other villagers had already left.

Wu Jianfu stayed standing by his father's grave, but the rest of us set off for home. We made our way down the road in the moonlight. Yang Yurong took the lead, striding along with Baoli skipping beside her. Renkai, Li Wei and I lagged. We turned and looked back at Wu Jianfu. The full moon hung like a new coin, crisp and bright above him. He stood there in the stinging wind, looking out over Ginkgo Village. What was he thinking, I wondered?

***

Now it's late afternoon the next day. I've been waiting in Wuhan's Tianhe International Airport, Terminal 3, for the past two and a half hours.

Wu Jianfu drove Renkai, Li Wei and me to Wuhan. Renkai is going back to university. Wu Jianfu himself will leave the village soon and return to work in Beijing. He wants to get a ticket for the high-speed train. It's expensive, he said, but so much faster than the ordinary one. He'd like to try it.[14]

I'm sitting at Gate 29, jotting down a few last fieldnotes and watching the people around me: families with bulging, multicoloured luggage and roly-poly kids munching snacks; a few slouching businessmen glued to their smartphones; a young woman with high heels and a figure-hugging dress. One other foreigner leans against a wall—a redheaded white guy with a daypack like mine. Probably a student.

Li Wei's flight boarded an hour ago. She's flying to Shenyang to visit her parents for a week, before returning to Australia. I'm flying home to Canberra via Guangzhou and Sydney. I have a long night ahead of me.

This will be my last stay in Ginkgo Village,[15] although I don't know that yet. Over the past few days, Li Wei and I have been eagerly planning another visit, returning for the New Year festivities next year. 'Will you pick us up from Wuhan again?' we asked Wu Jianfu in the car coming here.

'Of course!' he said with a laugh.

Boarding has just been announced. It's time to put away my notebook and pen. Time to hoist my daypack onto my shoulders once more.

---

14 The Xinyang–Beijing high-speed train takes four to five hours. The slow train takes 10–14 hours.
15 See the Appendix.

Epilogue

Early each morning, before the sun sneaks through my timber venetian blinds, I wake to the sound of Bob the rooster next door. I'm tucked in my cosy bed in my cosy suburban Canberra home, when suddenly the calm is rent apart.

I could complain; I'd be well within my rights. But my neighbour has told me Bob's story. He came in a batch of chicks and she couldn't tell he was different from the others. He's named after her favourite uncle. 'I'll have him put down if he's too loud,' she said.

I quickly demurred and shook my head. 'No, no,' I said, 'I like the sound.'

It's true. I pull my quilt up over my ears and imagine I'm back in Ginkgo Village. It's Aunty Gao's rooster I can hear. His crowing is coming to me across the paddy fields. Yang Yurong is in the kitchen and soon a warm *jiaozi* smell will drift up to me.

I imagine myself getting up, crossing to the window and looking over the paddy fields to the tree-covered hillside beyond. Everything's soft and foggy. There's a path running halfway up the hill and a dark old house. A ribbon of smoke rising from a chimney. I can just make out Aunty Gao, shuffling about in her yard. I can't see her rooster, but I know he's there.

I hear Bob and, in my mind's eye, I conjure the whole of Ginkgo Village. I see the old house across the paddy fields and smell the woodsmoke. I see the rooster and the hens pecking in the dirt and stooped old Aunty Gao feeding them. She'll beckon me into her home and I'll see the family altar and a small wooden stool. Or I imagine the paddy fields. I see a sinewy, bare-chested man, trousers rolled up, wading through the mud with a water buffalo and plough. Time stops. A stillness settles around me.

I get so mired in nostalgia,[1] I mix up everything. I lie in bed with tears in my eyes. My son's grown up and left home, I can't go back to Ginkgo Village and everywhere is climate change, disease, malevolence, war. Nostalgia is a refuge from rage and despair. I burrow deeper under my quilt.

But Bob is loud. He's not over the other side of the paddy fields. He's next door, just a small backyard and a falling-down fence between us. I feel restless and uneasy. My head aches. I long to share my story with you, but how?

'A rooster at dawn, a cold foggy morning, a thin trail of smoke rising from a chimney …'

'Is that all?' I imagine Yang Yurong cutting in. She stares. 'So much time you've spent in my house, so many questions you've asked,' she says. 'Even now you pester me for details. Did you get my WeChat message last night? What's the point of telling you things if this is all you write? Anyone could write that—it could be anywhere.'

Bob the rooster persists. I rage at him and at myself. I try to remember all the things that make Ginkgo Village real and not a thin sentimental fairytale. Like the fact that Aunty Gao is a nasty gossip, who's losing her marbles. And her house is a dump.

Yang Yurong's house is no cosy cottage either. And she doesn't have a rooster or even hens. Nor do her neighbours. In fact, there may be no more chickens in Ginkgo Village than in my Canberra suburb. And that paddy field? The first year Li Wei and I visited, I took pictures of a man out there with his water buffalo and plough. But later, the field lay abandoned. By 2018, it was full of dead weeds.

As the light grows, Bob finally stops crowing and the white cockatoos start to screech. I must get up. I feel sad and guilty going about my morning routine. Why do I have such a sentimental image of Ginkgo Village stuck in my head? It's not a new thing; even when I was in the village, it sometimes felt like a fairytale. Like when Li Wei and I stood by the pine tree in Old Pine Hamlet. It was all so wondrous I couldn't get over it.

---

1   My critique of nostalgia is inspired by Johannes Fabian, *Time and the Other: How Anthropology Makes its Object* (New York: Columbia University Press, 1983); and Svetlana Boym, *The Future of Nostalgia* (New York: Basic Books, 2001).

China is changing at a dizzying pace. It's what interests me most. Yet, in Ginkgo Village, something kept pulling me towards the exotic, the ancient, the different; towards long-held or revived traditions; to those faint traces of the lost or almost lost. Now I see it in my photographs: roadside shrines and paddy fields, a loom, a spinning wheel, a water buffalo pulling a harrow.

I took far fewer pictures of the modern and new. The only thing I photographed inside Yang Yurong's house was the kitchen with its traditional, wood-fuelled stove. I didn't bother with the couch, the chandelier and the enormous flat-screen TV in the living room. Or the carport with its roller door or the monster of a car—all the things in which Yang Yurong and Wu Jianfu take pride. I didn't want them to be proud of those things, I suppose. I didn't want them to be just like 'us' in modern capitalist societies. I wanted them to stay exotic and quaint. Stuck in the past. It makes me groan to think about it.

*

Now I sentimentalise even more. I forget how taxing I found living in the village. And how distressing sometimes, too. I forget my difficulties communicating; Li Wei's impatience with me and my impatience with her as well as with myself; my exhaustion and aching back; the humidity in summer and the frigid winter cold.

I didn't like some people and they didn't like me. I'd get angry with the cadres, who would use Li Wei and me as an excuse for a restaurant meal and a booze-up. I'd get frustrated with older villagers whose memory was fading or who chattered endlessly, scooting off on tangents when all I wanted was a simple answer to a simple question.

At times I hated myself for meddling in others' lives and being such a burden, especially to Yang Yurong and Li Wei. And I felt bad for being insensitive and blundering and having stupid accidents. Like the time I broke the toilet seat. Oh, I was so mortified by that!

And so often I didn't understand, even when Li Wei helped interpret for me. I was so demanding, asking so many maddening questions. Like a fledgling Australian magpie, opening my pink mouth wide, crying meee, meeee, meeeee.

I'd get so tired, too. Tired of all the people, all the talk. Tired of having to perform. Sometimes all I wanted to do was curl in a ball and hide.

And yet. I was such a clumsy outsider, but I felt I'd come home. What a gift to be in Ginkgo Village, to be accepted so generously and taught so much. Now I feel homesick. Lost in a fog. Afraid and feeling sorry for myself and the world. This battered, bloodied world, fouled by humanity's war with itself and other species and the planet.

But here I am at my desk, my mug of coffee warming my hands. I remember a short piece by Toni Morrison, addressing writers who feel overwhelmed by the darkness surrounding them: 'There is no time for despair, no place for self-pity, no need for silence, no room for fear. We speak, we write, we do language. That is how civilisations heal.'[2]

*

Here is my desk, my computer, my window. The sun-dappled green garden, the sulphur-crested cockatoos cracking seeds in the Chinese pistachio tree. My plump ginger cat is cross she can't catch them. I get up to refill my mug. Come back, sit down, put fingers to keyboard. Begin another tale.

To write, I must part the fog. I must sense anew each detail and fit it into place: each hand on knee, each toe-nudge of sunflower seed husk on concrete floor. Each birdsong, each rice seedling of freshly minted green. I must draw in each cloud, each rain shower, each car on the road, each creak of a door. Each scent that wafts across the courtyard towards Li Wei and me.

I sift through notes and memories. Sometimes I email Li Wei with a question and she contacts Yang Yurong or Wu Jianfu on WeChat. They in turn ask relatives or friends. I fabricate some things: the age of one woman and the types of flowers she grows; the gruff voice of one villager, the indulgent smile of another; what Li Wei and I are doing in a particular moment— sipping tea or scribbling notes or pulling on our gloves. I search for images and words, type them one at a time and build them into sentences.

I relish the process. The fog shifts, the colours and textures solidify: the warm gold of a hen picking grain, Baoli's toothy grin and Yang Yurong's ponytail. Wu Jianfu leaning towards the TV and turning his head. Renkai burning yellow spirit-money. The pink lanterns at the Dragon Parade and the explosions and smoke of the firecrackers. The strutting rooster with tail feathers of black and green.

---

2   Toni Morrison, 'No Place for Self-Pity, No Room for Fear', *The Nation*, [New York], 23 March 2015: 184–85, www.thenation.com/article/archive/no-place-self-pity-no-room-fear/.

This is me now: I'm busy crafting tales. Sometimes, I imagine I'm Gao Xiuhua curved over her loom, pulling the weft through, one line at a time. Or I'm Liang Anqin in her restaurant, frying up a storm. Or Zhang Hongren out there with the rice-transplanting team, sweating in thigh-high boots, leaning down through the water and plunging the seedlings into the mud, row after row.

This morning I belong to a community building a house—a spacious house with many rooms of different shapes and sizes. We're building from the soil and water and wood of the trees, from clay that's slapped into bricks and set in the sun. We're building from the hard ground all the way up to the dragon-gate frames and the dark curved roof tiles. The blossoming clouds above.

Each day we labour together. One of us bangs a thumb and curses. Another jokes, another sings, another weeps. The women rise long before the men to wash and clean and cook. At midday, they come with food in bowls and baskets, the children scampering and stamping the earth with their restless feet.

We pause beneath the ginkgo trees. Two trees stand side by side, fluttering their fan-shaped leaves and twining their roots together, deep in the rich, moist earth.

Here we are, chatting and gazing out across the village: over the patchwork of rice, canola and peanut fields, the sinuous rivers and roads, the ponds and tea plantations, the houses snug on the hillside, among the China fir and chestnut trees. Wild mountains rise beyond.

*

High in the sky, the clouds are forming new shapes. I feel a breath of rain on my face: another change is coming.

Appendix: Research and writing

Having read the tales in this book, readers might like to know more about the research on which they are based and the ways in which they combine fact and fiction. The first part of this Appendix gives details about the fieldwork that my research assistants and I conducted in Ginkgo Village, as well as information about other sources on which the tales draw. The second part explains which elements of the tales are factual and come directly from our research and which have been fictionalised. It also explains the function of aspects of the tales' storytelling mode, as well as the inclusion of snippets from my own and Li Wei's life histories and the use of fictionalisation, which distinguishes this book from conventional ethnographies and historical texts.

Research

Between 2014 and 2019, two research assistants and I made a total of 10 trips and spent altogether seven months in Ginkgo Village. Both research assistants were Chinese women doing postgraduate studies with me at The Australian National University. The primary assistant[1] made the first two trips in 2014 and early 2015. She spent a total of 20 days in the village and conducted semi-structured interviews with 40 Ginkgo Villagers. On these trips, she focused on her own research, which was separate from the joint project we carried out later, but what she learnt fed into the later project.

---

1   Each of the two research assistants made five trips to Ginkgo Village. I have identified one as 'primary' because she also helped with post-fieldwork research.

The main project, involving me as well as both assistants, began in 2015. It was carried out under the auspices of a Chinese university as part of a large collaborative project looking into the lives of the 'left-behind elderly'—older villagers whose adult children had left the village as migrant labourers. My university hosts chose Ginkgo Village as one of several rural communities involved in the project because of Xin County's history of large-scale rural outmigration and because they had previously forged ties with local officials.

During my first visit to Ginkgo Village, my assistant and I conducted semi-structured interviews focused on the current circumstances of those aged over 60 living in the village. But we also asked questions about the past. Over time, we became more and more interested in older villagers' life histories and asked more and more questions about how village life had changed over their life course. We also expanded our research to include interviews and conversations with middle-aged and younger villagers.[2]

I made five research trips to Ginkgo Village, accompanied by one or other of my assistants, in May 2015, March and December 2016, August–September 2017 and February–March 2018. Altogether, I lived for four months in the village.

I planned another trip for February 2017 and two more for 2019, but in February 2017, illness prevented me from travelling. I gave a long list of research topics and questions to my primary assistant and she went alone to Ginkgo Village for a few weeks. She conducted research both for our joint project and for her own separate project.

I also couldn't go in 2019. Through the preceding decade, Chinese state controls on foreign research had become tighter and tighter. By 2018, a non-Chinese person could obtain a research visa only if she collaborated with Chinese researchers on a state-approved project. The collaborative project in which I had been involved ended in 2018, so my trips to Ginkgo Village ended then, too.

---

2   Our interactions with those aged between 18 and 35 were limited by the prevalence of outmigration among this age group. However, in early 2018, we conducted several interviews with young migrant workers who had returned home to spend the Lunar New Year period with their families. Chapters 6 and 9 draw on these interviews, as well as numerous conversations with villagers who had worked elsewhere in China or overseas in the past.

Again, my assistants went without me. This time, they went together. They spent 40 days in the village in January–February 2019 and 23 days in August the same year. On each trip, they once more combined their own research with research towards our joint project.

*

While in Ginkgo Village, I paid for my assistants and myself to stay with Yang Yurong and her younger son, Baoli (Yang Yurong's husband, Wu Jianfu, and older son, Renkai, were present only for brief periods). The house in which we lived is described in Chapter 7.

As so often happens during ethnographic fieldwork, our hosts not only looked after and befriended us, but also became some of our most important informants. We spent much of the 2018 New Year period with the family, participating in most of their extended family get-togethers, their visits to temples and shrines, and other activities. At other times, too, we spent hours each day chatting with Yang Yurong over meals, gobbling up her wonderful stories and observations of villagers and village life, along with the delicious food she prepared for us. Sometimes, we also accompanied her on excursions within the village and nearby to visit friends and relatives or go shopping. A few times, we joined her picking tea, collecting chestnuts, foraging and harvesting peanuts. We tried to help her with domestic chores, too, but she commonly resisted these efforts.

Apart from this, my assistants and I walked around Ginkgo Village most days, looking around, chatting with passers-by, calling on people in their homes and conducting semi-structured interviews.

I always went out accompanied by an assistant. We would leave shortly after breakfast, again after lunch and occasionally after dinner, our daypacks loaded with a notebook and pens, typed-up sheets of questions and other paraphernalia. For security reasons, I always had my visa, passport and a USB drive containing all my fieldnotes on my person, rather than stored at Yang Yurong's house.

Aside from my first day in the village, when Village Accountant Wu introduced me and my assistant to one woman and accompanied us into her house, we chose all our villager interviewees and no cadres were present during our interviews. On some occasions, we talked with a single interviewee; on others, with a couple. But we rarely spent more than an hour at a stretch alone with our interviewees. Usually, a family member or a neighbour or two would drop by. Sometimes, we would find ourselves sitting with a large group of villagers talking among themselves.

Altogether, my research assistants and I conducted semi-structured interviews with 115 Ginkgo Villagers. I personally led interviews with sixty. With 23 of these people, my assistants and I held between two and six interviews. Usually these took place in the person's home and lasted between one and two hours. We got to know this core group also through shorter chats and casual encounters, often in group settings.

I haven't included the four village leaders in this count. Together with my assistants, I interviewed and chatted with each leader several times. Sometimes, they came to Yang Yurong's house; at other times, we visited them at their home. Only in 2017 did we talk with them in the village government offices. On other trips, these offices were closed most of the time.

We also chatted with a few cadres from other villages and from Red River Township—mostly at banquets in nearby restaurants. Ginkgo Village leaders invited us to at least one such banquet each time we visited. I volunteered to conduct English classes a few times in a nearby school and my assistants and I talked both with the headmaster and teachers there and with the headmaster of the Ginkgo Village primary school. We also talked with the Ginkgo Village doctor and visited the Red River Township elderly care home and talked with both its staff and its residents.

In all our interviews and conversations, my assistants and I spoke Mandarin Chinese. The villagers spoke a mixture of Mandarin and local dialect. Most middle-aged and younger villagers and I could understand each other enough for a simple conversation, but with villagers over the age of about 70, communication was more difficult. They sometimes couldn't follow my Mandarin and I had even more trouble understanding their dialect. Fortunately, though, my assistants were usually able to act as interpreters. Neither had grown up in Xin County, but they picked up the local dialect more quickly than me.

While in the village, we each carried lists of interview questions prepared in advance, but we referred to these only occasionally during interviews. At the beginning of each first interview, we explained who we were. We said we wanted to hear about villagers' life histories and how their everyday lives had changed over their life course. We explained that we might publish our research but, in doing so, wouldn't identify the village or any villagers. In later interviews, we reminded people about the purpose of our research. We sought villagers' oral consent for each interview we conducted.

At the end of each first interview, we gave most people a gift of an umbrella or a hand towel as a token of our appreciation for the time they spent with us. We also carried biscuits and small Australian souvenirs to give to children. To Yang Yurong and village leaders, I gave more substantial souvenirs: wallets, scarves and a pair of sheepskin boots for Baoli.

With interviewees' permission, I recorded the first few interviews we did in 2015, but I soon stopped that practice because villagers were less open when the recorder was going. Instead, both my assistant and I scribbled notes during each interview, which we would transcribe and add to in the evenings. Each night we spent a few hours talking together about our research findings, impressions, thoughts and questions, and typing copious fieldnotes into our laptops. Once a week or so, we fell behind and had to take a day off from research to catch up on our fieldnotes. Each of us wrote separate fieldnotes. Having these three sets of notes later proved invaluable, for it meant I could confirm details, fill in gaps and jog my memory by reading what my assistants had written.

*

The core source of information and inspiration for the tales in this book has been my own four months of fieldwork in Ginkgo Village. Thus, all the tales' villager characters are based on people with whom I personally interacted on at least two or, in most cases, several occasions.

Descriptions of these characters and their life histories, along with descriptions of Laoshi's and Li Wei's experiences and observations of life in the village, draw most heavily on my own fieldnotes, photographs and memories. In most cases, I have drawn on my research assistants' fieldnotes merely to jog my memory, confirm details or fill in gaps in my own notes; in instances when I couldn't understand our interviewees; or in relation to sensitive matters, such as birth planning, which villagers were not willing to discuss with me.

There are just two places in the tales where I draw extensively on research my assistants conducted with villagers I hadn't met. These are the account in Chapter 3 of the time women spent spinning, weaving and doing needlework during the Maoist period and the discussion in Chapter 4 of gender divisions of labour in agriculture. In these instances, I confirmed and supplemented my own research findings with those derived from a handful of interviews and a survey about women's work that my assistants conducted on my behalf during the two visits they made to Ginkgo Village in 2019. The survey involved short interviews with 48 women born before 1970, during which my assistants completed a questionnaire that I had prepared.[3]

Aside from fieldwork research in the village, the book draws to a lesser extent on information from three further sources. The first are conversations with Yang Yurong and Wu Jianfu on WeChat. These conversations, with my primary assistant and me, continued for a few years after we left Ginkgo Village. As well as keeping us updated about village affairs, they were a vital source of answers to questions that we had neglected to ask while in the village.

The second supplementary source are written materials from Ginkgo Village and surrounding regions. These include data for Ginkgo Village collected during the poverty alleviation campaign of 2014–20 and provided by Ginkgo Village leaders. Villagers also showed us several of their genealogies, portions of which we photographed. In addition, my primary assistant and I obtained several county-level statistical yearbooks and several prefectural, county and township gazetteers. These materials are the source of most of the figures in Chapter 1.

In 2019, my research assistants also gained access to internal Chinese Communist Party documents from the Maoist period contained in county archives. I have made brief references to these in Chapters 1 and 3.

Fact and fiction

How exactly do the tales in this book relate to the research that I have outlined here? What in the tales is factual and what is fictional? To answer these questions, I'll begin with the interviews that Li Wei and Laoshi conducted in Ginkgo Village.

My portrayal of these interviews includes myriad small details commonly left out of ethnographies, such as references to individuals' mannerisms, physical appearance, voices and body language, as well as brief descriptions

---

3   Forty-eight was the total number of women in this age group whom my assistants found in Ginkgo Village at the time of the survey and who were willing and able to participate.

of the weather and the place in which the interview is being conducted. Some of the details—instances, for example, of an interviewee getting up to fetch tea, the nature of the weather or a person's laughter or fidgeting at a moment in time—are fabricated. But in a broad sense, all such details mirror my real experiences in the village, as I remember them and as recorded in my fieldnotes.

My first aim in including these details has been to enable readers to hear and see in their mind's eye the tales' central characters in their surroundings. These concrete evocations of people and places play a vital role in storytelling. They are crucial to my efforts to enable readers to imagine, and from there to achieve an empathetic understanding of, Ginkgo Villagers and their lives.

My second aim has been to immerse readers in as evocative, realistic and representative a re-enactment of fieldwork practices as possible. My hope is that this will give those with little or no experience of conducting fieldwork in a Chinese village a good sense of what it entails.

But there's one way in which my descriptions are not realistic or representative: the interviews Li Wei and Laoshi conduct are far less messy than the reality. Our real interviews commonly involved more language difficulties and more hesitations, repetitions, confusion and gaps. They also meandered in a more disorderly manner across a wider range of topics than the tales might suggest. To make the tales more engaging, I've brought more focus to individual interviews. At the same time, I've condensed into a few encounters information we gleaned from several interviews, casual conversations and other sources.

*

What about Ginkgo Village and the characters in the book: In what ways are these fictional and in what ways are they factual? How representative are they of real places and real people? As mentioned in the Introduction, I've changed minor details about the village to protect the identity of its residents. Otherwise, my depiction is close to reality. This is not an 'average', 'typical' or 'representative' Chinese village; there's too much variety across China for such a thing to exist. But Ginkgo Village's society, culture and political economy share many characteristics with those of mountainous villages throughout eastern China's interior.

The book's characters are also not average or typical. They are representative of humans in their uniqueness. At the same time, though, each one shares similarities with other people similarly positioned in their community with respect to age, gender, socioeconomic and political status, and cultural and family background.

Take Laoshi: a stand-in for me, the researcher and author of this book, she's a comfortably well-off middle-aged woman with a characteristically Australian mixed heritage—British-Australian on one side, Baltic and Slav on the other. Key aspects of her life experiences, values and views are common among well-educated, middle-class, urban white Australian women of her generation.

As explained in the Introduction, I have fictionalised Laoshi's experiences and interactions in Ginkgo Village, but their overall tenor is true to life. Laoshi's views and opinions are my own and the key events in her life history match mine. I have taken a bit of poetic licence here and there but, in the main, Laoshi's past experiences are as I remember them.

In contrast, Li Wei is a fictional character. In terms of her personality, social position and world view—many aspects of which are common among well-educated, middle-class young Chinese women—she resembles my primary research assistant. But to protect that person's identity, I have altered her name and appearance and made changes to her parents' life history as well as her own. I have also fictionalised her interactions with Laoshi and others in the village.

Why weave short excerpts from my own and Li Wei's life stories into this book? My first aim has been to enrich readers' empathetic understanding of villagers and their lives by highlighting both particularities and universalities in their subjective experiences of trauma and transformation. In many respects, of course, Ginkgo Villagers' life experiences are light-years from Li Wei's and my own. For all this, though, there are common threads running through our stories and many resonances and connections between them.

I also want to underscore and provide concrete illustrations of a truth about anthropological research that is more usually glossed over or expunged from ethnographies—namely, when we go 'to the field', we don't leave our selves behind. Our personal histories and all the cultural and emotional baggage attached to them come too, and inevitably colour our research and what we take from it. I hope to demonstrate this basic truth by giving readers a glimpse into Li Wei's history and, in particular, writing about my personal life experiences and memories and showing how these bled into my thoughts and behaviour in Ginkgo Village.

Yet another motivation for including autobiographical snippets relates to Ruth Behar's observation that 'when readers take the voyage through anthropology's tunnel it is themselves they must be able to see in the observer who is serving as their guide'.[4] Following this, I suggest that making myself— the researcher-writer—vulnerable by revealing personal details helps readers to identify and connect with me. This in turn makes it easier for me to take your hand, metaphorically speaking, to guide you through Ginkgo Village and the lives of its inhabitants, so that you will come to empathetically understand villagers' lives almost as though experiencing them yourself.

*

To make myself vulnerable is one thing. To make other research participants vulnerable would be quite another. As with my assistants, I have fictionalised Ginkgo Villager characters to protect them from the potential harms associated with identification. For ethical reasons connected, once more, with my core aim of building empathy, the fictionalisation is unusually extensive.

To explain, let me first reiterate that a core aim of this book is to enable readers to imagine themselves immersed in Ginkgo Villagers' lifeworlds so they can empathetically understand villagers' experiences. Richly detailed portraits of individuals and individual lives are central to achieving this aim.

But it is not possible to provide such portraits and at the same time protect villagers from the risks associated with identification simply by changing their names and a few personal details, such as age. Suppose I had disguised individuals in this way but had truthfully described their physical appearance and mannerisms and given a detailed and truthful account of their life histories. Suppose I had also provided details, for example, of these individuals' conflicts with their spouses or had faithfully reported what they told Li Wei and me about corruption among village cadres. If I had divulged details such as these, locals could quite easily put two and two together and

---

4   Ruth Behar, *The Vulnerable Observer: Anthropology that Breaks Your Heart* (Boston, MA: Beacon Press, 1996), 16.

identify the individuals in question.[5] Potentially, that would risk damage to those people's relationships with family members or village cadres. And that, in turn, could result in all sorts of psychological, social, economic and political harm.

In addition, revealing truthful details about local village corruption would make it easier to distinguish Ginkgo Village from its neighbours in Xin County. Given the current political climate, such identification would risk punishment for the cadres who permitted my research in Ginkgo Village. It might also undermine other scholars' opportunities to conduct research in the county.

To ameliorate these potential harms, I have fictionalised not only the names and personal details of Ginkgo Villagers, but also their personalities and mannerisms, personal circumstances and life histories, and interactions with Li Wei and myself. My depictions of villager characters' thoughts and feelings are also fictional, of course. Even the direct speech I have included in each tale is mostly fictional.

I stress, however, that both in terms of what makes each individual unique and with respect to characteristics they share with other villagers, the villager characters in this book closely resemble real Ginkgo Villagers. All my descriptions of their personalities, appearances, behaviour, speech and even thoughts and emotions draw heavily on my perceptions of real people with whom my research assistants and I interacted. Similarly, the dialogue draws heavily on dialogue we recorded in our fieldnotes.

What's more, although I have changed a few details, all the major events recounted in the tales did in fact take place. Li Wei and I either witnessed them or heard about them from villagers. We heard, for example, from an older man about the death of his baby daughter, killed in exactly the manner I describe in Chapter 2. We also heard about a woman's suicide, as in Chapter 5 (I changed details about this woman and her death). A woman described her experiences in the core people's militia during the Cultural Revolution, as in Chapter 4. Another described the land redistribution of 1998 in the same manner as in Chapter 7. As in Chapter 3, I gave money to a very ill woman and, as in Chapter 5, Li Wei and I saw the charred ruins of a burnt house. Villagers did blockade an unfinished road as in Chapter 6,

---

5   It is unlikely, but nevertheless possible, that people in Xin County will learn the contents of this book indirectly or by reading a Chinese translation.

although the details of the dispute were not quite as I have described them. Li Wei and I were indeed repeatedly frustrated in our attempts to visit a woman with three children, as in Chapter 8. And I was overcome by the noise and fumes of firecrackers at New Year, as in Chapter 9.

While these events are 'real' in the sense that they did occur, each tale involves a lot of cutting and pasting. To disguise villagers, I have teased apart elements of people's identities, their life histories and our interactions with them, and combined them in new configurations. I've done something similar in the vignette recounted at the beginning of the Introduction, so I'll give this as an example.

My research assistants and I did meet an older man who would sit outside his small general store, weaving wicker baskets. But he was not a relative of Yang Yurong's. The incident with the racing bikes did happen as I have described it and my description of our emotional responses is true to life. An older man also told us about the trees being cut down in 1958 and, again, our emotional responses were much as I've described them here. But it was not Widower Yang who told us this story. I've spliced two encounters into one tale.

*

Though the details of individual villagers' characters and life histories are fictional, the general information I provide about key topics is factual. Information about the nature and extent of suffering and violence in the Maoist period (Chapters 2 to 5) was confirmed by many villagers. So, too, was information about land distribution and usage, and gender divisions of labour and patterns of work in the Maoist and post-Mao periods (Chapters 3, 4 and 6–8). In the case of the post-Mao period, my research assistants and I also confirmed details through our own observations around the village.

To protect villagers, I have changed or avoided details about recent cadre corruption, nepotism and coercion, as well as about social and family conflict among ordinary villagers. Broadly speaking, though, my descriptions (in Chapters 3 and 5–8) are representative of the range of corrupt and conflictual interactions that commonly occurred across rural China in the late twentieth and early twenty-first centuries. Such interactions were reported by many Ginkgo Villagers.

Information about New Year customs (Chapter 9) was pieced together from the accounts of several villagers as well as my own and my research assistants' observations. The details of the way in which the customs are carried out vary from one family to another but, in a broad sense, what I've described is representative of general practice. So, too, are the details I give about funeral rituals (Chapter 5) and housebuilding processes and rituals (Chapter 7). These details come from two or three villagers in each case. My assistants and I also confirmed some of them through our own observations as well as written sources.

Descriptions scattered through the book of other aspects of life in present-day Ginkgo Village draw on my own and my assistants' observations, as well as the accounts of numerous villagers. These include descriptions of the houses in which people live and the surrounding environment; the food they prepare and eat, the clothes they wear, their health and consumption of medical care; livelihoods and patterns of work; gender and intergenerational relations within a family; kinship, social networking and gift-giving practices; and incomes and expenditures. Of course, these core aspects of ordinary life vary from one family to another. Overall, though, my descriptions broadly reflect the situation in Ginkgo Village in the second decade of the twenty-first century.

Glossary

Pinyin	Characters	English
ba	爸	dad
bai hu	白虎	white tiger (righthand side)
baozi	包子	stuffed steamed bread bun
cai	财	wealth
caili	彩礼	bride price
Caishen	财神	the God of Wealth
chai	柴	firewood
changpao	长袍	a type of robe common before the 1950s
chaoji dao	超级稻	super rice
chi da guo fan shiqi	吃大锅饭时期	the time of eating from one big pot (a term Ginkgo Villagers used to refer to the Great Leap Forward)
chuandou	穿斗	pillars and transverse tie beams (a type of roof frame typical of southern Chinese architecture)
ciba	糍粑	glutinous rice cake
dangan	单干	working on one's own: (the return to) family farming
dibao	低保	minimum livelihood guarantee
didengxi	地灯戏	a type of Chinese opera specific to Xin County
doufu	豆腐	soybean curd
duilian	对联	rhyming couplets, pasted around doors and gates for the Lunar New Year
feng shui	风水	Chinese geomancy
fenjia	分家	to divide the family
ganbu	干部	cadre
gandi	干地	'dry' unirrigated land
gongfen	工分	work point
guanggun	光棍	bare sticks; bachelors

Pinyin	Characters	English
Guanyin	观音	Goddess of Mercy (China's female Bodhisattva Avalokiteśvara)
guo qiao	过桥	crossing the bridge (a ritual to help the soul of a deceased person cross into the otherworld)
hongbao	红包	small red paper packets containing gifts of cash
Hong Deng Ji	红灯记	*The Red Lantern* (a Cultural Revolution model opera)
Hong Weibing	红卫兵	Red Guard
Huangxiao pian	黄孝片	Huangxiao subgroup (of the Jiang-Huai dialect of Mandarin)
jianbing	煎饼	savoury egg pancakes
Jiangjun Xian	将军县	County of Generals (a nickname for Xin County)
Jiang-Huai	江淮	The region between the Yangtze River and the Huai River; a Mandarin dialect spoken in the Jiang-Huai region
jiahe xiqu	驾鹤西去	literally, 'to fly on a crane to the Western Paradise'; to go to Heaven
jiao hun	叫魂	to call a wandering soul back to a person's body
jiaozi	饺子	dumplings
jigan minbing	基干民兵	core people's militia
ji liang	祭梁	to sacrifice a beam
kaohuo de wuzi	烤火的屋子	heating-room (literally, a 'room for warming oneself by a fire')
laoshi	老师	teacher
laowai	老外	foreigner (an informal, sometimes derogatory term)
longmen jia	龙门架	dragon-gate roof frame
luopan	罗盘	*feng shui* compass
mantou	馒头	steamed bread bun
mapo doufu	麻婆豆腐	spicy Sichuan dish made with soybean curd
Meili Xiangcun Jianshe	美丽乡村建设	Construction of a Beautiful Countryside (state program)
mixin	迷信	superstition
mu	亩	unit of area
nan geng nü zhi	男耕女织	men plough, women weave (a traditional Chinese saying)
Pingfan de Shijie	平凡的世界	*Ordinary World* (the title of a novel and TV serial)
pinkun xian	贫困县	poor county (a state designation)
Po Si Jiu	破四旧	'Destroy the Four Olds' (a Cultural Revolution slogan)

Pinyin	Characters	English
popo	婆婆	mother-in-law
putong minbing	普通民兵	common people's militia
qi	气	vital energy; cosmic life force
qing	青	the colour green or azure
qing long	青龙	green dragon (lefthand side)
re'nao	热闹	warm and lively
san nian da jihuang	三年大饥荒	three years of great famine (villagers' term for the Great Leap Forward)
shang liang	上梁	raise the beam
shifu	师傅	master; a term of respect used when addressing craftspeople or others with valued skills
shou ling	守灵	to keep vigil over the soul of a dead person
shou mian'ao	守棉袄	waiting up for a cotton-padded jacket
shuitiandi	水田地	'wet land'; paddy fields
song long shang tian	送龙上天	sending the dragons back to Heaven (a ritual held on the sixteenth of the first lunar month to burn the paper dragons paraded earlier that month)
song qiao	送桥	seeing off at the bridge (a ritual to farewell the soul of a deceased person before it crosses the bridge to the otherworld)
Songzi Niangniang	送子娘娘	the Maiden Who Brings Children — a goddess of motherhood and children
tailiang	抬梁	pillars and beams (a type of roof frame typical of northern Chinese architecture)
tou liangmu	偷梁木	to steal wood for a beam
Tudi Gong	土地公	Earth God
Tudi Nainai	土地奶奶	Grandmother Earth God
Tudi Yeye	土地爷爷	Grandfather Earth God
Tuigeng Huanlin	退耕还林	Returning Farmland to Forest (program)
wubaohu	五保户	'five-guarantee' households (those entitled to state support because they need care but have no family to support them)
xiangchun	香椿	new leaves of the Chinese toon tree
xiao ming	小名	baby name
xiao wan	小湾	small riverbend (a term Ginkgo Villagers use to refer to hamlets)
xiaozu	小组	small group; hamlet
Xin Nongcun Jianshe	新农村建设	Construction of a New Socialist Countryside (campaign)

Pinyin	Characters	English
yanglou	洋楼	multistorey Western-style house
Yao xiang fu, xian xiu lu	要想富, 先修路	'If you want to get rich, you must first build roads'
xingzheng cun	行政村	administrative village
yiban	一般	ordinary; so-so
youtiao	油条	deep-fried pastry stick
yuan	元	Chinese unit of currency
yuanxiao	元宵	soft, sweet glutinous rice balls
Zao Nainai	灶奶奶	Grandmother Stove God
Zao Yeye	灶爷爷	Grandfather Stove God
Zhengjun	正君	Upright Gentleman (a person's name)
zhiqing	知青	educated youth (young urbanites sent to the countryside during the Cultural Revolution)
Zhongyuan Guanhua	中原官话	Central Plains dialect of Mandarin
zhuchi ren	主持人	master of ceremonies
zuo yuezi	坐月子	to rest for one month after childbirth
zuzong zhaomu shenwei	祖宗招募神位	a scroll to show reverence to the ancestors

Bibliography

Behar, Ruth. *The Vulnerable Observer: Anthropology that Breaks Your Heart*. Boston, MA: Beacon Press, 1996.

Benton, Gregor. *Mountain Fires: The Red Army's Three-Year War in South China, 1934–1938*. Berkeley, CA: University of California Press, 1992.

Bossen, Laurel. *Chinese Women and Rural Development: Sixty Years of Change in Lu Village, Yunnan*. Lanham, MD: Rowman & Littlefield, 2002.

Bossen, Laurel. 'Reproduction and Real Property in Rural China: Three Decades of Development and Discrimination.' In *Women, Gender and Rural Development in China*, edited by Tamara Jacka and Sally Sargeson, 97–123. Cheltenham, UK: Edward Elgar, 2011. doi.org/10.4337/9780857933546.00014.

Bossen, Laurel, and Hill Gates. *Bound Feet, Young Hands: Tracking the Demise of Footbinding in Village China*. Stanford, CA: Stanford University Press, 2017. doi.org/10.2307/j.ctvqsdshq.

Boullenois, Camille. 'Poverty Alleviation in China: The Rise of State-Sponsored Corporate Paternalism.' *China Perspectives* 3 (2020a): 47–56. doi.org/10.4000/chinaperspectives.10456.

Boullenois, Camille. 'The Self-Made Entrepreneur: Social Identities and the Perceived Legitimacy of Entrepreneurs in Inland Rural China.' PhD diss., The Australian National University, Canberra, 2020b.

Boym, Svetlana. *The Future of Nostalgia*. New York: Basic Books, 2001.

Breithaupt, Fritz. *The Dark Sides of Empathy*. Ithaca, NY: Cornell University Press, 2019. doi.org/10.7591/9781501735608.

Bruun, Ole. *Fengshui in China: Geomantic Divination Between State Orthodoxy and Popular Religion*. Copenhagen: NIAS Press, 2003.

Buck, John Lossing. *Land Utilization in China: A Study of 16,786 Farms in 168 Localities, and 38,256 Farm Families in Twenty-Two Provinces in China, 1929–1933*. New York: Council on Economic and Cultural Affairs, 1956 [1937].

Buck, Pearl S. *The Good Earth*. New York: Washington Square Press, 1931.

Chang, Zhaoqi, and Zhu Jiefan. 新县民俗志 [*Xin County Folk Customs Gazetteer*]. Zhengzhou, China: Xin County Bureau of Civil Affairs, 1991.

Chu, Julie Y. *Cosmologies of Credit: Transnational Mobility and the Politics of Destination in China*. Durham, NC: Duke University Press, 2010. doi.org/10.1515/9780822393160.

Coblin, W. South. 'Migration History and Dialect Development in the Lower Yangtze Watershed.' *Bulletin of the School of Oriental and African Studies* 65, no. 3 (2002): 529–43. doi.org/10.1017/s0041977x02000320.

Cohen, Myron L. 'Souls and Salvation: Conflicting Themes in Chinese Popular Religion.' In *Death Ritual in Late Imperial and Modern China*, edited by James L. Watson and Evelyn S. Rawski, 180–202. Berkeley, CA: University of California Press, 1988.

Domenach, Jean-Luc. *The Origins of the Great Leap Forward: The Case of One Chinese Province*, translated by A.M Berrett. Boulder, CO: Westview Press, 1995.

Erikson, Kai. *A New Species of Trouble: The Human Experience of Modern Disasters*. New York: W.W. Norton & Co., 1994.

Eyferth, Jacob. 'Women's Work and the Politics of Homespun in Socialist China, 1949–1980.' *International Review of Social History* 57, no. 3 (2012): 365–91. doi.org/10.1017/S0020859012000521.

Fabian, Johannes. *Time and the Other: How Anthropology Makes its Object*. New York: Columbia University Press, 1983.

Feuchtwang, Stephan. *Popular Religion in China: The Imperial Metaphor*. Richmond, UK: Curzon, 2001.

Geertz, Clifford. *The Interpretation of Cultures: Selected Essays by Clifford Geertz*. New York: Basic Books, 1973.

Guangshan County Histories and Gazetteers Compilation Committee. 光山县志 [*Guangshan County Gazetteer*]. Zhengzhou, China: Zhongzhou Guji Chubanshe, 1991.

Guo, Ruimin, Zhang Chunxiang, and Li Shui. 豫南民居 [*Southern Henan Houses*]. Nanjing, China: Dongnan Daxue Chubanshe, 2011.

Hartmann, William E., and Joseph P. Gone. 'American Indian Historical Trauma: Community Perspectives from Two Great Plains Medicine Men.' *American Journal of Community Psychology* 54, nos 3–4 (2014): 274–88. doi.org/10.1007/s10464-014-9671-1.

He, Suyuan, and Weiye Wang. 'Social Resources Transfer Program Under China's Targeted Poverty Alleviation Strategy: Rural Social Structure and Local Politics.' *Journal of Contemporary China* 32, no. 142 (2023): 686–703. doi.org/10.1080/10670564.2022.2109844.

Hershatter, Gail. *The Gender of Memory: Rural Women and China's Collective Past.* Berkeley, CA: University of California Press, 2011. doi.org/10.1525/california/9780520267701.001.0001.

Hollan, Douglas W., and C. Jason Throop. 'The Anthropology of Empathy: Introduction.' In *The Anthropology of Empathy: Experiencing the Lives of Others in Pacific Societies*, edited by Douglas W. Hollan and C. Jason Throop, 1–21. New York: Berghahn Books, 2011. doi.org/10.1515/9780857451033-002.

Hou, Zhiying. 大别山风云录 [*A Record of the Tempests in the Dabie Mountains*]. Zhengzhou, China: Henan People's Publishing House, 1990.

Jacka, Tamara. *Women's Work in Rural China: Change and Continuity in an Era of Reform.* Cambridge, UK: Cambridge University Press, 1997. doi.org/10.1017/CBO9780511518157.

Jacka, Tamara. *Rural Women in Urban China: Gender, Migration, and Social Change.* Armonk, NY: M.E. Sharpe, 2006.

Jacka, Tamara. 'Left-Behind and Vulnerable? Conceptualising Development and Older Women's Agency in Rural China.' *Asian Studies Review* 38, no. 2 (2014): 186–204. doi.org/10.1080/10357823.2014.891566.

Jacka, Tamara. 'Translocal Family Reproduction and Agrarian Change in China: A New Analytical Framework.' *Journal of Peasant Studies* 45, no. 7 (2018): 1341–59. doi.org/10.1080/03066150.2017.1314267.

Jacka, Tamara, Andrew B. Kipnis, and Sally Sargeson. *Contemporary China: Society and Social Change.* New York: Cambridge University Press, 2013. doi.org/10.1017/CBO9781139196178.

Jamison, Leslie. 'The Empathy Exams.' In *The Empathy Exams: Essays*, by Leslie Jamison, 1–26. London: Granta Books, 2014.

Kipnis, Andrew B. *From Village to City: Social Transformation in a Chinese County Seat.* Oakland, CA: University of California Press, 2016. doi.org/10.1525/california/9780520289703.001.0001.

Kipnis, Andrew B. *The Funeral of Mr Wang: Life, Death, and Ghosts in Urbanizing China*. Oakland, CA: University of California Press, 2021. doi.org/10.1515/9780520381995.

Lammer, Christof. 'Care Scales: *Dibao* Allowances, State and Family in China.' *The China Quarterly* 254 (2023): 310–24. doi.org/10.1017/S0305741023000309.

Lee, Hyeon Jung. 'Fearless Love, Death for Dignity: Female Suicide and Gendered Subjectivity in Rural North China.' *China Journal* 71 (2014): 25–42. doi.org/10.1086/674552.

Leung, Joe C.B., and Yuebin Xu. *China's Social Welfare: The Third Turning Point*. Cambridge, UK: Polity Press, 2015.

Li, Huaiyin. *Village China under Socialism and Reform: A Micro-History, 1948–2008*. Stanford, CA: Stanford University Press, 2009. doi.org/10.1515/9780804771078.

Li, Xiaoxuan. '成为 "洋工人": 河南省新县对外劳务输出机制研究 [Becoming an "Overseas Worker": Research into the Mechanisms for Exporting Labour in Xin County, Henan Province].' Master's diss., China Agricultural University, Beijing, 2019.

Li, Xiaoxuan. '移民时代: "流动基础设施"内部不断演变, 出国务工容易了吗 [The Era of Migration: With Constant Developments in "Migration Infrastructure", Has Overseas Labour Migration Become Easier]?' 澎湃新闻 [*The Paper*], [Shanghai], 11 July 2020. www.thepaper.cn/newsDetail_forward_8225916.

Liu, Shusha. '明代豫东南地区人口流动与社会变迁: 以汝宁府为中心 [Population Flows and Social Change in South-Eastern Henan in the Ming Dynasty: A Study Focused on Runing Prefecture].' Master's diss., Guangxi University for Nationalities, Nanning City, 2017.

Liu, Yanzheng, and Zhang Jie. 'The Impact of Negative Life Events on Attempted Suicide in Rural China.' *Journal of Nervous and Mental Disease* 206, no. 3 (2018): 187–94. doi.org/10.1097/NMD.0000000000000727.

Luo, Qiangqiang and Joel Andreas. 'Mobilizing Compliance: How the State Compels Village Households to Transfer Land to Large Farm Operators in China.' *Journal of Peasant Studies* 47, no. 6 (2020): 1189–210. doi.org/10.1080/03066150.2020.1822340.

McDonald, Tom. *Social Media in Rural China: Social Networks and Moral Frameworks*. London: UCL Press, 2016. doi.org/10.2307/j.ctt1g69xx3.

Morrison, Toni. 'No Place for Self-Pity, No Room for Fear.' *The Nation*, [New York], 23 March 2015: 184–85. www.thenation.com/article/archive/no-place-self-pity-no-room-fear/.

Mosher, Steven. *Broken Earth: The Rural Chinese*. New York: Free Press, 1983.

Mühlhahn, Klaus. *Making China Modern: From the Great Qing to Xi Jinping*. Cambridge, MA: Belknap Press of Harvard University Press, 2019. doi.org/10.4159/9780674916067.

Murphy, Rachel. 'Education and Repertoires of Care in Migrant Families in Rural China.' *Comparative Education Review* 66, no. 1 (2022): 102–20. doi.org/10.1086/717449.

Narayan, Kirin. *Alive in the Writing: Crafting Ethnography in the Company of Chekhov*. Chicago: University of Chicago Press, 2012. doi.org/10.7208/chicago/9780226567921.001.0001.

National Bureau of Statistics of China. 'China's Economy Realized a Moderate but Stable and Sound Growth in 2015.' Press release, Beijing, 19 January 2016. www.stats.gov.cn/english/PressRelease/201601/t20160119_1306072.html.

Nelsen, Harvey W. *The Chinese Military System: An Organizational Study of the Chinese People's Liberation Army*, 2nd edn. Boulder, CO: Westview Press, 1981.

Oxfeld, Ellen. *Bitter and Sweet: Food, Meaning, and Modernity in Rural China*. Oakland, CA: University of California Press, 2017. doi.org/10.1525/california/9780520293519.001.0001.

Pang, Lihua, Alan de Brauw, and Scott Rozelle. 'Working Until You Drop: The Elderly of Rural China.' *The China Journal* 52 (2004): 73–94. doi.org/10.2307/4127885.

Phillips, Michael R., Xianyun Li, and Yanping Zhang. 'Suicide Rates in China, 1995–99.' *The Lancet* 359, no. 9309 (2002): 835–41. doi.org/10.1016/S0140-6736(02)07954-0.

Pieke, Frank N. 'The Genealogical Mentality in Modern China.' *Journal of Asian Studies* 62, no. 1 (2003): 101–28. doi.org/10.2307/3096137.

Pieke, Frank N., Pál Nyíri, Mette Thunø, and Antonella Ceccagno. *Transnational Chinese: Fujianese Migrants in Europe*. Stanford, CA: Stanford University Press, 2004.

Red River Township Gazetteer [pseud.]. Unpublished draft, 2017.

Roughley, Neil, and Thomas Schramme. 'Empathy, Sympathy, Concern and Moral Agency.' In *Forms of Fellow Feeling: Empathy, Sympathy, Concern and Moral Agency*, edited by Neil Roughley and Thomas Schramme, 3–56. Cambridge, UK: Cambridge University Press, 2018. doi.org/10.1017/9781316271698.001.

Rowe, William T. *Crimson Rain: Seven Centuries of Violence in a Chinese County.* Stanford, CA: Stanford University Press, 2007. doi.org/10.1515/97815036 26195.

Santos, Gonçalo. *Chinese Village Life Today: Building Families in an Age of Transition.* Seattle: University of Washington Press, 2021.

Sargeson, Sally. 'Subduing "the Rural House-Building Craze": Attitudes Towards Housing Construction and Land Use Controls in Four Zhejiang Villages.' *China Quarterly* 172 (2002): 927–55. doi.org/10.1017/S0009443902000566.

Stafford, Charles. *Separation and Reunion in Modern China.* Cambridge, UK: Cambridge University Press, 2000. doi.org/10.1017/CBO9780511488931.

Steinmüller, Hans. *Communities of Complicity: Everyday Ethics in Rural China.* New York: Berghahn Books, 2013.

Thaxton, Ralph A., Jnr. *Force and Contention in Contemporary China: Memory and Resistance in the Long Shadow of the Catastrophic Past.* New York: Cambridge University Press, 2016. doi.org/10.1017/CBO9781316338094.

Thomason, Erin. 'United in Suffering.' In *Chinese Families Upside Down: Intergenerational Dynamics and Neo-Familism in the Early 21st Century*, edited by Yunxiang Yan, 76–102. Leiden: Brill, 2021. doi.org/10.1163/978900445 0233_005.

Tong, Yongsheng, Michael R. Phillips, Yi Yin, and Zhichao Lan. 'Relationship of the High Proportion of Suicidal Acts Involving Ingestion of Pesticides to the Low Male-to-Female Ratio of Suicide Rates in China.' *Epidemiology and Psychiatric Sciences* 29 (2020): E114. doi.org/10.1017/S2045796020000244.

Trappel, René. *China's Agrarian Transition: Peasants, Property, and Politics.* Lanham, MD: Lexington Books, 2016.

Tsai, Lily. *Accountability Without Democracy.* Cambridge, UK: Cambridge University Press, 2007. doi.org/10.1017/CBO9780511800115.

Walder, Andrew. 'Rebellion and Repression in China, 1966–1971.' *Social Science History* 38, nos 3–4 (2014): 513–39. doi.org/10.1017/ssh.2015.23.

Watson, James L., and Evelyn S. Rawski, eds. *Death Ritual in Late Imperial and Modern China.* Berkeley, CA: University of California Press, 1988.

Wemheuer, Felix. *A Social History of Maoist China: Conflict and Change, 1949–1976.* Cambridge, UK: Cambridge University Press, 2019. doi.org/10.1017/97813 16421826.

Whyte, Martin K. 'China's One Child Policy.' In *Oxford Bibliographies in Childhood Studies.* Oxford, UK: Oxford University Press, 2019. doi.org/10.1093/OBO/ 9780199791231-0221.

Wikan, Unni. *Beyond the Words: Resonance.* Chicago: University of Chicago Press, 2012. doi.org/10.7208/chicago/9780226924489.001.0001.

Wolf, Arthur P. 'Gods, Ghosts, and Ancestors.' In *Studies in Chinese Society*, edited by Arthur P. Wolf, 131–82. Stanford, CA: Stanford University Press, 1978. doi.org/10.1515/9781503620803-005.

Wou, Odoric Y.K. *Mobilizing the Masses: Building Revolution in Henan.* Stanford, CA: Stanford University Press, 1994. doi.org/10.1515/9780804766821.

Xin County Gazetteer Compilation Committee. 新县志1986–2005 [*Xin County Gazetteer 1986–2005*]. Zhengzhou, China: Zhongzhou Guji Chubanshe, 2012.

Xin County, Henan, County Committee. '关于缺衣群众用布的请示报告 [A Report and Request for Instructions Regarding the Use of Cloth Among the Masses Lacking Clothes].' Unpublished document, Xin County Archives, 1964.

Xin County People's Committee. '关于今多明春大力开展兴修农田水利和水 土保持工作的方案 [A Plan for the Major Development of Farmland Water and Soil Conservancy Construction and Maintenance Work this Winter and Next Spring].' Unpublished document, Xin County Archives, 1958.

Xin County People's Government. '我县召开扶贫开发暨农村改革试验区建设 工作会 [The County Holds a Work Meeting on Construction of a Trial Site for Developing Poverty Alleviation and Rural Reform].' www.hnxx.gov.cn, [page discontinued], 2015.

Xin County People's Government. 新县年鉴2016 [*Xin County Yearbook 2016*]. Zhengzhou, China: Zhongzhou Guji Chubanshe, 2016.

Xinyang Prefecture Local Histories and Gazetteers Compilation Committee. 信阳 地区志 [*Xinyang Prefecture Gazetteer*]. Beijing: Sanlian Shudian Chubanshe, 1992.

Yan, Yunxiang. 'Intergenerational Intimacy and Descending Familism in Rural North China.' *American Anthropologist* 118, no. 2 (2016): 244–57. doi.org/10.1111/ aman.12527.

Yang, Jisheng. *Tombstone: The Great Chinese Famine, 1958–1962.* New York: Farrar, Straus & Giroux, 2008.

Yang, Mayfair. *Gifts, Banquets, and the Art of Social Relationships in China.* Ithaca, NY: Cornell University Press, 1994.

Yang, Mayfair. *Re-Enchanting Modernity: Ritual Economy and Society in Wenzhou, China.* Durham, NC: Duke University Press, 2020. doi.org/10.1515/9781478 009245.

Yanow, Dvora, and Peregrine Schwartz-Shea, eds. *Interpretation and Method: Empirical Research Methods and the Interpretive Turn*, 2nd edn. New York: Routledge, 2015. doi.org/10.4324/9781315703275.

Ye, Jingzhong. 'Land Transfer and the Pursuit of Agricultural Modernization in China.' *Journal of Agrarian Change* 15, no. 3 (2015): 314–37. doi.org/10.1111/joac.12117.

Zhang, Yangyang, Xinye Zheng, and Lunyu Xie. 'How Do Poverty Alleviation Coordinators Help the Impoverished in Rural China? Evidence from the Chinese Poor Population Tracking Dataset.' *China Economic Review* 69 (2021): 101686. doi.org/10.1016/j.chieco.2021.101686.

Zhang, Yimou (dir.). 我的父亲母亲 [*The Road Home*]. Hong Kong: Beijing New Picture Distribution Company, 2000.

Index

Page numbers in **bold** indicate images.